The Power of Language

The Power of Language/ El poder de la palabra

Selected Papers from the Second REFORMA National Conference

Edited by

Lillian Castillo-Speed

and the

National Conference Publications Committee

Eddy Hogan	Romelia Salinas
Elissa Miller	Michael Shapiro
Vivian Pisano	Adalín Torres-Zayas
Rhonda Ríos-Kravitz	Judith Valdez

2001
Libraries Unlimited
A Division of Greenwood Publishing Group, Inc.
Englewood, Colorado

48014617   3-26-0

LIBRARIES UNLIMITED
A Division of Greenwood Publishing Group, Inc.
P.O. Box 6633
Englewood, CO 80155-6633
1-800-237-6124
www.lu.com

ISBN 1-56308-945-9

This book is dedicated to all Reformistas committed to serving Latino communities and especially in memory of Adelia (Deedie) Lines, mentor to many of us.

Contents

Part 1
The Power of Language

Part 2
Latino Leadership

Part 3
Issues in Latino Library Service

Part 4
Latino Programs and Models of Service

Part 5
Documenting Latino Lives and Creativity

Part 6
Conference Farewell Speech

About REFORMA
(National Association to Promote Library and Information Services to Latinos and the Spanish Speaking)

REFORMA is committed to the improvement of the full spectrum of library and information services for the approximately 31 million Spanish-speaking and Hispanic people in the United States. Established in 1971 as an affiliate of the American Library Association (ALA), REFORMA has actively sought to promote the development of library collections to include Spanish-language and Latino oriented materials, the recruitment of more bilingual and bicultural library professionals and support staff, the development of library services and programs that meet the needs of the Latino community, the establishment of a national information and support network among individuals who share our goals, the education of the U.S. Latino population about the availability and types of library services, and lobbying efforts to preserve existing library resource centers serving the interests of Latinos. Our Web address is http://www.reforma.org.

The organization is governed by an Executive Board that includes the officers, committee chairs, and presidents of chapters.

Nationally there are twenty-one REFORMA chapters. These function autonomously, working through their local library systems, state library associations, and local organizations to achieve local objectives.

One of REFORMA's most noteworthy activities is the annual scholarship drive. The association awards a number of scholarships to library school students who express interest in working with Latinos. Other activities that benefit the members include the publication of a quarterly newsletter, which keeps members abreast of the latest developments in the organization and in library services to Latinos; publication of an annual membership directory, which has, in effect, established a national network of librarians, library trustees, community and library school students with mutual concerns; and programs and workshops that focus on serving Latinos.

We warmly invite all interested persons to join us in our efforts.

Preface and Acknowledgments

It is with a great deal of gratitude and admiration that I want to thank the many people who put so much effort and work into making the REFORMA Second National Conference such a success. Special praise goes to the members of the RNCII Planning Committee, whose efforts resulted in wonderful and inspirational programs, heartwarming talks by local authors, and the very special gathering of our comunidad. This publication reflects the spirit of the conference and allows us to reach out and share our skills and expertise in serving the needs of the Latino/Hispanic communities.

—Susana Hinojosa, chair of the Conference
Planning Committee

We came together in the power of language and it changed us. And we ourselves became change agents. The inclusiveness of the conference made us feel we were part of the American fabric. We need to remember that feeling and keep that legacy going. We cannot forget that we are here because those before us struggled to retain their language and their culture.

—Toni Bissessar, REFORMA past president
(1999–2000)

Introduction

The essays in this book represent the collective knowledge and experience of an organization of dedicated library professionals and friends who met in Tucson, Arizona, for the group's second national conference, August 3–6, 2000. The members of REFORMA, the National Association to Promote Library and Information Services to Latinos and the Spanish-Speaking, share a deep commitment to serving the Latino population. That commitment is evident in these essays. Several overarching themes surface in these papers and proceedings, paramount among them the struggle to provide equity in service delivery and collections. Another theme is the quality factor. Excellence in programming and collections is a mantra of our profession, and we demonstrate this excellence in the programming and collections that we have organized during our thirty years of existence. Many of our conference presenters were chosen precisely for their reputations in their specific areas of expertise. The writings included here are but a sampling of the many programs and research projects that are routinely conducted by these outstanding Reformistas and supporters of the organization. Several of the authors have edited their oral presentations for these printed proceedings.

Sonia Ramírez Wohlmuth introduces our work with a scholarly literary essay infused with writings from Hispanic literature. Her essay reminds us that the power of language has long been a threat, from the days when Spanish *conquistadores* first subjugated the indigenous population of the New World up to the present.

The essay by Julia E. Curry Rodríguez addresses the importance of bilingual education and the impact that California's Proposition 227 and other such initiatives have had on English Learners. This chapter also presents the results of a two-year study by the Latino Policy Center at the University of California, Berkeley, on how school districts implemented Proposition 227. Dr. Curry Rodríguez articulately acknowledges that multiculturalism and multilingualism are the new American reality and that attempts to eliminate or reduce bilingual education are at best shortsighted and go against the powerful stream of our future endeavors as a nation.

In Isabel Espinal's quest for answers to the endemic racial problems that we as ethnic librarians encounter, she turns to other disciplines, namely anthropology and cultural studies, for solutions. Her thought-provoking analysis of "whiteness" theory as it could be applied to librarianship provides an excellent framework with which to better understand the inequities that exist in policies and services.

Jacqueline Ayala, Ron Baza, and Miguel Juárez document REFORMA's long-standing leadership in the library profession in their articles on professional development. Although Juárez's panel proceedings focus on our responsibility as library professionals to mentor those who are beginning their professional careers, Baza's and Ayala's serve as a record of our historical past and pay homage to those outstanding leaders who have served REFORMA as presidents and who continue to provide leadership while infusing their own institutions with the political muscle necessary to make the changes required. At the front end, educators who spoke on the panel on library education moderated by Loriene Roy invite Latino professionals in the field to work more closely with library schools to ensure that they are living up to their university diversity plans, thus encouraging more Latinos to enter the profession. Sara Martínez Tucker provides another perspective on library education, pointing out that the Hispanic Scholarship Fund and REFORMA share a common goal: to increase the number of Latinos enrolling in and completing library science programs. Her keynote speech, summarized here, provides key demographic data about the Latino population and gives us a vivid picture of the challenges facing both of our organizations.

Denice Adkins's new study on Hispanic demographics reminds us of the disjoint between the population that we serve and the ability of librarians to truly serve this group. The findings for children's services are the most striking and should serve as a wakeup call to the profession to move toward concrete, positive action on behalf of Latino children's services. Likewise, Bruce Jensen, through his analysis of library services to Latino prisoners, provides us with another lens through which to view the equity issue. His call for an ethnographic approach to library use and service provides us with the missing link that may well help us to better understand how we presently deliver services to Latino populations as a whole and to Latino prisoners in particular.

In his essay on independent distributors, Michael Shapiro invites us to widen our professional circle and embrace the professionalism of the work of Spanish language distributors. Susan Freiband's article on the state of libraries in Puerto Rico serves as a stark reminder of the need for the library profession as a whole to develop closer working ties with government to ensure the continued training and development of Spanish-language professional librarians. It also serves as a measure of how far we need to go to make sure that all U.S. citizens receive the full spectrum of library services.

On the digital end, the REFORMA Information Technology Agenda, written by the Information Technology Committee, is a comprehensive analysis of the issues associated with the digital revolution as they affect the Latino population that we serve. It is also a call to action, an organizational approach through which REFORMA members can engage in the civil rights issue of our time: the question of the digital divide. An important meeting on that topic took place at the conference and Lillian Castillo-Speed provides a report on the intense discussion that took place there.

Excellence in services is another theme that surfaces in the writings of the contributors. Josefina Gómez de Hillyer and Marie Flores Ortiz of the Carnegie Public Library in Puerto Rico provide a model of what can be accomplished with creativity and initiative even in the face of limited resources. Diana Borrego and Lorena Flores describe three variations of the bilingual story hour that can be utilized by librarians with bilingual children's audiences. The formats are derived from years of experience with bilingual children and storytimes.

There is very little literature in Spanish that provides support for gay youth. Ina Rimpau's critique of that literature is a valuable tool for librarians attempting to provide the best possible service to families in need of information.

Luis Alberto de la Garza and Horacio N. Roque Ramírez's contribution sheds light on another important area of collection: archives. It serves to remind us of how far we need to go to get institutions to recognize and make room for the communal and public history that continues to gather dust in the trunks and boxes of our closets and garages. Tatiana de la Tierra's literary essay is a journey through "Herstory." Her bibliography forges new pathways in the quest for the recognition and documentation of Latina lesbian literature that may otherwise be lost.

With the release of these writings, we carve a new niche in publishing. For the first time in the thirty-year history of the organization, REFORMA has assembled a record that, like the desert, will withstand the elements of time. We hope that these contributions will help practitioners in their immediate goal of serving the Spanish speaking. We also hope that these works will provide you, the reader, with the tools with which to better understand what it takes to be able to develop quality collections and provide effective services for 32 million Latinos living in the United States.

We also hope that this book serves to provide understanding and also to challenge and provoke us to create more democratic public institutions. May these works serve as a footprint that demonstrates the commitment and dedication of a special group of individuals who work daily to improve the lives of the people they serve.

Gracias, Lily Castillo-Speed and dedicated members of the publications committee for making this happen. Without you there would be no record.

Oralia Garza de Cortés
President
REFORMA
April 2001

Part 1

The Power of Language

Language and Identity in Contemporary Latin American Thought

Sonia Ramírez Wohlmuth

The problem of identity in the Spanish-speaking territories of the Americas begins with a name, the need to set apart those nations that have a distinct cultural legacy and different racial/ethnic profile from the United States. The "other Americans" who live south of the Río Grande confront their historical past with ambivalence: the prevalence of racial mixture, or *mestizaje,* and the hegemony of the Spanish language. These two factors, racial/ethnic identity and language, serve to marginalize U.S. Latinos and Latin American immigrants. To bring these communities into the mainstream and provide access to informational and recreational library materials, it is necessary to develop an understanding of the communities' self-identity. This study provides an overview of issues of language and race as expressed in modern Latin American writings.

Sonia Ramírez Wohlmuth is a lecturer in the School of Library and Information Science at the University of South Florida. She also teaches in the Division of Languages and Linguistics. She has interests in the development of curricular materials for Spanish-language instruction for information professionals, the study of technical and machine-assisted translation, and online library resources for the Spanish–speaking. At present she is also a doctoral student in Spanish linguistics at the University of Florida in Gainesville.

3

One may well ask what need librarians have to discuss issues of language and ethnic identity. However, in the best interests of those we serve—as well as the unserved and underserved—we must ask these questions. Do the materials we select for our collections provide a true and sensitive portrayal of the "other Americans," those whom eighteenth-century France designated *Latin* Americans out of the need to separate this continent into spheres of interest based on religion, that is, Protestantism versus Catholicism? Do we provide equitable access to informational materials and leisure reading by purchasing at least some items in the language of choice of one of seven residents of the United States? Have we adequately trained staff to be aware of subtle differences in social interactions among the different populations we serve? Is our knowledge of "American" history confined to events that occurred on this side of the Río Grande?

For those of us who have family roots on the other side of the divide, the Rio Grande, there is a struggle—even after decades or generations of residence within the confines of the United States—to define racial, ethnic, and linguistic identity. By having a multiplicity of names—Latin American, Spanish American, Hispanic American, Ibero American, Latino, not to mention the twenty adjectives of nationality of the former Spanish possessions—we have no name. We are not simply "Americans." Over time, the label that should rightly belong to all citizens of this hemisphere has come to designate the United States. We are a people in search of a name, an identity.

"Yo soy yo y mis circunstancias": I am myself and my circumstances. In these brief words the Spanish philosopher José Ortega y Gasset provided a working definition of identity in his 1923 essay, *El tema de nuestro tiempo*. What, then, are the circumstances peculiar to Latin America that have riven it from Anglo America, and in the process, imbued its citizens with a sense of inferiority, envy, and mistrust? A brief historical overview will demonstrate that the sense of identity of the colonizers, the colonized, and their descendants comes from three traits that characterize and often divide communities: race, ethnicity, and language. The three are intertwined and frequently inseparable.

We know that at some point mariners from Spain reached the Americas and established an enduring presence. Fray Bartolomé de las Casas provides a description of the inhabitants of the New World in the words of Columbus: "ellos son de la color de los canarios, ni negros ni blancos" [They are the color of the Canary Islanders, neither black nor white] (Casas 1997, 56). This is perhaps the first reference to race in the context of the New World. If one understands ethnicity to refer to collective customs that distinguish one community from another, Columbus also provides the first ethnic description when he relates that the autochthonous peoples are unclothed, and, lacking their own religion, can be easily converted to Christianity. Columbus also makes a chilling confession, that he has already taken prisoner several young men whom he plans to take to Spain "para que deprendan fablar" [so that they may learn to speak] (Casas 1997, 56). The Admiral's laconic description serves to dehumanize these newly encountered peoples: They are not of any known race, being neither black nor white; they lack the essential trappings of civilization, among them clothing and religion; and, finally, they must be taught a proper language.

The subsequent bands of adventurers who came from the Iberian Peninsula became literally the populators of the new world. History notes that there were very few women among the voyagers to the Indies during the first half of the sixteenth century. This, together with the fact that the Iberian Peninsula after nearly eight centuries of contact with Muslims and Jews presented a diverse ethnic profile, contributed to the mixture of races. Furthermore, the sons and daughters of Spaniards born in the New World were deemed to be somehow different—that is, inferior—and were designated as *criollos*. The term *criollo*, from the Portuguese *crioulo*, is documented within the first century of New World expansion. El Inca Garcilaso de la Vega (1539–1616), son of the Spanish captain Sebastián Garcilaso de la Vega and Isabel Chimpu Ocllo, a princess of the royal house of the Incas, describes at the end of the sixteenth century in his *Comentarios Reales* the origin of the term *criollo,* which modern lexicographical studies support: *Criollo* was a term given to the offspring of slaves whose children were felt to be inferior to those coming directly from Africa (Garcilaso de la Vega 1997, 115). El Inca Garcilaso also describes the different racial mixtures that the confluence of races produced in the Indies. According to him, *mestizo* is the term applied to the children of Spanish fathers and Indian mothers, and it is considered denigrating. However, Garcilaso adds that he bears it proudly: "me lo llamo yo a boca llena y me honro con él"—[I proclaim out loud that I am a *mestizo* and feel honored to be one] (1997, 115).

The text of el Inca Garcilaso finds a pictorial counterpart in the *pinturas de castas* of Mexico. These portraits of the family unit—father, mother, child—served two purposes: 1) to demonstrate the biological result of different racial mixtures and 2) to provide a ready reference for those in a position to classify an infant presented for the official register, namely the clergy. Today we may smile at the simplicity of such a scheme, as if human genetics could be summed up so neatly: $A + B = C$. However, identification with a "casta" limited many individual choices: with whom one could marry, what occupations one could hold, and where one could live. Racial classifications numbered between one and two dozen, including the following representative list of terms: *mulato, morisco, salta atrás, chino, lobo, gíbaro, albarrazado, cambujo, sambaygo, calpan mulato, ténte en el aire, no te entiendo, hay te estás* ("Negros" 1976, 739–42). It may be readily seen that issues of race in Latin America are anything but simple, and historical values have characterized as inferior the inhabitants of the new world whether white, black, indigenous, or of mixed race.

Moving forward 400 years, we see the continuing impact of questions of race and ethnicity. The Latin American writer of today is by choice or by circumstance socially engaged. The Uruguayan Mario Benedetti, in his evocatively titled *Letras del continente mestizo,* writes: "Para su bien o para su mal, el escritor latinoamericano . . . no puede ya cerrar las puertas a la realidad, y si ingenuamente procura cerrarlas, de poco le valdrá ya que la realidad entrará por la ventana" [To his benefit or detriment, the Latin American writer can no longer close the doors to reality, and if he naively tries to close them, it will do him little good because reality will enter through the window] (1967, 21). The reality of Latin America became increasingly apparent with the struggle for independence. The Bolivian essayist and educator, Mariano Baptista Gumucio, cites Bolívar in the introductory essay of *La cultura que heredamos*: "no somos europeos, no somos indios, sino una especie media entre los aborígenes y los españoles" [We are not European, we are not Indians but a species between the native peoples and the Spanish] (1973, 13). This vision of race parallels that of the Mexican José Vasconcelos, whose *La raza cósmica* predicts a fusion of the races. He responds to the ill-named October 12 holiday, El día de la Raza, thus: "¿De qué raza hablamos? ¿criolla? ¿quechua? ¿tupi-guaraní? ¿o por qué no aceptar de una vez por todas que somos un mosaico étnico en vías de muy lenta integración?" [What race are we talking about? Creole? Quechua? Tupi-guarani? Or why don't we accept once and for all that we are an ethnic mosaic in the process of very slow integration?] (Baptista Gumucio 1973, 12). Until that process of integration is complete and race no longer correlates with educational, economic, and social achievement, discussions of race will continue.

The involuntary immigration from Africa formed an important racial admixture in the Caribbean as well as the coastal areas of Mexico and Central and South America, extending from Colombia to Peru on the Pacific side. The Puerto Rican author Luis Rafael Sánchez describes in *La guagua aérea* (an allusion to the constant flow of traffic between Puerto Rico and New York) the reticence with which the Spanish-speaking Caribbean accepts its links to Africa (Sánchez 1994, 25–26). Sánchez also introduces the issue of language identity:

> Frontera de Puerto Rico ha sido el idioma español va a hacer, pronto, cien años. Frontera confirmadora de su diferencia frente a lo otro: el gringo y el idioma inglés que aquel quiso imponer de una vez. . . . Un obstáculo enfrenta el movimiento que promueve la incorporación de Puerto Rico a la nación norteamericana en calidad de estado cincuentaiuno. El obstáculo, hermoso hasta sofocar, imposible de fingir u ocultar, no es otro que el idioma puertorriqueño de cada día, el idioma español.
>
> [Puerto Rico has been the frontier of the Spanish language for nearly one hundred years, a frontier which confirms its difference in the face of the Gringo and the English language which he

sought to impose. . . . Only one obstacle stands before the movement which supports the incorporation of Puerto Rico into the United States as the fifty-first state. That obstacle, delightful almost to the point of dying of laughter, impossible to dissemble or hide, is none other than the Spanish language.] (Author's translation). (1994, 29–30)

The real threat of the persistence of Spanish, not only in Puerto Rico but among recent Hispanic immigrants to the United States as well as families of long standing in the West and Southwest, is that language has a unifying function. Under the umbrella of a common tongue, Hispanic Americans represent a cohesive force and part of the 350 million persons in the world who speak the Spanish language, the third most spoken mother tongue after Chinese and Hindi. The Spanish language is the one legacy of the Conquest that is beyond contention. Rosalba Campra, an Argentine scholar of the twentieth-century novel, affirms in her essay *América Latina: La identidad y la máscara:* "La unidad más evidente creada por la Conquista es la de la lengua: excepto Brasil, colonizado por Portugal. América Latina se expresa en una lengua única, el español" [The most evident unity created by the Conquest is that of language, except for Brazil, colonized by Portugal. Latin American expresses itself in one language, Spanish] (1987, 14).

In the United States, the early linguistic diversity of the colonies gave way to English hegemony. Westward expansion increased contact with Spanish-speaking settlers who lived north of the Río Grande and sowed the seeds of conflict, a conflict which is a leitmotif in Chicano literature in the twentieth century: the loss of land and the concomitant loss of language and cultural identity. Felipe [Phillip] Ortego comments on the paradoxical estrangement of the Chicano in territories where his ancestors dwelled: "La Raza came to this land over three hundred years ago. . . . And now we walk the earth as aliens in the land of our fathers" (1971, 294). The Mexican American has been reluctant to assimilate to Anglo American culture, both culturally and linguistically. Chicano literature is characterized by the alternation of languages.

The writings of U.S. Latinos provide valuable insight on the attachment to language as a hallmark of identity. The Puerto Rican author Esmeralda Santiago recalls her first entry into the Brooklyn public school system:

There were two kinds of Puerto Ricans in school: the newly arrived, like myself, and the ones born in Brooklyn of Puerto Rican parents. The two types didn't mix. The Brooklyn Puerto Ricans spoke English, and often no Spanish at all. . . . Those of us for whom Puerto Rico was still a recent memory were also split into two groups: the ones who longed for the island the ones who wanted to forget it as soon as possible. I felt disloyal for wanting to learn English. (1993, 280)

Santiago alludes to a major problem: the choice between education and upward mobility and abandoning the norms—linguistic and others—of the ethnic community. In a truly multicultural society, it should be possible to accomplish both. However, Richard Rodriguez's *Hunger of Memory: The Education of Richard Rodriguez,* with its controversial condemnation of bilingual education, describes the disintegration of family communication as he and his siblings became English speaking and his parents failed to achieve the same level of fluency:

> The silence at home, however, was finally more than a literal silence. Fewer words passed between parent and child. . . . I would have been happier about my public success had I not sometimes recalled what it had been like earlier, when my family had conveyed its intimacy through a set of conveniently private sounds. (1982, 25)

In an interview, Helen Valdez, one of the founders of the Mexican Fine Arts Center Museum, Pilsen, describes her early teaching experiences at Bowen High School in south Chicago:

> At Bowen I confronted the question . . . of what happens to the Mexican kids who are born here that makes them so alienated from mainstream American culture. I saw that deep alienation. . . . They don't see themselves as Americans. They hesitate to say they're Americans, but they don't feel Mexican either. In some cases, they begin to hate themselves, they hate each other, they hate the kids who speak Spanish, they hate the kids who speak English well. . . . There is no school today where the entire Mexican or Spanish-speaking population is in the bilingual program. It has always been a small percentage. In fact, the program really has not been about bilingual education, but about learning English, and the sooner the better. In the process, we give the kids the idea that the Spanish language is second-rate. By extension, we are also telling them that their parents, their religion, their entire culture is second rate. (Heyck 1994, 290)

Former Senator Paul Simon comments that the aversion to use of other languages in public life is paradoxical: "[W]e have this unusual, deep-seated phenomenon: a historical cultural barrier to the learning of another language in a land of great ethnic diversity" (1980, 12). He cites some of the contributing factors: the physical extension of the United States, the close proximity of another

English-speaking country of similar historical and cultural background, the perception of the southern border as a cultural/linguistic barrier, the widespread belief that acquisition of a second language requires a special gift, and the unavailability or inadequacy of foreign-language instruction in the public schools. Given these facts, the monolingualism of the United States is not surprising, and the drive to force all its citizens to use English exclusively is not only logical but comprehensible. The United States is ill-equipped to deal with linguistic diversity.

The fact that there are still Spanish-speaking enclaves in various locations throughout the United States may explain in part the political attacks against Spanish in the "English only" campaigns. The perseverance of the language is unnerving to those who believe that "one nation, one language" is the norm. However, the following summary of facts from the Linguistic Society of America (1996) shows that monolingualism is clearly not the natural state of affairs: Many of the nations of the world are bilingual if not multilingual, hundreds of languages were spoken in U.S. territory prior to the arrival of Europeans, immigrants to the United States brought with them many languages and traditions, and multilingualism presents many benefits and opportunities. Multilingualism will not threaten the role of English as a common language. Newcomers to the United States are eager to learn English because it is the ladder for educational attainment and economic success. There is a clear distinction between the vernacular language (spoken at home and among friends) and the vehicular language (required for employment and educational advancement) in immigrant communities.

Spanish has a wide geographic distribution in the United States and is present at all socioeconomic levels. Evidence of this wide diffusion is the proliferation of mass media in Spanish in the form of national and local newspapers, magazines, television, and radio broadcasting. Whether or not the 17.3 million speakers of Spanish are also competent in English is an important related issue. Clearly "English only" services will disenfranchise large numbers of limited English-speaking or non-English-speaking Latinos. A further consideration is the question of language of preference, that is, the preferred language for use in the context of family and close friends *as well as* for acquiring information and reading for enjoyment. After all, do not our collection policies provide for a wide range of materials to reflect the preferences of those we serve? Preference can extend beyond subject matter to include the language in which the topic is treated. For those library users whose primary or preferred language is Spanish, materials should be available that reflect a wide range of interests and reading abilities. In the realm of literary works, no one would suggest removal of Greek and Latin editions of classical authors because they are not in English. Likewise, the creative outpouring of Latin American authors should be available whenever possible in the original language. Literary production represents the culmination of a linguistic tradition, a vehicle to showcase the language. In the case of Spanish it is a language that has a long, historical attachment to the United States, the product of several centuries of coexistence. It is not going to go away as a result of antagonistic state propositions or national antipathy. Anglo Americans should embrace this opportunity to acquire a second language and broaden their horizons.

References

Arciniegas, Germán. 1945. *Este pueblo de América*. México, D.F.: Fondo de Cultura Económica.

Baptista Gumucio, Mariano. 1973. *La cultura que heredamos*. La Paz: Ediciones Camarlinghi.

Benedetti, Mario. 1967. *Letras del continente mestizo*. Montevideo: Arca Editorial, 1967.

Campra, Rosalba. 1987. *América Latina: La identidad y la máscara*. México, D.F.: Siglo Veintiuno Editores.

Casas, Bartolomé de las. 1997. Diario de a bordo: el primer viaje a las Indias. In *Huellas de las literaturas hispanoamericanas*, edited by John F. Garganigo, et al. Upper Saddle River, NJ: Prentice Hall.

Flores, Lauro, ed. 1998. *The floating borderlands: Twenty-five years of U.S. Hispanic literature*. Seattle: University of Washington Press.

Garcilaso de la Vega, el Inca. 1997. Tipos de hombre americano. In *Huellas de las literaturas hispanoamericanas*, edited by John F. Garganigo, et al. Upper Saddle River, NJ: Prentice Hall.

Heyck, Denis Lynn Daly. 1994. *Barrios and borderlands: Cultures of Latinos and Latinas in the United States*. New York: Routledge.

Linguistic Society of America. 1996. *Statement on language rights*. © 2000. Available: http://www.lsadc.org/web2/resolutionsfr.htm. (Accessed August 2, 2000).

Negros. 1976. *Enciclopedia de México*. Vol. IX. México, D.F.: Enciclopedia de México.

Ortego, Phillip. 1971. "The Coming of Zamora." In *The Chicano: From caricature to self-portrait*, edited by Edward Simmen. New York: NAL.

Rodriguez, Richard. 1982. *Hunger of memory: The education of Richard Rodriguez*. Boston: David R. Godine.

Sánchez, Luis Rafael. 1994. *La guagua aérea*. [San Juan, PR]: Editorial Cultural.

Santiago, Esmeralda. 1993. *When I was Puerto Rican*. New York: Addison-Wesley.

Simon, Paul. 1980. *The tongue-tied American: Confronting the foreign language crisis*. New York: Continuum.

Meeting the Needs of Linguistically Diverse Children

California's Legislation and the Future of Bilingual Education

Julia E. Curry Rodríguez

This paper addresses the importance of bilingual education as a holistic approach for multicultural children. California's 1998 Unz Initiative (Proposition 227) was passed overwhelmingly by California voters and here serves as a backdrop for our discussion. Proposition 227 has a bearing on bilingual education nationally; several states are now filing similar initiatives to curtail education to English learners. This chapter is based on empirical evidence from a two-year case study about how Proposition 227 affected the educational experiences of teachers and children in California. The study focuses on district implementation procedures for Proposition 227. We drew a stratified random sample from among the 905 school districts in the state. Forty districts were selected from all districts with 25 percent Limited English Proficient (LEP) students (N = 227). Our preliminary findings are divided into three categories of implementation: Structured English Immersion (4 out of 38), Elimination of Bilingual Education (9 out of 38), and Choice (25 out of 38). The Choice category addresses district variations in schools. It has three distinct strands: 1) Bilingual Education Maintained with Waivers (13), 2) Structured English Immersion with Diminishing Bilingual Education (7), and 3) True Choice—A variety of programs supported (5).[1]

Dr. Julia E. Curry Rodríguez received a Ph.D. in sociology in 1988 from the Department of Sociology at the University of Texas at Austin. Her research addresses immigrant women, immigration, racial and sexual stratification, and a variety of issues pertaining to Chicanos and Latinos in the United States. She has taught at Arizona State University, UCLA, and UC Berkeley. Currently she is on the faculty of the Mexican American Studies Department at San Jose State University.

Introduction

In 1998, the people of the state of California followed the lead of businessman millionaire Ron Unz and voted favorably for Proposition 227, known as the "English for the Children Initiative," with a 61 percent majority. Presumably this initiative was a response to apparent widespread discontent with the state's policies regarding the education of language minority children in public schools. However, Proposition 227 followed a systematic pattern of resolutions that constructed barriers for many of California's racial/ethnic and linguistic group members. For example, Proposition 187, the "Save our State Initiative" of 1994, attempted to curtail the rights of immigrants to receive public education and public assistance and, in general, to intimidate both legal and undocumented immigrants. A major feature of this legislation was the implication that children attending public schools whose immigrant status was suspect were drawing undeserved benefits from our society.

In the 1990s the retrenchment over civil rights was extended to the anti-affirmative action efforts of Ward Connerly, with his infamous Proposition 209. Proposition 209 prohibited public institutions from providing access to higher education on a "preferential basis" to members of historically underrepresented and institutionally discriminated against groups such as racial and ethnic minorities and women.

After Proposition 209 came another assault on the children of racial/ethnic and linguistically diverse groups, Proposition 227. This proposition continued a plan dating from the 1980s of taking back an English-only America that had been introduced with the English-only initiatives. The intent of Proposition 227 was to instill more English instruction for LEP students in the public schools of the state of California. California had 904 districts in 1997 (the most recent data when the initiative went into practice in 1998). Of these, 227 had at least 25 percent students who were classified as LEP, English Language Learners (ELL), and/or as Language Minority students. California Department of Education statistics identify ninety non-English languages among its student body. Of these language groups, twenty require language instruction in that language.

Proposition 227 was informed by the assumption that teaching children in their native language served only to hold them back in their acquisition of English and therefore in their future success. Therefore, the initiative changed the California Education Code to require schools to teach English and content areas in English, as rapidly and effectively as possible.

Immediately upon its passage, Proposition 227 became a part of the California Education Code (#300-340). The districts were given sixty days to implement Proposition 227. Children entering California public schools who were identified as having very little English proficiency were to be "observed" for a period of thirty calendar days and then placed in programs meeting the regulations of the new law. In general, districts interpreted the observation period as taking place in an English-language classroom. However, the law did not specify how it should be interpreted.

After the initial thirty days of observation, school personnel were to determine if children were fluent enough in English to function in a mainstream English classroom. If the school personnel did not judge the child to be able to perform in a mainstream classroom, they issued a waiver allowing the child to receive one year of "Sheltered English Immersion" (SEI), also referred to as "Structured English Immersion." The SEI program of English-language instruction, like other elements of the law, was not clearly delineated. Rather, educational personnel were directed to provide instruction so that "nearly all" was in English. The term "nearly all" was left up to the district's discretion. The law assumed that children would be proficient enough in English after one year to be integrated into mainstream English classrooms. Such classrooms are characterized as having instruction "overwhelmingly" in English, again with definition of the term "overwhelmingly" left up to the district's discretion. An important feature of this law was the enabling of parents or legal guardians to sue for damages if they found that district or school personnel, including classroom teachers, willfully and repeatedly refused to provide the language instruction in other than English, as required.

The only legal alternative to SEI and/or mainstream English classrooms found in Proposition 227 is the parental waiver process. According to the law, children who have special language needs, or whose parents specifically request it, can be placed in "alternative programs." These programs have some form of bilingual instruction, including instruction in the child's primary language. The law requires that the parent or guardian must go to the school annually to request and sign a waiver for the child to be enrolled in an alternative program. This right notwithstanding, every child who enters a California school for the first time must go through a thirty-day "observation" period in an English-language classroom. Only after the thirty-day observation period is completed can the child be enrolled in an alternative program. To ensure that the law can be implemented with local and federal government regulations in mind, Proposition 227 included a clause stating that any conflicts between its requirements and federal, state, or constitutional law could be addressed while non-conflicting portions must be implemented.

Two areas of the California State Board of Education's policy regarding the instruction of Language Minority children that were not at all affected by Proposition 227 were teacher credentialing and the requirement regarding the assessment of LEP children in English and in their native language. Schools and districts must still communicate with language minority families in their primary language whenever necessary. Children who are identified as Special Education and operate under an Individual Education Plan are not affected by the changes, nor in any real sense are students in secondary schools.

However, Proposition 227 certainly altered basic elements of policy toward Language Minority children in California's public schools. Since the 1970s, California Language Minority groups had enjoyed policies that were supportive and encouraging. In addition, in the 1970s, bilingual education programs were mandated. The United States Supreme Court ruling in *Lau vs. Nichols* in 1974 stated that offering instruction only in English to students who did not speak English was a violation of their civil rights. In addition, § 1703(f) of the Equal Education Opportunities Act (EEOA) required every school district to take "appropriate action to overcome language barriers that impede equal opportunity by its students in its instructional programs." This was followed by the Castañeda Standard, which set criteria for special programs serving LEP students. In 1987, the Castañeda Standard and § 1703(f) were sunsetted, making the provision of these mandates less clear in the state of California. Nevertheless, after 1987 there was a climate of increasing openness toward bilingual programs and other special services for Language Minority students in California schools. Proposition 227, however, brought about a reversal of the state's position with its amendment to the Education Code as dictated by the voter initiative.

In the fall of 1998, the Center for Latino Policy Research at the University of California, Berkeley began a study of how districts implemented Proposition 227. We examined the outcome of this reform by investigating the implementation procedures on a small scale with a pilot study of eight districts immediately following the vote in 1998. This study focused on three educational levels to discern a frame for assessing the future impact of the new law vis-à-vis students, states, and federal educational mandates. The data we collected in our pilot phase provided us with an empirical base, which we used to develop a more detailed study of the impact of Proposition 227, conducted in 1999. The 1999 study consisted of forty randomly selected California school districts that had a minimum of 25 percent students who were English Language Learners (ELL) and where Spanish was the language of at least 10 percent of the students.

Methodology and Sample Practices

This research uses qualitative research techniques. We conducted in-depth interviews using structured, open-ended interviewing protocols designed for each of three groups of educators: district personnel, principals, and teachers. We conducted the interviews over the telephone. In our protocols we asked questions in four categories: implementation, professional development, school culture, and external policy agents. Participants were informed that their answers were confidential and all our data were coded. No identifying information was recorded in our interviews. We used codes to link clusters of participants by district, school/principal, and teacher/classroom to be able to analyze the relationship between the district's stated form of implementation of Proposition 227 and the eventual classroom practices used at a sample site.

Our sample consisted of 80 principals (two per district) and 160 teachers (four per district, two per school). Forty districts in our sample were randomly selected to be representative of school districts in terms of size, region, Spanish, and "Spanish *plus* 10 percent other native language." The sample was drawn from eligible districts by controlling for the specified characteristics of LEP percentage and size. We identified a total of seventy-seven districts eligible to participate in our study, which represented approximately 51 percent of the total eligible districts.

Summary of the Sample

Total Sample:	40 districts serving English Language Learner (ELL) Students
Actual Respondents:	171 (39 district personnel, 56 principals, and 76 teachers)
District Selection Criterion/Characteristics:	25 percent ELL student enrollment
Distribution by Language:	Spanish-ELL 25 districts
	Spanish *plus* 10 percent Other Languages 15 districts
District Size:	29 > 5000 (10 *"Spanish plus"*)
	10 < 5000 (5 *"Spanish plus"*)

Summary of Findings

Our findings suggest that ideology, previous district position on bilingual education, and attitudes toward ELL students were important factors in shaping the district response to Proposition 227. We found that teachers do not necessarily respond to Proposition 227 in terms of their own cultural background. That is, being members of a group that sustains a language other than English does not mean that a teacher will support bilingual/bicultural teaching. Many teachers support the idea of English proficiency as a primary task of school settings. Several teachers stated that culture ought to be taught at home and not at schools. By the same token, for some teachers, ELL students do best when they are proficient in their native language—but now they have diminishing support for such schooling.

The districts in our sample implemented Proposition 227 in one of three outcomes: 1) eliminated Bilingual Education (9 out of 39), 2) developed Structured English Immersion Programs (4 out of 39), and 3) provided choices for the district (26 out of 39). These implementation categories are described in the following section.

Implementation Categories Used by Districts

Eliminated Bilingual Education, Moved to SEI or SE: Several of these districts had bilingual education programs prior to Proposition 227. Proposition 227 enabled these districts to establish what they refer to as SEI or "Sheltered English" (SE) programs. These programs have become English Only Instruction, with some support for transition.

Structured English Immersion (SEI): Some districts had SEI prior to Proposition 227. Thus, very little change has taken place.

Choice: Three distinct types of choices were offered:

1. Choice with push for waivers; maintains strong bilingual education programs (14 out of 39).

2. Choice with push for SEI; bilingual programs in these districts are diminishing (7 out of 39).

3. True choice: A variety of programs, all supported (5 out of 39).

Although touted as a voter mandate ushering in the end to bilingual education, Proposition 227 included enough ambiguity to enable districts to determine how exactly the new code would alter their practices. As stated previously, we found that ideology played an important role in how a district defined its implementation policy. Sixty-six of the districts in our study provided for "choice" as defined by the district schools. Among these "choice" districts, eleven went for diminishing bilingual education in a quasi-structured English Immersion program. Only three districts provided for "true choice," allowing principals and teachers to implement parental and their own pedagogical wishes. Three of these districts defined their program implementation plan as SEI without that meaning diminishing bilingual education (there may have been no bilingual education previously).

Teachers, principals, or district personnel did not always make the waiver option known to parents. We found that in several cases information about such waivers was given only in English and sent home in the form of flyers instructing parents to go to the district or school offices to sign such waivers. Some teachers reported being instructed not to speak to the parents at all about the waiver options.

On a day-to-day basis, Proposition 227 and the district implementation definition affected teachers and students most. Students, finding themselves in English-Only classrooms (even though this was not the overwhelming response from our study), were faced with the reality of a classroom in which they could not use their native language and were instructed in a language in which they did not understand what was being taught. Asked what students did in this case, teachers replied that sometimes students tried to help each other; at other times they just sat in confusion. For many teachers this was a source of profound distress. One teacher stated that she told her students that they could speak their language at home, but that the law said that they had to try to learn English at school. She wanted to make them understand that it was the law, not she, that made the English-Only classroom.

Teachers coupled Proposition 227 with assessment and their ability to teach effectively. Overwhelmingly, they cited increasing state-required assessment as a major detractor from their ability to teach. Teachers had been asked to keep an abundance of records on student performance, which drew them away from actual teaching time. It is important to recognize that this inordinate amount of recordkeeping was largely the result of standardized testing and not necessarily of Proposition 227, but both were initiated at the same time.

Teachers cited still another problem with fulfilling their teaching role in terms of resources. Many teachers expressed dismay over a lack of adequate literacy resources for their transition students. Others discussed how they figured out ways to prompt students, encouraging them to follow the reading plan so that at least they would learn to respond in English. They figured that in the absence of understanding, practicing (that is imitating a behavior) would somehow at least help students to figure out what they were supposed to be learning.

One outcome of the assessment/Proposition 227 challenges was addressed by some districts in terms of the redefinition of literacy resources available to teachers. Overwhelmingly the teacher sample in our survey cited Hampton Brown as the most often-cited literacy resource used in their district. However, we found an array of other literacy resources used, including Harcourt (12), Open Court (5), Macmillan (11), Results Reading Program (4), Estrellitas (2), Direct Instruction (1), Scholastic (11), Reading Recovery (3), Solares (5), Houghton Mifflin (2), Rigby (2), Ace (1), Success for All (3), Addison Wesley (3), Sullivan Reading Readiness (1), and Silver Burdett (2). Sixteen teachers did not indicate any literacy resource, which does not mean they didn't have one. They simply did not respond with any resource.

An amazing finding, even if not too frequent, was that some teachers stated that they were actually totally unaware of Proposition 227. Our sample design relied on nomination for teacher and principal respondents. When the initially nominated teacher was unavailable, we resorted to asking someone else at the school to give us another referral. Even after explaining the characteristics that we wanted to use, that is, teachers representing the district response to Proposition 227, or knowledgeable teachers having their own plan for Proposition 227, we still were sometimes given teachers as potential respondents who were unaware of Proposition 227. Although these respondents were of little use to our study, they were in charge of ELL students and therefore should have known about changes in educational law pertaining to their pupils.

The principals in our study either strongly supported English Only or strongly supported the ideal of bilingual education. The latter group worked hard to ensure that parents were informed about the use of waivers so that their ELL students would be instructed in their native language. Regardless of ideological position, principals demonstrated that they were very much in a leadership position and that their role was to ensure that the best pedagogy was implemented for all students, not only ELL students. Their challenge was to figure out how to comply with the district implementation decision if it did not square with their beliefs. Just as some teachers faced emotional hardships in implementing English Only, some of the principals who would have wanted to continue with a bilingual program were challenged in districts where the plan called for the elimination of bilingual education.

District personnel also ran the gamut as far as their role in implementing Proposition 227. Some agonized individually while setting out a plan to be followed with little assistance. Others convened task forces or paid staff to discern the best way to implement this proposition. District personnel were also divided in terms of supporters and critics of bilingual education. The struggle faced by these respondents was to garner the support for whatever decisions and implementation plans they developed.

What Does the Future Hold?

As we prepared this chapter, many popular media sources were speaking and writing about the end of bilingual education in the state of California. In the state of Arizona, the Unz initiative was about to be introduced in its local version. Having learned that waivers had the possibility of preventing the full implementation of English-Only education, the Arizona Unz initiative removed the parental waiver provision and went farther than the California initiative, including the languages of native peoples in addition to those of immigrant groups.

The California initiative allowed for the possibility of suing teachers, principals, and districts that did not pursue English-Only mandates. Although this aspect of the law has not yet been fully tested in the courts, it is an important measure of control for teachers, parents, and advocates of bilingual education.

Meanwhile, the children of the cohort of 1998 who were not English-language proficient when they began their public education continue to face a myriad of troubles that are reminiscent of those faced by children in the pre-civil rights United States. The state of California, and many other states in the United States, will become increasingly multicultural as we fully enter this millennium. Indeed, according to preliminary census reports, certain major cities in which Latinos and Asians have settled promise to become as multilingual and multicultural as these umbrella terms indicate. We are only now learning that children in bilingual classrooms perform better in schools than children in monolingual English-Only classrooms (Crawford 1999). We also know that youth, that is, children in middle school and high school, are also in need of bilingual education if they are to rise to their occupational and intellectual promise. Yet this group is largely left unattended by initiatives like "English for Children" (Proposition 227), "Save Our State" (Proposition 187), and Proposition 209 (the anti-affirmative initiative that has also erupted in the states of Washington and Texas and is quickly taking root in other states).

Although existing scholarship and programmatic changes regarding race and ethnicity have made it difficult to maintain the idea that the United States is a homogenous society with only one language and one cultural heritage, initiatives such as Proposition 227 continue to deny that multiculturalism and multilingualism are the new U.S. reality. In effect, to not be conversant in more than one language in the modern "global reach" society goes against the stream of all that is part of future human endeavor involving many nations and many cultures.[2]

Notes

1. This research project is housed at the Center for Latino Policy Research at UC Berkeley: Research Principal Investigator, Dr. Eugene E. García, Graduate School of Education, UC Berkeley; Research Director, Julia E. Curry Rodríguez, Ph.D., San Jose State University. This research was supported by The Stuart Foundation, Spencer Foundation, UC-LMRI, Department of Education—OBEMLA, UC Berkeley Faculty Research Grant, ISSC, and the Graduate School of Education. We thank our graduate student researchers: Sara Paredes, Betty Pazmiño, Tom Stritikus, Deborah Palmer, Celia Viramontes, and Laura Alamillo. Thanks also to Octavio Estrella, Paloma Esquivel, and Elena Tinker-Valle for general assistance. For information, contact Dr. Julia E. Curry Rodríguez, Mexican American Studies, San Jose State University, One Washington Square, San Jose, CA 95192-0118. E-mail: jcurryr@email.sjsu.edu.

2. This chapter draws on research conducted by my colleague, Eugene E. García, the graduate student researchers listed in the note 1, and my discussions with Betty M. Pazmiño in preparation for the REFORMA National Conference presentation. I am grateful to all of them for their collaboration.

Selected Print and Web Resources on Bilingual Education and Proposition 227

This list was compiled collaboratively with Betty M. Pazmiño.

Our objective was not to provide a complete list of all research available on bilingual education but rather to provide a pathfinder of sorts for any interested parties, in particular those who provide services to Latinos.

Books

August, Diane, and Kenji Hakuta, eds. 1997. *Improving schooling for language-minority children: A research agenda.* Washington, DC: National Academy Press.

Crawford, James. 1999. *Bilingual education: History, politics, theory and practice.* 4th ed. Los Angeles: Bilingual Educational Services.

Krashen, Stephen. 1999. *Condemned without a trial: Bogus arguments against bilingual education.* Portsmouth, NH: Heinemann.

———. 1996. *Under attack: The case against bilingual education.* Culver City, CA: Language Education Associates.

Professional Organizations, Research Centers, and Agency Web Links

Center for Applied Linguistics. [No copyright date given]. Available: http://www.cal.org. (Accessed June 11, 2001).

Center for Bilingual Education & Research at Arizona State University. [No copyright date given]. Available: http://www.asu.edu/educ/cber. (Accessed June 11, 2001).

Center for Latino Policy Research, UC Berkeley. [No copyright date given]. Available: http://www.clpr.berkeley.edu. (Accessed June 11, 2001).

Center for Multilingual, Multicultural Research. © 2001. Available: http://www.usc.edu/dept/education/CMMR/. (Accessed June 11, 2001).

English for the Children-Arizona. [No copyright date given]. Available: http://www.angelfire.com/az/english4thechildren. (Accessed June 11, 2001).

James Crawford's Language Policy Web Site and Emporium. ©2001. Available: http://ourworld.compuserv.com/homepages/jwcrawford. (Accessed June 11, 2001).

Joint National Committee for Languages. [No copyright date given]. Available: http://www.languagepolicy.org. (Accessed June 11, 2001).

Linguistic Minority Research Institute (LMRI). [No copyright date given]. Available: http://lmri.ucsb.edu. (Accessed June 11, 2001).

Mexican American Legal Defense and Educational Fund (MALDEF). [No copyright date given]. Available: http://www.maldef.org. (Accessed June 11, 2001).

National Association for Bilingual Education (NABE). © 2000. Available: http://www.nabe.org. (Accessed June 11, 2001).

National Clearinghouse on Bilingual Education (NCBE). [No copyright date given]. Available: http://www.ncbe.gwu.edu. (Accessed June 11, 2001).

Office of Bilingual Education and Minority Languages Affairs (OBEMLA). [No copyright date given]. Available: http://www.ed.gov/offices/OBEMLA. (Accessed June 11, 2001).

Proposition 227—English for the Children. © 1997. Available: http://www.onenation.org/index.html. (Accessed June 11, 2001).

Teachers of English to Speakers of Other Languages (TESOL). [No copyright date given]. Available: http://www.tesol.edu. (Accessed June 11, 2001).

Part 2

Latino Leadership

The Hispanic Scholarship Fund and REFORMA

Highlights from the Conference Keynote Speech

Sara Martínez Tucker

The keynote speech during the opening session of the Second REFORMA National Conference was an inspiring success story and at the same time a sobering reminder of the difficult challenges both REFORMA and the Hispanic Scholarship Fund (HSF) face in our shared goal to increase the number of Latinos earning degrees in library science.

Sara Martínez Tucker is the president and CEO of the Hispanic Scholarship Fund. A native of Laredo, Texas, she received her undergraduate degree in journalism and her master's degree in business administration from the University of Texas at Austin. Prior to joining HSF, she became the first Hispanic female to reach the executive level at AT&T. In 1998 Ms. Martínez Tucker received *Hispanic Magazine's* Heritage Achievement Award for Education. She was also included in *Hispanic Business Magazine's* 100 Most Influential Hispanics for a second consecutive year.

The HSF Story

The mission of the Hispanic Scholarship Fund (HSF) is to double the number of Hispanics earning their college degrees by 2006 and to be the premier Hispanic scholarship fund in the United States. It was founded in 1975 and its purpose is to strengthen the United States by advancing Latinos in higher education. HSF has raised more than $60 million and awarded more than 45,000 scholarships to Latino students in all fifty states and Puerto Rico. HSF scholars have majored in all disciplines and attended more than 1,300 colleges and universities across the United States.

In its original mission, HSF tracked the dollars raised and the level of scholarships awarded. The new mission is to ask whether scholarships make a difference in college retention. The 1998 evaluation revealed that 97 percent of HSF's scholars earned a bachelor's degree, 43 percent are either in graduate school or have earned their advanced degree, and 85 percent did so in five years or less. Many overcame significant financial obstacles, with 77 percent working and 66 percent relying on student loans. Forty-one percent of the scholars' fathers and 36 percent of their mothers did not graduate from high school. In one generation, we went from non-diploma to college degreed.

HSF's theme is "Opening American Minds." It utilizes public awareness campaigns, Web sites, and town hall meetings to inform potential students of its programs. Students already in college have noted by a 2-to-1 ratio that a lack of financial resources is the number one reason for dropping out. Students in high school have stated that they need more outreach efforts, information on what they need to get to college, how to apply, where they can get money, what support they will need, and what college is like. We need to tell students our stories and be visible role models.

Latinos, Higher Education, and Employment

Latinos continue to be severely underrepresented in our nation's colleges and universities. Only about half (56 percent) of our students graduate from high school, compared with 83 percent for all other students. Less than one-third (31.5 percent) of our recent high school graduates chose to go to college, compared with 45.5 percent of non-Hispanic whites; less than 11 percent of the adult Latino population has a college degree, compared with 28 percent of non-Hispanic whites.

Undereducation leads to inadequate employment, and inadequate employment leads to lower median income. Although Latinos exceed the U.S. labor participation rate of non-Hispanic whites, they are underrepresented in managerial jobs and overrepresented in "service" jobs. Although the U.S. median household income has continued to climb steadily to around $40,000, the Latino population has stayed relatively flat, at around $30,000. In 1987, Latinos earned 70 cents to the dollar and by 1996, that level had dropped to 64 cents to the dollar.

Latino families cannot afford to support their children's higher education dreams with lower median incomes. In 1980, the cost of attending a four-year public college was 39 percent of a low-income family's annual budget. In 1990, that had escalated to 50 percent, and by 2000 it was 61 percent. A private education in 2000 was unimaginable, representing 162 percent of a low-income family's budget.

HSF exists to break this cycle. Its goal is to double the rate of Hispanics earning their college degrees by 2006. A college education empowers the Latino community by preparing our population for today's jobs. More important, a college education for Latinos strengthens the United States. Businesses benefit from the increasing buying power in Latino households. Government benefits from the increased tax base. Communities benefit from stronger Latino participation and from the reduced consequences of an undereducated Latino population. Above all, everybody benefits from the development of a skilled future workforce.

Demographics

Latinos are the fastest-growing segment of the U.S. population. The population has doubled from 6 percent in 1980 to 11 percent today and is projected to be 25 percent of the U.S. population by 2040. Latinos are already a majority in many parts of the country. And we are very young: 40 percent of our population is under the age of eighteen.

Therefore, the need for HSF's work continues to escalate as our population has grown exponentially. Let's examine the class of 1996. Approximately 2 million Latinos graduated from high school and 1.3 million "dropped-out." Of the 700,000 who started college, 400,000 went to a community college. Only about 32,000 got their associate degree, and fewer than 8,000 transferred to a four-year college to join the 300,000 who started there. Ultimately, only 68,000 got their bachelor's degree. We cannot help but ask, what is the cost to this country for turning out 1.93 million Latinos ill-prepared to enter the workforce, ill-prepared to support their children's higher education?

REFORMA and HSF

As organizations, REFORMA and HSF are concerned with connecting students to our programs and their fields of interest, and we share the common goal of attracting *and* retaining Latinos in the field of library science. Because the number of Latinos in library science is so small, we need to unite to remove all roadblocks to the completion of degrees.

Since 1975 HSF has awarded only three scholarships worth $3,900 to students pursuing a library science degree, and we received only two applications in 1999–2000.

REFORMA and HSF need to ensure that applicants for the REFORMA scholarship also apply for the HSF scholarship. In our outreach efforts to Latinos in accredited schools, we need to let them know that we are both out there for them.

We can use the power of language to engage and attract students of color and gain impetus from the conference theme, "The Power of Language: Planning for the 21st Century."

Mentoring *con Ganas* (Mentoring from the Heart)

Bridging the Mentoring Gap for Latina/o Librarians

Miguel Juárez

Following is a report of a panel presentation that explored the shared experiences of Latina/o mentors and their approaches to mentoring others. Panelists, most of whom were experienced managers at major academic and public institutions, were invited to offer their personal experiences of mentoring and being mentored in their professional lives. They offered suggestions for mentoring and being mentored, including being mentored by someone other than a Latino/a mentor.

Miguel Juárez is an assistant librarian at the University of Arizona Library and at the Center for Creative Photography Library in Tucson, Arizona. He received his M.L.S. from the State University of New York, Buffalo, in 1998. In addition to articles and reviews in journals and newspapers, his publications include a chapter in *Diversity in Libraries: Academic Library Residency Programs* (Greenwood Press, in press); a chapter in *Ordinary Women, Extraordinary Lives: Women in American History* (Scholarly Resources Inc., 2000), and *Colors on Desert Walls: The Murals of El Paso* (University of Texas at El Paso Press, 1997).

In the fall of 2000, librarian Selina Gómez-Beloz was working with the Connecting Libraries and Schools Program (CLASP) at the New York Public Library. We began a mentoring relationship following her posting on the REFORMA electronic mailing list, REFORMANET. In her message, Selina stated she was in search of a mentor; I responded to her request by offering to mentor her via electronic mail.

As librarians, we typically find ourselves in predominantly white institutions. How do those of us outside the ethnic mainstream locate mentors who are sensitive to diversity and who value who we are and where we come from? How do we peer mentor when there is a lack of mentors around us? How can we create mentoring relationships with others who are different from us? Mentoring opportunities for Latina/o librarians are also limited by the dearth of Latina/os entering the profession. As a result, we often have to go out of our cultural group to locate a mentor.

From my experience mentoring Selina "electronically" came the idea for us to co-moderate a session on mentoring Latina/os at the REFORMA National Conference II, which we called "Mentoring *con Ganas* (Mentoring from the Heart): Bridging the Mentoring Gap for Latina/o Librarians." We invited as speakers seasoned and high-level Latina/o librarians who were all past presidents of REFORMA. Our panelists included Dr. Camila Alire, Dean of Libraries at Colorado State University; Martín Gómez, Executive Director of the Brooklyn Public Library; Al J. Milo, Director of the Fullerton Public Library; Sandra Ríos Balderrama, Diversity Officer for the American Library Association; and Edward Erazo, Head of Reference at Florida Atlantic University.

Panel members explored the elements needed to mentor Latina/os in public and academic libraries. We asked them to address the following questions: Why is mentoring necessary? How do new and junior librarians find a mentor? What are your experiences with formal versus informal mentoring? What are the challenges for mentors? What are the challenges for those being mentored? What is the role of coaching in the mentoring mix? What are some alternate forms of working with a mentor? What is expected in the mentor/mentee relationship? How have various REFORMA chapters organized projects for mentoring librarians?

The panelists discussed the experiences they had with mentoring in their careers and work. Al Milo has been involved with two formal mentoring programs, with the UCLA Department of Information Studies and the San Jose State University School of Library & Information Science program in Southern California. Milo recounted how the Orange County Chapter of REFORMA, along with librarians Ron Rodriguez and Susan Luévano-Molina, approached the dean of UCLA's Department of Information Studies and created a program called "Escalera" Mentoring Program. Milo said the program had a three-fold purpose: 1) to recruit and retain students in the library profession, 2) to match mentors and protégés, and 3) to develop programs on a variety of issues such as management and how to do interviews. The program included a steering committee. To document the program, Sandra Tauler, a UCLA student, wrote a manual as her MLS thesis, *REFORMA/UCLA Mentor Program: A Mentoring Manual.*[1]

This program was successful for several years and continued throughout the terms of subsequent deans. When the UCLA program came to an end, Milo and the Orange County Reformistas developed a subsequent program with the San Jose State University School of Library & Information Science in Fullerton. The second mentoring program, called the "Meta-program," was aimed at potential library science students.

Reformistas formed a steering committee to shape the program and created a brochure to market and promote it. They also collected student profiles, designated students as "protégés" and assigned librarians to act as "mentors." Milo cited a key ingredient to the program's success: "There was also involvement from the library school and not only from REFORMA." Milo emphasized the importance of involving the library schools to ensure that "it would not be only us talking to ourselves." In addition to the mentoring program, Milo said, Reformistas developed special workshops and presentations for students to augment their experiences. He said it was important to have students look beyond their first jobs and envision themselves in future positions of leadership as librarians.

Dr. Camila Alire has been involved heavily in both formal and informal mentoring. Before becoming a member of REFORMA, she designed a mentoring program for all library minority staff in her state (for paraprofessional as well as professional staff). Dr. Alire said she did not create a program from scratch, but used the Southern California program developed by Al Milo and others as a base to tailor the Colorado program. Most recently, Dr. Alire designed a formal national mentoring program as part of the REFORMA Education Committee, which was used as a model for the American Library Association's Spectrum Scholarship program.

Dr. Alire stated that mentoring is extremely important. "I see a mentor passing a gift to the protégé—a gift of experience, a gift of wisdom, knowing when you've made a mistake and being able to get past that." Dr. Alire said she herself was a recipient of mentoring (although not from a formal mentoring program). She cited three mentors early in her career, and it was these experiences that allowed her to "fast track" into the profession.

Mentoring is also necessary in our profession, said Dr. Alire, "because we need to change the demographics of our profession." The profession needs to retain Latinos in libraries, encourage paraprofessionals to become professional librarians and, if they are librarians and they have the *ganas* (will), "it's our professional obligation to mentor these individuals and change the demographics in the leadership."

For Sandra Ríos Balderrama a key to successful mentoring is the personal relationship and rapport that is established and that is so important in this time and age. Mentoring is reciprocal, and mentors and mentees must have something to offer each other. It is also important, Balderrama noted, to have many different types of mentors in one's life. "At times, it is important to have someone from what you define as your community—that may mean that that person is a Latino, a woman, or it may mean someone of the same sexual orientation. At other times it's important to cross over, to discover a mentor who is the most different from who you are because often you will learn from someone who you least expect to learn from."

Balderrama further stated that to secure a mentor it is important to attend conferences, such as this REFORMA National Conference, and observe and take note of who excites you. She recommended seeking individuals with whom you "click" or those from whom you would like to learn. People are usually agreeable to mentoring, but you must decide what you want from this mentor. Balderrama sees mentoring as an open, two-way, reciprocal learning process. She encouraged mentees not to enter mentoring relationships with predetermined judgments and to keep in mind that the mentoring process is one of exchanging opinions and advice. It is based on the experience of what "has gone well and what has bombed." There is a tendency in the Latino culture, said Balderrama, not to accept constructive criticism and good coaching. But as mentors and mentees, "we have to be conscious of where people are with accepting that level of constructive critique."

Ten years ago, after graduating from the University of Arizona, Ed Erazo attended his first ALA and REFORMA conferences, and it was at these meetings that he met his mentors. These individuals encouraged his involvement in committee work.

In Erazo's experience, formal mentoring provides an accelerated track for those new to the profession. Mentors, however, may not have much time to mentor. Although they may be willing, mentors are often very busy people. E-mail now provides a useful mentoring vehicle for mentors with heavy schedules. E-mail mentoring doesn't have to involve lengthy correspondence, but it must be consistent. Erazo believes that by helping someone's career along, mentors get a sense of giving something back to the profession.

Martín Gómez stated that his approach to mentoring is more informal than formal. For him, mentoring is important because it helps to develop the potential in people, both in those who are mentored and in those they see as mentors. It is important to have mentoring as part of your personal vision. It is also important to align your mentoring goals with your mentees' realization of their careers. Having a mentor, said Gómez, is necessary for demographic reasons as well. His mentors, for example, have helped him acculturate to what is a very white community. They have made it possible for him to learn the different mindsets, rules, and expectations.

Furthermore, Gómez said, mentoring helps one's chances for success, improves the sense of community and belonging, and helps to create a network. And, he said, "it helps you to benefit from your mentor's experience." But where can one find mentors? Gómez offered several suggestions. First, you should attend organizational conferences where you will see, hear, and meet people who offer some spark or chemistry and where you can speak to them on a more personal level. Second, look at the library literature. Third, mentees should be "willing to be found."

What should you look for in a prospective mentor? Gómez recommended looking for mentors who have some common values, whether they are cultural or professional, or perhaps someone you just admire for the way he or she speaks or what he or she has presented on a certain topic.

There are some deterrents to mentoring, and Gómez cited some. Time and availability are prime deterrents. Where there may be an appearance of a conflict is another. For example, a mentoring relationship between members of the opposite sex may deter a prospective mentor. Another situation that can impede successful mentoring is being mentored by someone in the same chain of command, as in the case of a branch manager being mentored by the director of the library system.

Gómez said the mentor should be clear about the relationship and its goal. The relationship should be based on honesty and a sense of ethics. It's important that people being mentored understand their own strengths and weaknesses and recognize the strengths and weaknesses of their mentors as well. We all have baggage, and it's important to know what one is getting into before starting a mentoring relationship. Gómez stated that it is important to have a network of mentors and not to "hang your star on one mentor" and also to know when mentoring is working and when it is not. He said that it might be easy for someone new to the profession to get attached to one person, but this is not healthy. You need "to know when it's time to create some space for you and the person who's mentoring you." Gómez cautioned against putting mentors in awkward positions, such as expecting mentors to create or provide a position or a promotion. People need to maintain some perspective in mentoring relationships; one must not mistake friendship for mentoring nor mentoring for friendship. Sometimes they overlap, and sometimes they don't.

Following the individual presentations, the panel took questions from the audience. One of the questions was: How do you find mentors in predominantly white institutions? Dr. Alire gave a thoughtful answer. She said that a mentor does not have to be Latino or Latina. It's great if you can find one "but you may be in a situation where there are no other Latinos in that organization. I'm also convinced that our white colleagues can serve as successful mentors no matter the situation. In every organization, in my experience, there have been white colleagues and administrators who have been extremely sensitive to cultural differences and to the need for recruiting and in wanting to retain their minority librarians in the academic environment." How they relate to other people is what is important when looking at potential mentors. But when Latina/o mentors can be found, relationships are fruitful, Dr. Alire said, "because we're all great role models for each other and for other minority librarians in our profession."

Another question posed to panel members was: What is the definition of a mentor, and what skills are needed to be an effective mentor? Gómez said he saw a mentor as someone who "realizes a person's potential, and mentoring is a process of trying to help them realize their potential." Dr. Alire stated that the skills vary: "The mentoring role is very informal and the relationship usually takes the form of conversations and e-mail. What is most important is that there be the desire or *ganas* to want to mentor, and not even know that you're doing it, and the *ganas* to want to be mentored." Mentoring is a win-win situation. "I give and I give back, it's good and it's the right and professional thing to do."

The "Mentoring *Con Ganas*" panel proved to be an insightful, educational and inspirational experience for both the panel and audience members. It helped to demystify the mentoring process and bring it to a level to which people could relate. It gave experienced librarians and directors an opportunity to share their successes in establishing mentoring relationships and the effects they had. It also made it possible to continue discussion on this much-needed topic for Latina/o librarians and those who will work with them.

Notes

1.   *REFORMA/UCLA Mentor Program: A Mentoring Manual*, by Sandra Tauler, UCLA, 1989. Available as an ERIC Document. The program was established to help recruit bilingual-bicultural students into the library profession. One-to-one matching of prospective/current library school students with professional bilingual-bicultural librarians is the basis for the program. Besides acting as a support system, the program offers educational experiences and provides a forum for professional networking. Approximately eighteen mentor/mentee relationships were initially established in the program, and mentees who graduated from the program became mentors themselves. The program was designed to serve as a training guide for participants and as a model for the development of similar programs. The manual 1) provides background on the school and the program, 2) outlines the roles and responsibilities of both mentors and mentees, 3) offers guidelines for coordinating a mentor program, and 4) presents the program's activities since its inception.

The Future for Latinos in Library Education

A Panel Presentation

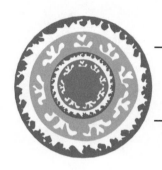

Loriene Roy[1] ✦ *Clara Chu*
Ann O'Neill ✦ *Carla Stoffle*
Elaine Yontz

Leaders in library and information science education gathered at the REFORMA Second National Conference to discuss strategies for how information professionals, professional organizations, and library and information science (LIS) schools might cooperate to create more diverse library school programs and student bodies. Key among the suggestions were involvement in the accreditation process and participating in LIS programs as instructors, recruiters, and advisory board members. Panelists highlighted several exemplary programs. Dr. Loriene Roy moderated the panel. Panelists included: Dr. Clara Chu (Associate Professor, Department of Information Studies, UCLA), Dr. Ann O'Neill (Director of the Office for Accreditation at the American Library Association), Carla Stoffle (Dean of the University Library at the University of Arizona and Acting Director of the School of Information Resources & Library Science), and Dr. Elaine Yontz (Assistant Professor at the School of Library and Information Science at the University of South Florida). Dr. Loriene Roy (Professor in the Graduate School of Library and Information Science at the University of Texas at Austin) moderated the session.

Loriene Roy is Professor in the Graduate School of Library and Information Science at the University of Texas at Austin. She is the Director of "If I Can Read, I Can Do Anything," a program promoting reading at schools on reservations. Her other research involves creating a National Virtual Museum of the American Indian, conducting a study of Spectrum Initiative scholars for the American Library Association, and co-developing an intelligent agent for making book recommendations.

The American Library Association (ALA) identifies diversity in education and continuous learning as two of its five key action areas. The Spectrum Initiative, a program to provide scholarships to students from underrepresented groups, exemplifies ALA's commitment to diversity. Similarly, the Association for Library and Information Science Education (ALISE) has identified increasing diversity in LIS education as a goal for LIS education. The establishment of its Multicultural, Ethnic, and Humanistic Concerns Special Interest Group reflects this concern. In spite of these efforts, we are reminded that LIS education continues to lag behind in diversity efforts (McCook and Lippincott 1997).

At the REFORMA Second National Conference in Tucson a panel of individuals assembled to discuss the future of Latinos in library education. Panelists were selected based on their demonstrated commitment to addressing the educational needs of individuals who come from underrepresented backgrounds or who want to serve multicultural populations. The panelists' discussion, summarized below, provides ideas on how individuals, LIS schools, and professional associations can help further the goals of educating Latinos in the library and information science professions.

How Individuals Can Contribute to Diversity in LIS Education

The panelists identified several strategies that information professionals could employ to become more involved in local LIS schools and their programs. Chu, O'Neill, and Stoffle recommended that information professionals of color volunteer to mentor students. They also noted that LIS programs often seek people to teach courses. Chu advised librarians from underrepresented ethnic backgrounds interested in teaching to submit a resume indicating their areas of expertise and identifying specific courses they would like to teach. Stoffle asked that professionals unable to commit to designing and teaching an entire course consider volunteering as a guest speaker or help identify good speakers who can help LIS environments be more hospitable to students of color.

Stoffle reminded LIS professionals of their responsibility to assist in recruitment of new librarians of color by identifying prospective students and encouraging them to apply for admissions and financial aid. Chu and Stoffle stressed the need for practitioners to work toward providing LIS students with information about available financial support. As acting dean of an LIS program, Stoffle has heard from practitioners in varied work settings that they consider it a very high priority that the University of Arizona turn out a diverse workforce. Their request implies shared mutual responsibility among employers and LIS schools. Practitioners must be willing to assist their employees through tuition reimbursement and/or paid leave time. She identified two potentially productive recruitment communities: student workers in libraries and undergraduate Gates Millennium Scholars.

O'Neill commented that her office frequently hears from LIS students who want to see diverse people on the faculty, advisory boards, and external review panels. She also outlined how individuals could participate in the accreditation process by serving as members of external review panels. Members of panels travel to the LIS schools, review them, and write reports for the Committee on Accreditation. The Committee needs up to sixty panelists annually. Each six-member review panel visits one of ten LIS master's degree programs scheduled for review. Panels usually include three educators and three practitioners and usually have one member who has not previously served as a panelist. The schools can request panelists with special subject expertise. Chu added that the ability to speak and/or read Spanish was a desirable skill for some site visits. O'Neill pointed out that even though her target is to increase the diversity of the panelist pool, the proportion of people of color on the panels is still very small. She aims also to make training more accessible by providing more flexible training opportunities, including Web-based training on the office's Web page (http://www.ala.org/alaorg/oa/) and training scheduled as preconferences to local or regional professional conferences. Roy pointed out that alumni of schools also have the opportunity to assist in the preparation of an LIS school's self-study report, which is required for the accreditation process.

A Call for LIS Association Involvement in LIS Education Programs

Ethnic organizations can be involved in socializing students into the profession. LIS schools are logical forums for ethnic library associations. Chu described how representatives of organizations at UCLA provide short presentations and staff information booths at new student orientation. LIS programs can also encourage students to form student chapters of national associations.

Ethnic organizations can also be involved in program planning, design, and policy making. At UCLA, REFORMA members offered suggestions for curriculum changes. Stoffle saw a role for REFORMA to be a force in the development of standards for ALA and for the LIS schools. O'Neill noted that individuals and their organizations can encourage LIS schools to develop equity programs and plans to achieve diversity. Chu and Stoffle stressed that LIS schools should have diverse advisory boards. Panelists commended REFORMA on the establishment of the Library School Excellence Award, which they saw as an effective incentive for LIS schools to be involved in Latino librarian education.

How LIS Programs Might Become More Diverse

Roy cited a recent article by Jane B. Robbins that stated, "there is little evidence in External Review Panel (ERP) reports [of accreditation visits] that [LIS] schools have developed equity programs and action plans to achieve diversity" (Robbins 2000). Chu noted that this statement concurred with results of a study she conducted in 1993; representatives from forty-eight of seventy-two accredited and non-accredited LIS programs supplied her with data (Chu 1994). She found that although schools voiced support for diversity, they expressed this support as a general philosophy and not as a detailed plan for action. Chu suggested that LIS programs might make progress in diversity efforts incrementally. She felt that action plans did not need to be sweeping or include multiple components of a program but instead could make progress in a piecemeal fashion. Stoffle, on the other hand, advocated programs with fully developed equity plans so that a critical mass of students would enroll at one time.

O'Neill disagreed slightly with Robbins's statement. She observed that some schools, including the GSLIS at the University of Rhode Island and the GSLIS at the University of Texas at Austin, were setting up aggressive diversity programs. She agreed with Chu that diversity was reflected in the schools' philosophies and that strong programs may be particularly dependent on the philosophy of the dean or director of the school and the commitment of the faculty. She warned that schools in areas with diverse populations did not necessarily have aggressive diversity programs, whereas schools located within less ethnically diverse populations might have stronger diversity efforts. She reminded the audience to encourage, reward, and publicize the efforts of smaller LIS schools, such as those at the University of South Florida and the University of South Carolina, that engage in interesting and noteworthy diversity efforts.

Stoffle indicated that she did not see much evidence of active recruiting on the part of the schools. Nor did she witness many efforts to build diversity in the curriculum and in the student body. She identified several schools she thought had stronger reputations for encouraging diversity than most: the University of Texas, the University of Rhode Island, and the University of Pittsburgh.

LIS schools may also need to provide more options for employed library workers to pursue advanced degrees. Stoffle indicated that her school volunteers to design special courses to meet the needs of practitioners and to offer the classes on site, away from the main campus in Tucson.

Another way that LIS schools could meet the needs of students interested in serving diverse clientele is to provide flexible programs. The School of Information Resources and Library Science at the University of Arizona now requires LIS students to take coursework in other disciplines. Representatives of the LIS schools at UCLA, South Florida, the University of Texas at Austin, the

University of Illinois, and Dominican University all indicated that they provided flexible options for students to enroll in coursework across departments. Some LIS schools, including UCLA and the University of Texas at Austin, offer joint-degree arrangements with other departments. The University of Arizona program also encourages students to engage in more field experiences and internships. Their students may soon be able to receive certifications in specialized areas.

Roy added that schools with reputations for supporting diversity should not rest on their reputations but instead continue to develop strong and innovative plans. She pointed out the need for coordinated efforts among LIS schools. Several panelists and audience members offered suggestions and examples of such collaborations. Chu suggested that LIS programs might investigate how to collaborate to provide a national certification program that would permit students to take courses from different LIS programs to earn specializations, including a specialization in Latino librarianship. Representatives from Dominican University and the University of Illinois described their collaborative effort to attend career days together at universities in the Chicago area. A librarian from the University of Michigan relayed how her LIS school has learned successful recruitment strategies from a school of social work. A representative of the Institute of Museum and Library Services challenged the LIS representatives to consider writing a National Leadership Grant application that would provide funding to support collaborative efforts. The University of Illinois representative suggested that a future collaboration could partner LIS schools with public libraries willing to offer college undergraduates with paid summer internship opportunities and mentoring by LIS professionals.

Several panelists focused on models of practice currently employed at LIS schools. Chu shared how UCLA's school expresses its support for cultural diversity and social justice through diversity recruitment and mentoring. They coordinate their efforts with the School of Library and Information Science at San Jose State University, assisting potential students through the application process. These efforts resulted from a campus diversity summit and now are formalized through the establishment of a number of committees focusing on diversity in faculty recruitment, student recruitment and retention, and curriculum. Roy briefly mentioned that Texas students are integral participants in "If I Can Read, I Can Do Anything," a reading promotion program for schools on reservations.

Yontz summarized some of the successful endeavors at the University of South Florida. It offers distance education through on-site courses away from the South Florida campus and through Web-delivered classes. The university established the Miami cohort program with the Miami-Dade County School Board and the Miami-Dade Teacher's Union. This program provided prospective school media specialists with tuition and on-site and Web-based instruction. The

LIS school also has an initiative to help new librarians serve migrant families. In addition, the school recruits students through undergraduate service courses.

Summary

There is much work to be done to create a representative workforce. This goal will require efforts involving multiple partners employing various strategies. We have many strengths on which to rely. O'Neill echoed the sentiments of many: "I would say that all of the programs care about the profession. And I think that in most, a vast majority of the faculty care about the profession" (Chu et al. 2000). Expressing guarded optimism, Chu cited cooperation as the key to progress:

I think the success of trying to address multicultural education, whether it's serving one particular group or a diverse group, is to work together; to rely on each other in terms of the different library and information science programs; to talk about what kinds of things we can do collaboratively; or to build on each other's successes and to work with the professional community. Without that, I think that the efforts will require a lot more resources than any one program has available. (Chu et al. 2000)

Notes

1.   I wish to acknowledge Antony Cherian's careful editing of the transcript of the panel session. He vastly improved the manuscript.

References

Chu, Clara. 1994. Education for multicultural librarianship. In *Multiculturalism in libraries,* edited by Ruhig Du Mont, Rosemary, Lois Buttlar, and William Caynon. Westport, CT: Greenwood.

Chu, Clara, Anne O'Neill, Loriene Roy, Carla Stoffle, and Elaine Yontz. 2000. The future for Latinos in library education. Panel presented at the REFORMA Second National Conference, August 4, in Tucson, Arizona.

McCook, Kathleen de la Pena, and Kate Lippincott. 1997. Library schools and diversity: Who makes the grade? *Library Journal* 122 (April 15): 30–32.

Robbins, Jane. B. 2000. Library and information studies education: Diversity/equity, *Prism* 8 (2) (Summer): 6–7.

Developing Female Leadership

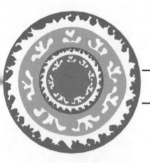

Jacqueline Ayala

This chapter captures the warmth and openness of a panel presented at the REFORMA National Conference. Focusing on what it means to be a female leader in a national organization and also to lead a dynamic organization such as REFORMA, the panel participants were very willing to share their experiences, observations, and advice. The author also gives us a glimpse into the process of planning a panel with such accomplished and engaging participants. A selective bibliography on women and leadership compiled by Ronald L. Baza is included.

Jacqueline Ayala is an information specialist at the law firm of Christensen, Miller, Fink, Jacobs, Glaser, Weil & Shapiro, L.L.P. in Century City, California, where she manages the Library Services Department. Ms. Ayala received her B.A. in Chicano Studies from Loyola Marymount University and her M.L.I.S. from the University of California at Berkeley. She served as REFORMA National President from 1998 to 1999 and is a proud member of the Los Angeles chapter.

All Ethnic Caucuses of the American Library Association have male and female leaders, but the easiest leadership role to identify is the office of president. As an elected officer, the president of an organization is a figurehead who also serves as the spokesperson for the membership that voted her or him into that office. As we discussed possible programs to present at the Second National REFORMA Conference, Sandra Ríos Balderrama and I thought of a panel that would showcase female presidents of color. Official and unofficial mentors, officers and non-officers, men and women came to mind as we hoped to recruit a panel of individuals who could enlighten us with their experiences and provide the substance of a program that all would find beneficial. We agreed that there was a host of female leadership within the ranks of REFORMA. The presidents of female gender were Susan Luévano-Molina, Elena Tscherny, Elizabeth Rodríguez Miller, Ingrid Betancourt, Rhonda Ríos Kravitz, Camila Alire, Gilda Baeza Ortego, Judith Castiano, Sandra Ríos Balderrama, Jacqueline Ayala, Toni Bissessar, and Oralia Garza de Cortés.

We decided to concentrate on the past and the future of female leadership within our organization. For our panelists, we would draw on a pool of past national presidents of REFORMA. Very graciously, Sandra agreed to be a panelist while I accepted the role of moderator.

Next, we felt that some empirical research on the topic of female leadership, and specifically Latina leadership, should be included. Ron Baza, a doctoral student, came to mind as a resource. He was enthusiastic about participating in the conference and particularly in a program on female leadership. Ron was particularly interested because he had conducted a research project the previous year on REFORMA's past and present leadership development capacities.

We then wrote a working description of the program:

> Designed to acknowledge the past and present contributions of female librarians in REFORMA's growth and development. REFORMA past presidents will reflect upon first hand experiences of mentoring, nurturing and leading in REFORMA. Historical perspectives and future aspirations of key Reformistas will be highlighted. Models, concepts, and competencies of female leadership will be commented on and discussed by panel participants and presenters.

We wanted the panel to include individuals from various geographical regions and ethnic backgrounds, as well as represent REFORMA's twenty-nine-year existence. Luis Herrera (Los Angeles Chapter), Ingrid Betancourt (Northeast Chapter), and Judith Castiano (LIBROS Chapter–San Diego, CA), along with Sandra (ALA Diversity Officer, Chicago) and Ron Baza, completed the panel. An abstract paper by Susan Luévano-Molina (Orange County Chapter-CA), the first female president (1985–1986), entitled "Following the Leader," was made available at the program. (Ms. Luévano-Molina had declined to be on the panel because she was unable to attend the conference.) The panelists were to limit their remarks to no more than ten minutes due to time constraints. With so much collective insight the participants told a tremendous story.

Luis Herrera (Term: 1982–1983)

Luis offered the unique perspective of a past male president. He spoke about the perception that the leadership of the organization was primarily male during the first decade, and he acknowledged that the organization still had a long way to go as far as being inclusive—not just in the sense of gender. There was a struggle for the organization to gain recognition and there was an emphasis on peer networking. Al Milo provided Luis with key support as vice-president, and Al's transition from vice-president to president went smoothly. Luis believes that there is a core value of REFORMA that views participation and involvement as important for both the individual and the organization. REFORMA can give the individual a personal and professional training ground, and in turn the individual's volunteerism strengthens the organization. Luis credited the female leadership of REFORMA with specific leadership traits such as strong organizational skills, attention to detail, the ability to formalize structure, and a support system based on *la familia*. Sharing with us how he has benefited from mentoring, including learning a great deal from those he mentors, Luis accepts the fact that leading is a lifelong endeavor. He gave great praise to the Spectrum Scholarship Initiative of ALA for its emphasis on training. Luis mentioned a leadership development training proposal within REFORMA that has not yet materialized. As challenges for the future, he gave high priority to instilling the core value and recruiting leaders from an incredible pool of talent. He is grateful for his individual accomplishments but realizes that he has learned to acknowledge the potential within himself largely because his colleagues in REFORMA have encouraged him.

Ingrid Betancourt (Term: 1988–1989)

Ingrid began her talk by sharing some statistics with the audience. In the almost thirty years of REFORMA, twenty-six presidents have served. For the first fourteen years these presidents were exclusively male. Beginning with Susan Luévano-Molina in 1985, twelve female presidents have been elected. Ingrid was elected in 1988; she was the second East Coaster, the fourteenth person and fourth female to be elected to a developing national organization's leadership. During the time she served as president, REFORMA's role was one of advocacy, which was at the time necessary in ALA and on the state level in those states where Reformistas resided. Organizational issues included the dues structure (both national and chapter), a national agenda, and growth. Chapters had organized throughout the country and there was a growing concern about disenfranchisement. Ingrid felt that Latinas in many organizations are initially hesitant to assume powerful positions, but once they are reassured, these same women square their shoulders and lead boldly. Ingrid had questioned her own abilities but found strength in her wealth of experience and network of friends. She was a founding member of the Northeast Chapter, where she served as treasurer, and she felt that the women who preceded her as national REFORMA presidents influenced her the most as she became a leader. Ingrid marveled at Elena Tscherny's skills and energy and at Liz Rodriguez Miller's ability to keep countless balls in the air and maintain open lines of communication. Ingrid underscored the importance of direct and indirect peer mentoring. As we bring newcomers to our events and functions, she suggested, we also entrust them with the future of our organization. She believes that leadership training must be implemented at the chapter level. Her advice to us is that clarity of vision and focus are priceless. Her hope for REFORMA lies within the commitment, drive, and passion that she and others have modeled for their successors.

Judith Castiano (Term: 1995–1996)

Judith is the first non-Latina to be elected by the membership to the presidency. She belongs to the Laguna Pueblo Tribe, which is located in New Mexico. She confessed that she didn't think that she was going to win the election and, once she did, she wondered why she had agreed to run in the first place. It was Camila Alire, one of her mentors, who convinced her that REFORMA was inclusive and accepting of anyone who wished to further the collective goal of service to the underserved. Judith's initial experience with REFORMA was with the LIBROS San Diego (CA) Chapter, where she served in various offices, including president. She had heard wonderful stories of REFORMA and its unusual ability to recruit leaders, especially female leaders. She found that once a potential volunteer was identified, that person was taken under the wing of mentors and at the same time challenged to grow. Mentors strongly encouraged involvement in other organizations such as state library associations, PLA, and ALA so that an impact could be made both in REFORMA and outside REFORMA. Reflecting on her leadership experience, Judith said that she began learning management skills when she was put in charge of her younger siblings. She learned to mediate and impose a semblance of order. Later, she was formally educated as a National Urban Fellow to develop her problem-solving skills. Two of the mentors who played a critical part in her development were Luis Herrera and Al Milo. She expressed thanks to them and others for the interest they took in her and for their unfailing support. Judith sees the organization as being in the forefront of similar organizations and acknowledges that there is awesome potential in our ranks among both females and males. She advises that as we mentor we make sure that we are willing to give support, technical expertise, or a shoulder to cry on as the situation demands. Our organization is growing and getting better, and its strengths are inclusiveness and the passion of its members. She is grateful for the opportunities REFORMA has provided and she has much hope for not only the organization but the future of our profession.

Sandra Ríos Balderrama (Term: 1997–1998)

Sandra applauded her colleagues for the road that they paved in REFORMA. She credits her grandmother and mother for advice that made her a strong Latina and a strong feminist. When she was first approached in the 1980s to be a leader in REFORMA she felt such a patronizing attitude from the person who promised to groom her that she lost interest. However, she was impressed favorably by Ingrid Betancourt and Rhonda Ríos Kravitz and their welcoming manner, *su manera de ser*. Later in the 1990s, when she received a call from Judith Castiano and Luis Herrera asking her to run for president, she was courageous *and* she was ready. They told her that if she decided to run she would not be alone. Sandra felt that it was an honor just to be on the ballot, and if she were the successful candidate she would have an incredible opportunity and platform for female leadership. Our collective experience in the presidency of REFORMA, she said, allows those of us who have served to package political, coalition-building, and communication skills and transfer them to our work arenas, be they corporate, academic, or public library and non-library settings. We celebrate the gender diversity that exists in REFORMA and thrive on it. The significance of inclusiveness and representation in REFORMA is that we are accepted with equity. We must always be careful not to recreate the discrimination we fought so hard against. Sandra felt that her presidential term was a turning point for REFORMA because it was a time when we were diverse regionally, culturally, and in gender and were striving for inclusiveness. During her term, there were retirements of a long-time treasurer and the newsletter editor. The Orange County Chapter continued the momentum from the first national conference and provided REFORMA with an electronic business card via the World Wide Web. Sandra felt it necessary to have increased participation by the constituents in the leadership of the organization. She did a lot of recruiting and made very strategic appointments. It might be just good business sense, or perhaps it has something to do with inherent female traits, she said, but our leadership has had the ability to pass on information and make important connections that have allowed smooth successions from herself to Jacqueline Ayala to Toni Bissessar to Oralia Garza de Cortés and to Susana Hinojosa. This is a key practice that needs to be continuously cultivated.

Ron Baza

Ron Baza is a doctoral candidate in Leadership Studies and Administration at the University of San Diego and currently a human resources management consultant and practitioner. He reported on the preliminary results of a pioneer leadership research project he conducted in the spring of 1999 under the auspices of national REFORMA and the University of San Diego. Ron identified a number of common leadership themes and issues that emerged from his videotaped interviews with seventeen female and male REFORMA leaders, past and present. Ron concluded his presentation by providing a cursory overview of various leadership competencies and qualities from selected scholarly surveys and sharing brief profiles of prominent national and international female leadership role models. [In the next chapter of this book, Ron discusses the outcomes of his groundbreaking research.]

Author's Note

I would like to thank our distinguished and accomplished panelists for participating in this program. You are to be commended for the tremendous amount of work that you so graciously volunteered (and continue to volunteer) to REFORMA. Additionally, I acknowledge the work of the Program Committee of the REFORMA National Conference, the moral support, and invaluable behind-the-scenes assistance of Jean Marie Ayala and Jo Ann Ayala. *¡Que Dios las bendiga siempre!* Finally, I wish to thank REFORMA itself for inspiring those of us who have served so faithfully to continue the momentum by sharing the power of *our* language and *our* experience with one another.

Selective Bibliography on Leadership and Female Leaders

Compiled by Ronald L. Baza

Books

Astin, Helen S., and Carole Leland. 1999. *Women of influence, women of vision: A cross-generational study of leaders and social change.* San Francisco: Jossey-Bass.

Block, Peter. 1993. *Stewardship: Choosing service over self interest.* San Francisco: Berrett-Koehler.

Bonilla-Santiago, Gloria. 1993. *Breaking ground and barriers: Hispanic women developing effective leadership.* San Diego: Marin.

Bruhns, Karen Olsen. 1999. *Women in ancient America.* Norman: University of Oklahoma Press.

Brunner, C. Cryss. 1999. *Sacred dreams: Women and the superintendency.* Albany: State University of New York.

Cantor, Dorothy W., and Toni Bernay. 1992. *Women in power: The secrets of leadership.* Boston: Houghton Mifflin.

Chipman, Donald E. 1999. *Notable men and women of Spanish Texas.* Austin: University of Texas Press.

Collins, Nancy W., Susan K. Gilbert, and Susan H. Nycum. 1988. *Women leading.* Lexington, MA: Stephen Greene Press.

De La Pena McCook, Kathleen. 1998. *Women of color in librarianship: An oral history.* Chicago: American Library Association.

Dunlap, Diane M., and Patricia A. Schmuck. 1995. *Women leading education.* Albany: State University and New York Press.

Enkelis, Liane, and Karen Olsen. 1995. *On our own terms: Portraits of women business leaders.* San Francisco: Berrett-Koehler.

Frick, Don M., and Larry C. Spears. 1996. *On becoming a servant-leader: The private writings of Robert K. Greenleaf.* San Francisco: Jossey-Bass.

Garcia, Mario T. 1989. *Mexican Americans: Leadership, ideology, & identity, 1930–1960.* New Haven, CT: Yale University Press.

Gardner, Howard, and Emma Laskin. 1995. *Leading minds: An anatomy of leadership.* New York: Basic Books.

Gilligan, Carol. 1983. *In a different voice.* Cambridge, MA: Harvard University Press.

Heifetz, Ronald A. 1994. *Leadership without easy answers.* Cambridge: Belknap Press.

Helgesen, Sally. 1990. *The female advantage: Women's ways of leadership.* New York: Doubleday/Currency.

———. 1995. *The web of inclusion: A new architecture for building great organizations.* New York: Currency/Doubleday.

Hesselbein, Frances, Marshall Goldsmith, and Richard Beckhard. 1996. *The leader of the future: New visions, strategies, and practices for the next era.* San Francisco: Jossey-Bass.

Jamieson, Kathleen Hall. 1995. *Beyond the double bind: Women and leadership.* New York: Oxford University Press.

Kostner, Jaclyn. 1996. *Virtual leadership.* New York: Warner Books.

Kouves, James M., and Barry K. Posner. 1995. *The leadership challenge: How to keep getting extraordinary things done in organizations.* San Francisco: Jossey-Bass.

Lipmen-Blumen, Jean. 1996. *The connective edge: Leading in an interdependent world.* San Francisco: Jossey-Bass.

———. 1999. *Connective leadership: Managing in a changing world.* New York: Oxford University Press.

Luke, Jeffrey S. 1998. *Catalytic leadership: Strategies for an interconnected world.* San Francisco: Jossey-Bass.

Marshall, Judi. 1984. *Women managers.* New York: John Wiley.

Miller, Jean Baker. 1986. *Toward a new psychology of women.* Boston: Beacon Press.

Morrison, Ann M. 1992. *The new leaders.* San Francisco: Jossey-Bass.

Pearson, Carol S. 1991. *Awakening the heroes within: Twelve archetypes to help us find ourselves and transform our world.* New York: HarperCollins.

Powell, Gary N. 1993. *Women and men in management.* Newbury Park, CA: Sage.

Rodriguez, Victoria E. 1998. *Women's participation in Mexican political life.* Boulder, CO: Westview Press.

Rosen, Robert. 2000. *Global literacies: Lessons on business leadership and national cultures: A landmark study of CEOs from 28 countries.* New York: Simon & Schuster.

Senge, Peter M. 1994. *The fifth discipline: The art and practice of the learning organization.* New York: Doubleday/Currency.

Book Chapters

Avilio, Bruce J. 1988. Developing transformational leaders: A life span approach. In *Charismatic leadership*, 276. San Francisco: Jossey-Bass.

Conger, Jay A., and Rabindra N. Kanungo. 1988. Conclusion: Patterns and trends in studying charismatic leadership. In *Charismatic leadership*, 324. San Francisco: Jossey-Bass.

De Pree, Max. 1993. Followership. In *Contemporary issues in leadership*, edited by William E. Rosenbach and Robert L. Taylor, 137. Boulder, CO: Westview Press.

Kanter, Rosabeth Moss. 1975. Women and the structure of organizations: Explorations in theory and behavior. In *Another voice: Feminist perspectives on social life and social science*, 382. Garden City, NY: Anchor Books.

Miller, Jean Baker. 1991. The development of women's sense of self. In *Women's growth in connection: Writings from the Stone Center*, 11. New York: Guilford Press.

Rosenbach, William E. 1993. "Mentoring: Empowering followers to be leaders." In *Contemporary issues in leadership*, edited by William E. Rosenbach and Robert L. Taylor, 141. Boulder, CO: Westview Press.

Journal Articles

Bennis, Warren. 1999. The leadership advantage. *Leader to Leader* 12 (Spring): 18.

Bordas, Juana. 1999. Latino leadership: Moving into the future. *Selected Proceedings 1999 Annual Meeting International Leadership Association,* 31.

Conger, Jay. 1999. The new age of persuasion. *Leader to Leader* 12 (Spring): 37.

Hunt, Michele. 1999. Leading with vision and values. *Leader to Leader* 12 (Spring): 11.

Langone, Christine A. 1999. Search and evaluation strategies for effective use of World Wide Web in leadership education. *The Journal of Leadership Studies* 6 (3/4): 110.

Lipmen-Blumen, Jean. 1999. Connective leadership: Leading in a new era. *Selected proceedings 1999 annual meeting International Leadership Association,* 10.

Rosen, Robert H. 1999. Global leaders, world class companies, and national cultures. *Selected proceedings 1999 annual meeting International Leadership Association,* 16.

Sachs, Stephen M. 1998. LaDonna Harris, founder of Americans for Indian Opportunity: Leadership in the tradition of American Indian women's voices. *A Leadership Journal: Women in Leadership-Sharing the Vision* 3 (Fall): 77.

Santora, Joseph C., William Seaton, and James C. Sarros. 1999. Changing times: Entrepreneurial leadership in a community-based nonprofit organization. *The Journal of Leadership Studies* 6 (3/4): 101.

Discovering Common Leadership Experiences and Perspectives among Latino Librarian Leaders Involved with REFORMA

A Leadership Research Project Report and Project Summary

Ronald L. Baza

The following description of a research study of REFORMA leadership reveals several overarching "themes" or perspectives unique to REFORMA. Seventeen leaders were interviewed and videotaped as they described their leadership experiences. This study may lead to a more extensive video documentary and oral history of REFORMA's organizational history and contributions to the field of librarianship.

Ronald L. Baza is currently a doctoral candidate in Leadership Studies and Administration at the University of San Diego and a human resources management consultant. Mr. Baza received his B.A. in social science from San Diego State University and his M.A. in human behavior from the United States International University.

Overview

The purpose of this Leadership Research Project was to conduct a preliminary survey of Latino librarian leaders involved with REFORMA with the goal of recording, analyzing, and ascertaining what they do, how and where they do it, and what and who benefits from their work and voluntary services. Within the scope of a Doctoral Leadership Internship Course (University of San Diego, EDLD 361, Spring 1999), the study was primarily intended to provide me (the Leadership intern) and the broader community with a deeper understanding of the organization's history, leadership capabilities and capacities, and advocacy record; sufficient baseline information with which to undertake further organizational research, assessment, and documentation; and a pilot study to explore the feasibility of extending this research into a dissertation.

Additionally, there was a broader anticipation that the proposed research would 1) enable REFORMA to conduct an organizational assessment of its experience and capabilities in leadership development and succession planning; and 2) produce written and video documentaries of REFORMA's organizational history and contributions to the field of librarianship, the Hispanic community, and society in general.

Because of the gracious organizational support extended to me, as well as the genuine encouragement and willingness to contribute by many dedicated Reformistas around the United States, I was able to go forward with this research effort from March 1999 through June 1999. Through analysis of recorded interviews with seventeen REFORMA leaders (ten women and seven men) from around the country (Arizona, California, Illinois, Massachusetts, Nevada, New York, and Texas) as well as personal observations from a general membership meeting (New Orleans) and a local chapter meeting (Los Angeles), this chapter examines and identifies common leadership experiences and perspectives shared among REFORMA's distinguished past and present leaders.

Overarching Themes

Preliminary results from examination and analysis of the seventeen videotaped interviews reveal several overarching themes that merit discussion. The first significant theme that surfaced frequently among the interviewed participants was a high level of expressed personal fulfillment with librarianship as a career choice and with REFORMA as a voluntary advocacy activity. With rare exceptions, the study participants expressed considerable satisfaction with their choice of vocation and profound gratification with their involvement and association with REFORMA.

The second theme is the widely held opinion that REFORMA's mission and objectives remain unchanged and align well with the personal views and commitments of virtually all of the interviewees. In toto, the research participants overwhelmingly supported the underlying premise that, throughout the past twenty-five years, REFORMA has remained true to its original organizational mission and objectives.

Another prevalent theme that surfaced during the interviews is the strong notion that although substantial progress has been made, there still remains the need for more Latino librarians, as well as improvements in library materials, services, and programs delivered to Spanish-speaking communities. Clearly, a general consensus shared among the interviewees strongly supports REFORMA's joint mission of increasing Latino librarianship as well as improving materials, programs, and services to Spanish-speaking communities.

The final theme is the firm belief that although REFORMA's leadership development and mentorship efforts have been successful, there still remains room for continuous process improvement and broader inclusion. With adroit balance and modest conviction, the interview respondents invariably suggested that REFORMA could greatly benefit from concerted leadership development programs and activities.

Leadership Themes

In addition to the themes cited above, preliminary analysis of the recorded interviews disclosed several important leadership issues that appear to guide and inform REFORMA's ongoing internal discussion of the efficacy of its leadership development and mentorship programs. Ranking highest among these emergent leadership issues was the frequently expressed need for the formalization of broad-based and inclusive leadership development and mentorship programs. As alluded to previously, a large majority of the research subjects expressed genuine interest in systematic, organization-wide leadership programs and symposia.

The second leadership issue was widespread support for the efforts of REFORMA's Information Technology Committee and its recent achievements in improving REFORMA's information technology resources. These information technology advances (i.e., the electronic list REFORMANET and the REFORMA Web page) are viewed as important tools for the continued evolution of REFORMA's future leadership development initiatives.

The next-highest-scoring leadership issue was the high degree of approval and encouragement for REFORMA's continued collaboration with other local and national organizations. The survey respondents specifically cited recent collaborations with the American Library Association (ALA), the ALA Ethnic Caucuses, and the California Library Association, as well as potential partnerships with such organizations as the National Council of La Raza and other local and national organizations.

Another leadership issue consistently expressed by the study participants was the perception that individual experiences in local and/or national levels of REFORMA are very rewarding and beneficial to the development of leadership skills. In particular, many of the respondents praised their REFORMA supporters and colleagues for the invaluable leadership opportunities and challenging assignments that contributed to the development and evolution of their own unique leadership styles. Another notable item was the expressed need and desire to establish a national headquarters office and staff with which to support REFORMA's anticipated growth and ever-increasing programs.

Finally, a careful review of the recorded interviews yields other potential leadership issues and other valuable organizational resources, including a long list of exemplary male and female role models or potential mentors and, indeed, a very rich oral history.

Concluding Acknowledgments and Final Comments

In closing this summary report, I would like to express final reflections and acknowledgments on this unique experience. First, I would be remiss if I failed to convey how impressed I was with the incredible dedication and commitment of each and every participant interviewed. Second, I am grateful for the tremendous support and encouragement that I received from Mr. Luis Herrera (director, Pasadena Public Library and internship supervisor) and Dr. Mary Scherr (faculty advisor and leadership internship instructor). Indeed, without these individuals, this internship would not have been the rich and insightful experience that it ultimately became. Finally, I look forward to continuing my efforts to bring this worthwhile project to a successful completion: the production of a video documentary and oral history of REFORMA's organizational history and contributions to the field of librarianship, the Latino community, and society in general.

Bridging the Leadership Divide

REFORMA, ALA, and Democracy

Lillian Castillo-Speed

The REFORMA Information Technology Agenda was formally introduced at a conference plenary session intended to bring leaders of the American Library Association and leaders of REFORMA together on the topic of the Digital Divide. The following is a record of the dialogue they began and that they must continue.

Lillian Castillo-Speed is the head librarian of the Ethnic Studies Library at the University of California at Berkeley. She is also the database manager of the Chicano Database and the series editor of the Ethnic Studies Library Publications Unit. She has compiled the *Chicana Studies Index* (Berkeley: Chicano Studies Library Publications Unit, 1992) and is the editor of *Latina: Women's Voices from the Borderlands* (New York: Simon & Schuster, 1995).

"The digital divide is a big dirty house but we have to start somewhere."

—Ana Alvarez, Seattle Public Library, during the questions and comments session of the RNC2 Plenary on the Digital Divide

With all the exciting events and panel discussions that captured our attention at the Second REFORMA National Conference, we should not forget that an important discussion took place there at the Saturday plenary session on "REFORMA and the Digital Divide: A Strategic Planning Session." Moderated by Oralia Garza de Cortés, the panel included speakers representing ALA, REFORMA, and academia at high levels of leadership. Richard Chabrán, director of the Center for Virtual Research at the University of California, Riverside, made several direct proposals to the ALA leadership to promote cooperation between ALA and REFORMA and REFORMA's own technology agenda. Jorge Reina Schement, professor of Telecommunications at Penn State and co-director of its Institute for Information Policy, stated that the Digital Divide issue is a discourse that is not about technology but about democracy. The combination of access plus participation equals democracy, he said, and librarians, not academics, have to figure out how to deliver that access. Nancy Kranich, president of ALA, agreed that ALA would need REFORMA's help to define information equity in the Information Age. Saundra L. Shirley, telecommunications specialist for the ALA Office for Information and Technology Policy (OITP) and ALA's point person on the Digital Divide issue, stressed that the key issue for her was building partnerships and collaboration. Bill Gordon, executive director of ALA, described his own personal Digital Divide story, a story about his family moving from a rural area to a city and how they wanted to bridge the information divide. He now wants to fight to give all people the simple ability to get the information they need to make their lives better, regardless of technology.

Before the conference each of the speakers had been given a copy of REFORMA's Information Technology Agenda, a document that had been recently drafted by the Information Technology Committee. Richard Chabrán's proposals to ALA were based on that document's recommendations and were an attempt to bring firm commitments to the discussion. He proposed that an issue of *American Libraries* be devoted to the Digital Divide; that an ALA conference presidential program focus on the Digital Divide; that ALA co-sponsor with REFORMA a forum on the development of digital content; that an OITP Fellow do research on the Digital Divide; that ALA co-sponsor with REFORMA a forum to discuss how library schools can prepare librarians to face the Digital Divide; and finally, that REFORMA's voice be preserved in the national dialogue on this issue. Stating that she was, "delighted to see the ITC document" because it calls for digital content and skills and not just for selling computers, Kranich stated that ALA hopes to move forward to further the dialogue and needs REFORMA to help define information equity. She did agree to have her presidential program at the ALA conference to be about the Digital Divide and suggested that Professor Schement would help with this. She also mentioned that incoming ALA President John Berry had included the Digital Divide issue as part of his initiatives and will include it on his presidential program at the 2002 ALA conference. In addition, a meeting at an IFLA conference (the International Federation of Library Associations and Institutions) on this topic was arranged with G8 librarians. Kranich concluded by asking for our stories, stories about what is going on in Latino communities because of the e-rate issue, for example. ALA needs more surveys and to do more outreach, she said. ALA needs REFORMA members to talk about this issue among ourselves and in our Latino communities.

The reaction from the audience was strong, lively, and sometimes heated. The first voice was that of Isabel Espinal, who brought up her objection to one of the speakers' use of the phrase "information poor" when referring to Latinos and other ethnic minorities. She felt it was misleading and insulting, a comment that was echoed by Oralia Garza de Cortés, who compared it to the phrase "culturally deprived." The point was made that our ethnic minorities have a great deal of information as well as culture, but that it has been devalued in our society. The phrase "digital repatriation" was mentioned in reference to the recovering of Native American digital artifacts that might otherwise be buried or lost. Another person challenged ALA and REFORMA to focus on the relationship to libraries in Mexico, especially near the border, and not just the wealthier G8 libraries. Both Bill Gordon and Nancy Kranich reacted positively to this challenge, stating that ALA needed REFORMA's help in reaching out to the Spanish-speaking world and that IFLA is working toward making sure there is participation from Spanish-speaking countries. In an eloquent rebuttal, Reformista Diana Rivera stated the issue of access in simple terms: "We'd like to come to the table, but we don't have the money for the meal. We'd like to come to the banquet, but we don't have the resources." Stating that REFORMA doesn't have the resources to provide ALA with the information it is calling for or to do the groundwork for ALA because we are all busy in our jobs, she also objected to the talk about "globality and inclusiveness." To her it was impossible to reconcile that senti-ment with the situation of what is available to U.S. Latinos. "There are pockets of population, such as the barrios of Michigan, that will never have access because REFORMA doesn't have the money" to help ALA on the Digital Divide issue. Saundra Shirley responded by stating that the cost of services will depend on how strongly voices are raised to telecommunication companies that services must be affordable. Nancy Kranich pointed out that REFORMA's voice itself was valuable in articulating the needs of Latinos and that this is how REFORMA contributes to the goal of access for all. Tension was in the air as Diana Rivera shot back, "What would ALA be doing if REFORMA didn't exist?" At that point, Satia Orange tried to tone down the discussion by reminding us that ALA is not just the 300 staff persons in Chicago but an organization of 60,000 members who do the work of the association in committees. Nancy Kranich is not an ALA staff member, for example, but an ALA member just like any Reformista who belongs to ALA. To this Oralia Garza de Cortés responded by asking, "Does that mean we have power?" To which Satia Orange answered with an emphatic "Yes!" Then Gladys Smiley Bell from the Black Caucus brought up the work of the five ethnic caucuses on ALA's Goals 2000. "After we contributed, we never heard from anybody. We wanted to go to the room and write more about the issues. We've heard the same rhetoric for the last three years. I'd like to see some action and I'd like to see people of color at the table. I'd like to hear a response to that. Can we update that document?" Bill Gordon said that a report on Goals 2000 was issued at last year's conference and that, since the time the document was released, ALA had hired a literacy officer as well as a diversity officer. At that point Richard Chabrán tried to bring a final word to the dialogue: "respeto." One discussion can't begin to resolve all the issues, he said, but some positive actions can be taken while other problems at least have the possibility of being solved. However, keeping "respeto" in mind, he said, we want ALA to come back and talk to us and we want to make sure that REFORMA remains a part of the dialogue and is acknowledged for its contributions. Addressing the ALA leadership, he asked, "Are you willing to work with REFORMA on the Digital Divide? Are you willing to work with us as an organization and not with just a few individual REFORMA members?" Both Nancy Kranich and Bill Gordon answered yes, with Bill Gordon going on to say that ALA expects to have REFORMA's involvement as well as the involvement of the other ethnic caucuses. It was then that Oralia Garza de Cortés, after emphasizing once more that appointing a few Reformistas to a few committees would not be sufficient, brought this historic planning session to an end.

REFORMA's Information Technology Agenda

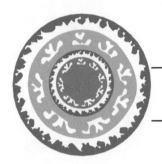

The REFORMA
Information Technology Committee

In June 2000, the REFORMA Information Technology Committee (ITC), whose members at the time were Mario Ascencio, Selina Gómez Beloz, Iván E. Calimano, Lillian Castillo-Speed, Richard Chabrán, Isabel Espinal, Carlos Rodriguez, and Romelia Salinas, wrote this document as REFORMA's response to the challenge of providing equitable service to Latinos and the Spanish speaking in the digital era. The REFORMA Board of Directors accepted it at its July 2000 meeting in Chicago. Minor editing changes have been made since that date.

Because of REFORMA's unique position as a national organization involved with literacy, information, libraries, and underserved populations, it is important for it to put forward an information technology policy agenda. This means monitoring government and corporate policies that affect access to information technologies, as well as formulating and advocating public policy that furthers our overall agenda. Some of the current technology policy areas are universal service (often called "e-rate"), communications policy concerning cable television and direct broadcast satellites, and national legislation that authorizes grant monies for technology projects. *Public Space in Cyberspace* (Schuler 1999), a publication of Libraries for the Future, provides information on how organizations like REFORMA can go about working on information technology policy at the local, state, and national levels.

Demographics of the Divide

The secretary of the Department of Commerce, William M. Daley, recently commented: "In a society that increasingly relies on computers and the Internet to deliver information and enhance communication we need to make sure that all Americans have access" (National Telecommunications Information Administration 1999). A number of recent studies reveal that there are disparities in access to telephones, personal computers, and the Internet. These disparities are marked by race, ethnicity, income, education, physical disabilities, and place of residence. They signal not only lack of access to technologies but, more fundamentally, access to resources that are becoming critical in today's society. It is in this larger sense that we refer to a "Digital Divide" between the haves and the have-nots. The use of high technology among Latino communities is only now beginning to be investigated. Currently we do not have a demographic profile of Latinos that includes key technology and communication variables. At the national level the *Falling Through the Net* series, published by the National Telecommunications and Information Administration (NTIA), has provided the most useful information. This influential series has noted that there is not only a persistent but also an increasing gap in computer and online use among Latinos and African Americans. The Tomás Rivera Policy Institute has also made important contributions to our understanding of these issues, especially in the areas of computer ownership and school use. Regional trends are beginning to be tracked by research organizations such as the Center for Virtual Research at the University of California, Riverside.

Early studies on high technology in Latino communities focused on computer ownership (see, e.g., Wilhelm, 1997b). Although the initial studies began to make the case that a "Digital Divide" does exist, they told us little about how and where people were using these new technologies. More recent surveys include questions about types of computers, modems, online access, and use and have begun to track where people use computers. More targeted studies such as those that focus on media use (Henry J. Kaiser Foundation 1999) and civic participation (Baldassare 1999) have also found evidence of a Digital Divide. Some recent industry-based surveys (see, e.g., Cheskin Research 2000) suggest that the divide is disappearing. Although these industry-based studies suggest higher Internet use by minorities, they are often based on very small sample sizes, target only individuals with phone access, and focus almost exclusively on access versus use. Relying on phone surveys to measure the Digital Divide is fraught with problems, as Jorge Reina Schement's (1999) work documents, because segments of the Latino population do not have telephones in their homes. Moreover, we need to measure quality of connections and use rather than just quantity. For example, possession of a 486-based computer with a 14.4 K modem means only marginal participation on today's Information Highway. We will also need to track the introduction of other digital devices such as digital assistants (e.g., pagers) and monitor digital television as these innovations begin to broaden the ways in which people use high technology. Most important, we need to move beyond tracking access and focus on measuring what the National Research Council (1999) describes as "information fluency." Information fluency includes the ability to use today's computer applications and to apply information technology immediately; it requires people to understand the basic principles of computers, networks, and information that underpin technology and to possess the intellectual capabilities to apply information technology in complex and sustained situations (National Research Council 1999). Reformistas can contribute to public understanding in this area by becoming aware of the issues, sharing that awareness with others, commenting on national studies, and advocating local surveys in their region that document the use of high technology in low-income communities. We must advocate and work for the construction of a Latino demographic profile that includes relevant technological variables. Only then can we begin to more adequately plan for the future.

Impact of New Technologies

Although the introduction of new technologies is not new for libraries, the introduction of personal computers and the Internet as resources for patrons presents new challenges and opportunities. Libraries are recognized as strategic sites that can help address the inequities in access to technology resources. In fact, libraries have been specifically identified as potential recipients in many federal programs aimed at employing high technologies in local communities, such as the e-rate. REFORMA supports the expansion of the e-rate to include broadband access for libraries. Libraries have also been the recipients of funds from private donors such as the Gates Foundation.

As Reformistas, we are particularly interested in exploring what impact new technology resources in libraries, such as Internet access, CD-ROMs, scanners, or word processing, have had on Latino communities. As practicing librarians, we know that many libraries started offering Internet access without a thought about their Latino communities. Evidence of this was the lack of advertising of these Internet resources and/or programs directed to the Latino communities and the paucity of Internet classes conducted in Spanish and/or with culturally relevant examples. Often it took a Reformista to provide the appropriate outreach and services to Latinos.

The failure of many public libraries and public academic libraries to provide technological resources to Latino communities must be documented and addressed. More research needs to be done to ascertain the extent to which the library community is making technology resources accessible and relevant to Latinos. To that end, in March 1998 Isabel Espinal of REFORMA's ITC produced a draft of a library survey, "Survey of Technology Service to the Spanish-speaking and Latinos" (available on the ITC Web site, http://www.reforma.org/ITC). In addition, the GCTA Spanish Language Public Access Computing Project, a partnership between the Gates Center for Technology Access and public libraries throughout the country, has begun to address how librarians can support public access computing for Spanish-speaking patrons. REFORMA can serve as an independent monitor and resource for such projects that have corporate origins and, when appropriate, may also serve as a partner.

But once Latinos gain access to technology, whether through libraries or through personal efforts, the question arises as to what impact the technology actually has on our economic, cultural, and personal lives. Rather than viewing that access as a panacea, it will become even more important to understand what obstacles and opportunities these new technologies hold for Latinos. There are many important questions for REFORMA to address. Does technology bridge the gap between immigrants and their countries of origin? We have to recognize the impact, in the words of librarian Oralia Garza de Cortés, "of free access to e-mail for those without means; the ability to reconnect with homeland while trying to make sense of this new place called home" (1999). Will Internet technologies, such as "cookies" or "agents," which pose a general threat to individual privacy, place immigrants at increased risk? Does technology help keep distinctive Latino cultures alive, or does it lead to greater homogenization? Does technology help keep Latino families united or help tear them apart?

The workplace is another area where the impact of technology on Latinos must be investigated. Specifically, the impact of technology on the working conditions of Latino librarians should be examined and addressed. Information technology holds many exciting promises but also many dangers. It has often led to greater democratization of the workplace. For example, through electronic communication, such as e-mail, employees have a level of access to administrators that was seldom possible before. Also, there is often much greater communication laterally. In addition, for some Latinos electronic communication is preferable to oral communication in the workplace because they are less likely to be judged by their spoken accent. E-mail for Latinos also allows communication across geographic boundaries and reduces the isolation that many Latino professionals face in their work environments by facilitating daily communication with other Latino professionals in their field. This is evident on REFORMANET, the REFORMA national electronic discussion list. Yet for some Latinos the new reliance in organizations on e-mail as a communication tool instead of phone communication may lead to greater discrimination against them because e-mail is text and therefore literacy-based.

For all the areas listed above, research, discussion, and advocacy should be developed. REFORMA has an important role in gathering, using, and furthering the research of those who are studying these vital questions.

Awareness and Instruction

How will our communities be made aware of new technologies such as digital television, digital phone lines, cable modems, online banking, virtual reality, electronic books, and information appliances? Recent media coverage of the Internet has helped contribute to misunderstandings, misconceptions and, at times, unrealistic expectations. REFORMA has an important role in promoting awareness of new technologies and instruction on how to use them. It can assist in promoting non-biased, informative, relevant, and up-to-date information about these new technologies. This information should be non-threatening, easy to understand, and straightforward about hidden costs and possible social ramifications (such as privacy issues) associated with these technologies. It should also be focused on our current understanding of the demographic characteristics of Latinos.

From recent studies (National Telecommunications Information Administration 1999) we know that there are correlations among educational attainment, computer ownership, and Internet use. Latinos as a group have low educational attainment and low literacy rates. Literacy is a serious issue that must be more fully addressed in our communities. Many Latino households have little or no experience with technology. Many lack basic information technology skills such as keyboarding and mouse use. Instructional programs should take into account demographic background such as language, education level, literacy, age, and access to technology.

Emphasis should also be placed on instructing users how to critically evaluate the information they find on the Internet as well as reminding them that the Internet is only one source of information. Traditional sources such as books and print reference works still contain useful information and often are the only sources on a particular subject. Although it is important to acknowledge that many libraries and librarians have begun to provide instruction to their communities about these technologies, much more needs to be done. In addition to libraries, other places offering access to technology, including community technology centers, K–12 schools, community colleges, and local universities, should be encouraged and supported in these efforts. Productive partnerships are being formed between librarians and outside agencies to promote information fluency to Latinos. These efforts should be multiplied and extended. REFORMA should gather data on these instructional programs and partnerships, illustrating best practices.

Tomorrow's technologies that are under development today should also be investigated and shared with REFORMA's constituents. REFORMA should continue to be an advocate for educating our communities about the strengths, benefits, opportunities, effects, and limitations of these new technologies. The issue of awareness and instruction applies not only to patrons but also to librarians and library staff. Librarians and staff must be prepared to both operate new technologies and be aware of Latino digital resources. Finally, it should be a crucial concern for the library profession as a whole to improve recruitment of librarians and other staff, especially Latinos, who will be most knowledgeable and effective in conducting instruction programs. We must insist that library schools and programs produce many more professionals with a blend of technical, linguistic, and cultural skills that can make a difference in helping our Latino communities understand and use technology.

Digital Collections

In the same way that Latino print and audiovisual collections had to be rescued from neglect, ignorance, and efforts to downplay their significance, so must we think about what we need to do to preserve Latino digital collections. For example, at the beginning of the Chicano Movement, mainstream libraries either discarded or did not collect materials about Chicanos that were written from the Chicano perspective. They were considered too political, too ephemeral, or too specialized. Activist students who foresaw the need to document and preserve this information established Chicano libraries in the Southwest. The same was true for Puerto Rican, Dominican, and other ethnic collections. In the digital age we are faced with the same imperative to make sure that Latino materials are included in digitization projects; that the separation of important from trivial materials is done from the Latino perspective; and that the long-term preservation of Latino digitized materials, including images, electronic list messages, text, audiovisual materials, Web sites, and other materials, is planned for. For all we know, digitized documents may be the historical documents of the future, perhaps the only historical documents of the future. Our Latino identities and heritage must be represented in that future. Current large-scale digitization efforts must include Latino materials. We cannot assume that governmental, educational, or privately developed aggregators will automatically consider them. Total reliance on approval plans has never served the building of core Latino collections, and the same will be true of an over-reliance on aggregators. Nor can we leave Latino digital collection and preservation to the vagaries of marketing decisions. Instead, REFORMA should support efforts that focus only on Latino or other ethnic materials and work with them to establish common goals in this area. An example is CLNet in the University of California system. We must also remember that the particular technological tools that are used for preservation are not as important as the content itself or the ultimate users of that content. The title of the Children's Partnership's recently released report, *Online Content for Low-Income and Underserved Americans: The Digital Divide's New Frontier* (Lazarus and Mora 2000), is one indicator of the significance of content, documenting the need to develop relevant content for these populations.

Categories of Digital Preservation That Merit Special Attention

Special Collections That Document the Presence of Latinos in the United States

These collections include newspapers, journals, personal papers, films, videos, historical documents, flyers, posters, photographs, and audio materials relating to the political and social history and conditions of all Latino groups in the United States.

Production by the Digital Small Press

This includes alternative digital products, for example, Web sites with a Latino perspective or alternative electronic journals or books.

Collaborative Digital Projects

These include large-scale governmental or educational collaborative digital efforts that include Latino digital materials appropriately, with the guidance of experts in Latino materials and with their inclusion at a high level of decision making. There should be a balanced representation of Latino cultures and histories.

Aggregation by Commercial Digital Publishers

This covers collections made by commercial digital publishers who include Latino digital materials appropriately in their inventories, with the guidance and consultation of experts in Latino materials. There should be a balanced representation of Latino cultures and histories.

Digital Latino Collections

These include libraries with important Latino collections that need to be preserved through digitization. By identifying and collaborating with such libraries, we can establish procedures for requesting support from third parties. Third parties would include grant-making organizations, such as the National Endowment for the Humanities. REFORMA would serve as a "monitor" of the programs and make the information accessible through REFORMA and ALA channels.

Materials for Specific Population Sectors

Materials relevant for farm workers and children are often lacking on the Internet, so we must advocate their development.

Access to Digital Collections

The preservation and creation of Latino digital collections is imperative, but access to these collections is also essential to the needs of REFORMA's constituency. We as librarians have always utilized a range of access tools. This will continue to be true in the digital era, whether using digitized finding aids to peruse archives or Internet search tools to access the variety of digitized media (audio, video, images, and text). During the 1980s and 1990s Latino librarians made critical advances in the development of digital access tools. Some examples are online catalogs of Latino and ethnic collections, indexes to periodical literature such as the *Chicano Database* and the *Hispanic American Periodicals Index* (HAPI), and subject vocabularies such as the *Chicano Thesaurus* and *Bilindex*. It is not often acknowledged that library catalogs were the first access tools on the Internet. The further development and growth of the Internet offers librarians another opportunity to develop culturally relevant access tools.

There are many possible ways for new tools to be developed. However, before developing these new tools we should ask ourselves some important questions. Are the existing access tools meeting the needs of the Latino community? Can existing tools be modified to include Internet resources? How is the Latino community currently accessing information on the Internet? How successful are Latinos in locating the information they are seeking? What will be the criteria for the inclusion of resources provided by access tools? Will we continue to use our existing culturally relevant subject vocabularies? Will subject specialists be responsible for selecting, describing, and indexing these new resources?

Although the Internet is growing at a rapid pace, we also need to teach the Latino community that not everything can be found on the Internet nor is it just a mouse click away. In fact, it is this exponential growth that will provide the challenge for librarians to create and provide these access tools. Because many Reformistas over the years have been engaged in the development of analog as well as digital access tools for a wide variety of materials, REFORMA is in a good position to make important contributions in this area. The first step is to begin a dialogue about the best way to proceed. In any case, REFORMA should support existing access projects while at the same time determining steps for the future. We must also keep in mind the following criteria.

Relevant, Specific, and Non-Biased Subject Headings

Inclusion of Latino digital material in large collaborative or commercial efforts can be negatively affected by the continued use of subject headings that are general, biased, or non-specific to the topics covered by the materials. For example, a listing of all Latino materials under the term "Hispanic" or "Hispanic Americans" is not adequate to provide access to the wide range of topics in the Latino experience. The use of the term "Illegal Aliens" is not acceptable in referring to "Undocumented Workers." Also, specific cultural terms should always be used (with scope notes if needed) rather than translations, for example, "Quinceañeras" and "Curanderos."

Emphasis on Public Use Rather Than Private or High-Cost Use

Digitization does not automatically imply access. Some private or institutional organizations may launch projects to digitize valuable segments of our cultural heritage with the intent of keeping access to these materials restricted or with the intent of charging prohibitive fees to use them.

Inclusion of Spanish-Language Interfaces and Materials

There is widespread digitization of Spanish-language materials in the Latin American world. Although we encourage and promote access to these materials in the United States, for example by lobbying for Spanish-language interfaces, our emphasis must be on what is most likely to be lacking in the digital arena, that is, culturally relevant materials centered on the Latino experience in the United States in any language.

Partnerships

In an effort to provide the best service to our constituents, REFORMA must collaborate with organizations that are committed to supporting information technology research, education, preservation, access, and legislation. With the advent of new technologies, REFORMA must make contact with research and educational institutions, such as the Tomás Rivera Policy Institute, to find new and creative methods to collaborate on addressing the Digital Divide. REFORMA's ITC has identified several organizations as potential partners. Although many of these organizations do not target Latino communities or Latino collections specifically, it is REFORMA's role to make sure that our organization's stand is known when decisions relating to, for example, grant opportunities and legislation, are made. Furthermore, local chapters should participate by identifying local partners, such as local Latino media (for example, *La Opinión* in Los Angeles and *El Tiempo Latino* in Washington, D.C.). And of course, we should also reach out to the other ethnic caucuses within ALA and work with them to speak with a strong, united voice. Reformistas are encouraged to help the ITC identify possible foundations and organizations with which to form partnerships. These may be organizations that support research and education, provide grants for preservation and access, or lobby for library and information policy.

Advancing the Organization Through Technology

The effective integration of technology into the core processes of business firms dominates the thoughts of today's managers. Technology that only fifteen years ago was considered back office administrative overhead has been revolutionized into the key ingredient determining a company's strategic direction and defining its ability to compete in a global marketplace. The concept of leveraging technology in the twenty-first century has become a priority in the business world. The nonprofit sector of our society has not been untouched by this phenomenon, recognizing the value in harnessing technology to advance an organization. Over the course of the last few years REFORMA has successfully integrated technology into its organization by various methods such as e-mail communication among members, the creation of the national electronic list REFORMANET, and the development of a Web presence at the national and chapter level. REFORMA should continue to integrate appropriate technologies into the organization in a conscious and resourceful manner.

ITC should investigate how REFORMA National and REFORMA Chapters use technology in their organizational and procedural processes and identify areas that can be improved or facilitated through technology. These areas should then be prioritized and a plan for implementation created. Areas may include communication, publications, education, recruitment, and administration. The integration of technology in an effective and appropriate manner should be identified, encouraged, and facilitated by the ITC.

Recommendations

Demographic Profile

* Contribute to public understanding by becoming aware of the issues and sharing that awareness with others.

* Comment on and participate in national studies.

* Advocate local surveys that document the use of high technology in low-income communities.

* Advocate and work for the construction of a Latino demographic profile that would include relevant technological variables.

* Incorporate access and use of digital technologies into the census and current population surveys.

Impact of Library Technologies

* Survey the extent to which library technology resources have been made available, relevant, and accessible to Latinos.

* Monitor the Gates Center for Technology Access and other similar projects.

* Define and pursue areas of research about the effects of technology on Latinos, including:

> Impact on communication and interaction between immigrants and home countries;
>
> Impact on transition to new country;
>
> Impact on cultural homogenization/cultural diversity;
>
> Impact on Latino families;
>
> Impact on economic lives of Latinos;
>
> Impact of technology available in libraries versus technology available in private homes; and
>
> Impact of Latino digital collections on Latinos.

- Within the library community, advocate research to be done in these areas. In particular, advocate that the following groups conduct such research:

    ALA

    LITA

    ALISE

    ALSC

- Support ITC in keeping in touch with other organizations that are conducting this research. Serve as a clearinghouse for Reformistas to see what the current research is. Support a Web site/bibliography on this research.

- Identify and promote those uses of information technology that improve the lives of Latinos.

- Identify and take a strong stand against uses of technology that have negative impacts on Latinos.

- Support the identification of the needs of Latino communities and find ways that library information technology can address those needs, such as:

    Reducing unemployment

    Economic empowerment

    Education in general

    Literacy

    Math and science education

    Cultural support

    Political participation

    Communication across geographic boundaries

    Spanish language maintenance

    English-language instruction

    Instruction in other world languages

    Communication

    Alliances with other ethnic groups

Awareness and Instruction

- Identify, support, and partner with local community information technology instruction programs.

- Promote and publicize programs and information sources that promote information literacy, through the use of appropriate electronic lists, such as REFORMANET.

- Evaluate new technologies and their potential effects (negative and positive) on the Latino community.

- Evaluate existing information technology awareness programs and measure their effectiveness.

- Sponsor programs to inform and educate the Latino community about new technologies and how they will potentially affect their lives.

- Partner with other information technology organizations such as LITA, ASIS, and ACM to promote information technology careers among Latinos.

- Create social networks and mentoring to introduce Latinos into information technology careers.

- Keep abreast of information technology policies and legislation that will affect libraries, communities, and individuals; create summaries and distribute.

- Develop information technology programs to promote literacy.

Digital Collections

- Support collaborative preservation projects that include Latino digitized materials.

- Identify collections of and create priorities for the preservation of Latino cultural materials.

- Support the digitization and preservation of local and national Latino cultural materials.

- Support the inclusion of all Latino cultures and heritages in digitization projects.

- Advocate the inclusion of minority librarians and underserved voices in high-level decision making relating to the development, cataloging, and preservation of Latino cultural materials.

- Support the production of Spanish-language materials that meet the cultural needs of the Latino population.

- Support the development of practical content that meets the basic needs of the Latino community in the areas of education, employment, housing, legal assistance, health, and political representation.

- Encourage the development of culturally appropriate subject headings and categories for Latino digitized materials.

- Support the creation of government online information resources in the Spanish language.

- Encourage and support the Latino publications produced by the digital small press and the digital alternative press.

Access to Digital Collections

- Support the development of culturally relevant electronic access tools.

- Encourage and assist projects to survey and evaluate the needs of the Latino community in terms of electronic and Internet access.

- Survey current Latino-focused Internet finding tools and evaluate their effectiveness and usefulness. Evaluate content, quality, size, frequency of updates, level of indexing and/or cataloging, search interface, and experience/background of content provider.

- Sponsor programs to educate and inform the Latino community about what is available on the Internet and what is not.

- Sponsor further discussions and programs on the issue of electronic access to information for the Latino community.

- Support the development of Spanish-language interfaces.

- Support and encourage the development and use of culturally appropriate subject headings and categories for Latino digitized materials and other electronic information.

- Withhold support from electronic information projects or services that will have exclusive access or prohibitively high costs.

◆ Support the use of metadata standards, such as Dublin Core, in Latino-based digital collections.

Partnerships

REFORMA should create collaborative efforts with the following organizations.

Research

Julian Samora Research Institute

Tomás Rivera Policy Institute (TRPI)

Inter University Program for Latino Research (IUPLR)

Center for Virtual Research at the University of California at Riverside

Preservation and Access Grants

Gates Center for Technology Access

Getty Grant Program

Institute for Museum and Library Service (IMLS)

National Endowment for the Humanities (NEH)

Smithsonian Center for Latino Initiatives

Legislation

ALA's Office for Information Technology Policy

Education and Library Networks Coalition (EdLiNC)

Hispanic Association of Colleges & Universities (HACU)

National Commission on Libraries and Information Sciences (NCLIS)

National Council of La Raza (NCLR)

National Information and Telecommunications Administration (NTIA)

Benton Foundation

Community Technology Centers Network (CTCNet)

Computers in Our Future (CIOF)

Libraries for the Future

League of United Latin American Citizens (LULAC)

Society of Hispanic Professional Engineers (SHPE)

Nonprofits' Policy & Technology Project (a Project of OMB Watch)

Education and Instruction

K–12 schools

Community colleges

Universities

Community technology centers

Outreach

Television networks

Local and national newspapers

Cable television

Radio

Advancing the Organization Through Technology

- Investigate how national-level REFORMA uses technology in its organizational procedures.

- Identify areas in which technology can be applied to improve or facilitate internal processes, for example, keeping membership records and collecting dues.

- Prioritize areas and create a plan for implementation.

- Encourage active participation on REFORMANET regarding issues that relate to REFORMA's Information Technology Agenda.

- Expand and report on the national survey titled "How Reformistas Use Technology."

- Investigate how chapters use technology in their organizational procedures.

- Identify areas in which technology can be applied to improve or facilitate communication such as using online discussion rooms.

- Make recommendations/suggestions to chapters about areas of improvement such as the development of chapter Web sites.

- Develop resources for facilitating the integration of technology by chapters (for example, "how to establish an electronic list") .

- Identify how REFORMA committees can leverage technology (for example, the creation of bilingual Web-based tutorials/guides).

- Publicize the organization through the use of promotional materials such as bookmarks.

References

Bagasao, Paula. 1999a. *Challenges to bridging the Digital Divide: Building better on ramps to the Information Highway*. Claremont, CA: The Tomás Rivera Policy Institute.

———. December 1999b. Knowing about who has access: A matter of strategy. *IMP Magazine*. Available: http://www.cisp.org/imp/december_99/12_99bagasao .htm. (Accessed June 9, 2001).

Baldassare, Mark. 1999. *Californians and their government*. San Francisco: Public Policy Institute of California Statewide Survey.

Bertot, John Carl, and Charles McClure. 1998. *The 1998 national survey of U.S. public library outlet Internet connectivity: Final report*. Washington, DC: American Library Association.

Carnevale, Anthony P. 1999. *Education = success: Empowering Hispanic youths and adults*. Princeton, NJ: Educational Testing Service.

Cheskin Research. April 2000. *The digital world of the US Hispanic*. Available: http://www.cheskin.com/think/studies/ushisp.htm. (Accessed June 9, 2001).

Chow, Clifton, et al. 1998. *Impact of CTCNet affiliates: Findings from a national survey of users of community technology centers*. Newton, MA: Education Development Center.

Computers In Our Future. 1999. *A policy agenda for community technology centers: Assuring that low-income communities benefit from technological progress in the Information Age*. Los Angeles: Computers In Our Future.

Cummins, Jim, and Dennis Sayers. 1995. *Brave new schools: Challenging cultural illiteracy through global learning networks*. New York: St. Martin's Press.

Digital Divide Network. Available: http://www.digitaldividenetwork.org/content/sections/index.cfm. (Accessed June 9, 2001).

Escobar, Arturo. 1994. Welcome to Cyberia, notes on the anthropology of cyberculture. *Current Anthropology* 35 (3) (June): 211–231.

———. 1995. Living in Cyberia. *Organization* 2 (4): 22–26.

Garza de Cortés, Oralia. 1999. E-mail correspondence, November 16.

Henry J. Kaiser Family Foundation. 1999. *Kids & media at the new millennium.* Menlo Park, CA: The Henry J. Kaiser Family Foundation.

Hoffman, Donna, and Thomas Novak. 1999. *The evolution of the Digital Divide: Examining the relationship of race to Internet access and usage over time.* Nashville, TN: Owen Graduate School of Management, Vanderbilt University.

Institute for Health Policy Research. 1999. *Work and health survey.* San Francisco: Institute for Health Policy Research, University of California.

Kominiski, Robert, and Eric Newburger. 1999. *Access denied: Changes in computer ownership and use: 1984–1997.* Washington, DC: Population Division, U.S. Census Bureau.

Lazarus, Wendy, and Francisco Mora. 2000. *On-Line content for low-income and underserved Americans: The Digital Divide's new frontier.* Santa Monica: The Children's Partnership.

Moller, Rosa. 2000. *Profile of California computer and Internet users.* Sacramento: California Research Bureau.

National Center for Education Statistics. 1999. *Internet access in public schools and classrooms: 1994–1998.* Washington, DC: National Center for Education Statistics.

National Public Radio, Kaiser Family Foundation, Kennedy School of Government. 2000. *National survey of American adults on technology and national survey of American kids on technology.* Menlo Park, CA: National Public Radio, Kaiser Family Foundation, Kennedy School of Government.

National Research Council. Committee on Information Technology Literacy. 1999. *Being fluent with information technology.* Washington, DC: National Academy Press.

National Telecommunication Information Administration. 1995. *Falling through the net: A survey of the "have nots" in rural and urban America.* Washington, DC: U.S. Department of Commerce.

———. 1998. *Falling through the net II: New data on the Digital Divide.* Washington, DC: U.S. Department of Commerce.

———. 1999. *Falling through the net: Defining the Digital Divide.* Washington, DC: U.S. Department of Commerce.

Neiman, Max, and Richard Chabrán. 1999. *Cyber access in the inland empire.* Riverside, CA: Center for Social and Behavioral Science Research.

Schement, Jorge Reina. December 1999. Of gaps by which democracy we measure. *IMP Magazine.* Available: http://www.cisp.org/imp/december_99 /12_99schement.htm. (Accessed June 9, 2001).

Schuler, Douglas. 1996. *New community networks: Wired for college.* New York: Addison-Wesley.

———. 1999. *Public space in cyberspace—Library advocacy in the Information Age.* New York: Libraries for the Future.

Wilhelm, Anthony. G. 1996. *Latinos and information technology: Preparing for the 21st century.* Claremont, CA: The Tomás Rivera Policy Institute.

———. 1997a. *Buying into the computer age: A look at the Hispanic middle class.* Claremont, CA: The Tomás Rivera Policy Institute.

———. 1997b. *Out of reach? Latinos, education and technology in California.* Claremont, CA: The Tomás Rivera Policy Institute.

———. 1998. *Closing the Digital Divide: Enhancing Hispanic participation in the Information Age.* Claremont, CA: The Tomás Rivera Policy Institute.

———. 2000. *Democracy in the digital age.* New York: Routledge.

Part 3

Issues in
Latino Library Service

The Cárcel
and the Biblioteca

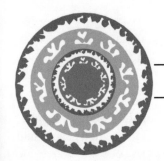

Bruce Jensen

Bruce Jensen is a former jail English as a Second Language instructor and now a graduate student in information studies and Latin American studies at the University of California, Los Angeles. The chapter printed here had its genesis in a failed attempt to get books and magazines to a family member being held in a U.S. immigration jail. Jensen maintains the SOL (Spanish in Our Libraries) Web site, newsletter, and electronic resource bank.

Introduction

La cárcel de Granaditas
Es pura Inquisición
Donde humillan a los hombres
Sin tenerles compasión

"De la prisión de Granaditas," Mexican corrido

W hat follows is part of an ongoing investigation into the slender, developing branch of librarianship that serves prisoners of detention centers and correctional facilities. The focus here is on a narrow aspect of such service: the needs of linguistically marginalized inmates, especially speakers of Spanish.

Correctional facility libraries are poorly understood even within the library profession. Librarians and the public at large are aware that such entities exist, but very few information professionals have ever seen one outside of films such as *The Shawshank Redemption*. Although these libraries employ complex specialized practices, are becoming increasingly professionalized, and serve a potential patron base of some 2 million prisoners in the United States alone, they are generally ignored within library education programs. When I told a library school student about my interest in correctional library service to this country's 200,000 Hispanic inmates, she responded authoritatively—but erroneously— that *those people* are, with few exceptions, illiterate.

Library services to linguistic minorities, although receiving more attention than prison library practices, are similarly plagued by gaps in understanding and training as well as a lack of historical momentum. What is more, both subfields are increasingly remote from the digit-driven core of modern information studies education. What follows then, is a call to arms—necessarily flawed, tantalizingly incomplete—for those who recognize the value of anthropological librarianship, an idea that blossomed and faded a generation ago but remains as vital as ever as an alternative to current practice.

Inside/Outside

El otro día hubo un concierto
hubo un concierto en la prisión
en la cárcel de Santa Marta
los internos se divirtieron
y se olvidaron de sus blues

—El TRI, "Santa Marta"

Many on the outside—inmate argot denotes everything beyond the walls of one's prison, jail, youth camp, or detention center as *the outside*—seldom stop to think that prisoners take an active interest in popular culture. The prevailing stereotype is that convicts are immersed in dangerous and violent subcultures of their own making. It is well to recognize that as this population grows, arguably as a result of policy rather than any increase in criminal behavior, it necessarily becomes more like the rest of us, here on the outside.

No matter how much time one is allowed to lift weights, play cards, or do production work for a private-sector contractor, what most prisoners face are twenty-four-hour days within the confines of the high walls. They have time on their hands, and quite naturally this fuels a hunger for diversion and distraction. Unlike jails and detention centers with their quick turnaround rate, the prison social circle is stable and limited. Eventually one runs out of things to talk about and seeks other ways to occupy the mind. Some convicts turn to movies on video, some to pulp Western novels, others to institutional education programs.

This array of options varies greatly from one site to another, but largely excludes the prisoner who speaks little or no English. How institutional programs in education and library services address, or decline to address, the needs of foreign-language speakers is the focus of this report.

It bears mentioning that prisoners are here discussed without regard to the nature of their offenses or speculation about their guilt, innocence, or suitability for incarceration. This is not to imply that their crimes are of no consequence to society at large, but frankly such issues are not the concern of librarianship. By the same token, sentencing policies, racial inequities, or prison management practices in a climate of privatization are not addressed in much depth here; again, the intent is not to deny their importance but rather to hold the focus tightly on library practices. This perspective is based on a principle that is no universal tenet of library service but rather a personal opinion forged in the crucibles of correctional education and library work: *The role of the librarian is to think and operate on behalf of users, without being judgmental about their information needs or the events that brought them to the library.*

Among the factors that *do* matter to librarians, on the inside and the outside alike, are the needs and, by extension, the well-being of their patrons. This demands recognition of their personal interests as well as their particular barriers to accessing materials. In the case of users with limited English skills, the obvious obstacle separating them from the holdings of most U.S. libraries is language; however, as we shall see, there are more subtle barriers that may be equally important.

Librarians are responsible not only to patrons—whose wishes can sometimes be ignored—but also to agents who exercise direct control over their work. In a public library this might be a board or municipal government; in a university library, regents and chancellors. Prison librarians must answer to supervisors who have compelling concerns about security, safety, budgets, and intellectual content.

This chapter begins with selective historical overviews of two fields of library service in the United States: correctional facility librarianship and what is sometimes referred to as "Latino librarianship," that is, service to users with roots in Hispanic cultures.

The next section seeks to explain the connection and overlap I see between these two fields, discussing the role behavior and cultural frictions that help shape both. Next, I briefly examine foreign-language material selection in prison libraries, focusing on one very popular item in particular. This is followed by interviews and site descriptions of a pair of libraries in facilities holding a large number of Hispanic inmates. I conclude with a brief appraisal of one of the alternatives here presented, a prototypical model of needs assessment and service design rooted in anthropology and the Chicano movement of the late 1960s and early 1970s.

This study is far from complete; indeed, it can scarcely be said to have begun. What is certain is that librarians have for too many years been lamenting shortcomings in services to linguistic minorities while simultaneously taking part in practices that serve to deepen and widen the gaps between their libraries and these potential users. One factor that allows this to continue is a kind of plausible denial. In many correctional settings, such denial would not even be worth trying; the facts are plain to see, hidden from those on the outside but not the people who live and work within. Although it is unlikely that prison librarianship, given its marginal status, could ever serve as a petri dish for wide change in professional practices, it is itself an area crying out for change. Furthermore, it presents interesting parallels to familiar problems with services to cultural and linguistic minorities in public libraries. Many of the ideas presented here would apply equally well to libraries on the outside or on the inside.

Evolution of the Prison Library

It would seem that any institution daring to use the term "corrections" would require all of its charges to participate in educational programs for how else is one "corrected?"

—Mumia Abu-Jamal, "Campaign of Repression"

Books have been finding their way into American jails since colonial times, and this country's first true prison library, with a budget and a book acquisition plan, was founded just over 200 years ago in Philadelphia (Coyle 1987, 10). Variety of reading matter was not the spice of prison life in the late eighteenth and early nineteenth centuries. Prison library historian Austin MacCormick writes: "Even in the dungeon-like cells of the early 19th century, where silence waged continual war on sanity, prisoners were permitted to read. Their reading, to be sure, was restricted to the Bible and other religious works, but they could read" (1970, 3).

The prevailing view that inmates, as demonstrably flawed sinners, should be force-fed a steady diet of morally uplifting texts shaped convicts' reading habits until after the Civil War. The 1870s were revolutionary times in American librarianship, with the advent of the American Library Association and the rise to prominence of Melvil Dewey, inventor of the venerable decimal classification system and founder of the nation's first library training school. The era brought a new orientation to prison libraries, acknowledging their educational and recreational role. Still, according to Brenda Vogel, the next hundred years were marked by a series of fits and starts: "Articles appeared in professional journals, though not many. The movement did not take hold. This stall in progress is due in part to the lack of acceptance and agreement by the narrow-visioned corrections community and in part due to the ambivalent, disinterested library community" (1995, 5).

In 1967, the U.S. Congress for the first time directed substantial funding to correctional libraries through the Library Services and Construction Act. LSCA funds have financed important library projects across the country. The program began in the 1950s as the LSA, originally to build rural libraries, and is now called the LSTA, where the *T* stands for "technology." The act channels federal money to state libraries to be distributed, through a competitive grant process, to local agencies. The new financing for prison libraries enabled the establishment of facilities where none had existed before and facilitated the improvement of existing sites through the hiring of trained professional staff. The legitimization of the prison library had begun, but it was a Supreme Court ruling ten years later that gave such libraries, for better or for worse, the shape they have today.

Bounds v. Smith, 430 U.S. 817 (1977), forced prisons to provide inmates with "meaningful access to the courts." In practice, this was widely interpreted as a mandate to assemble libraries of law books and make them available to prisoners. Although *Bounds v. Smith* ensured for two decades that inmates had library service in some form, there has been serious debate about its value. Law books, like lawyers, are expensive; Vogel has estimated recently that complete sets cost roughly $35,000 to purchase and some $6,000 yearly to update and maintain (1977, 37). During an expansion of the jail where I worked, I watched a counselor spend one lonesome work week unpacking and shelving box after box of heavy leather-bound volumes, most of which, he told me despairingly, "haven't even been cracked open."

And none of those books, of course, was in a language other than English. This oversight—indeed, inequity, for how can an inmate unable to read a law book be said to have the same access to the courts as one who can?—has not escaped the notice of inmates and their advocates. This was in fact one of the elements of *Lewis v. Casey,* 116 S. Ct. 2174 (1996) which reached the Supreme Court in 1996. Among the effects of the lower court's ruling, had it stood, would have been the employment of multilingual legal staff to assist non-English speakers. The high court's reversal is an apparent setback for minorities and inmates in general, but Vogel is among those who are optimistic about what the decision, which continues to send ripples through the correctional library community, will mean for prisons. She argues that a "communal misinterpretation" of *Bounds* has led correctional institutions to install expensive, little-used law libraries as a matter of course, ignoring the fact that the creation of such a library was but one possibility suggested by the 1977 ruling (1996).

The changes resulting from *Lewis v. Casey* have not yet settled out. An August 1999 memorandum from the California Department of Corrections Library Services office notes that courts are "CURRENTLY IMPLEMENTING THE *LEWIS V. CASEY* DECISION" but that the state's prison libraries will maintain the programs they had in place before the ruling, pending written notice ordering changes (California Department of Corrections 1999, 2). This might seem surprising, more than three years after the ruling. As people who work on the inside are fond of saying, *if it takes a year to get something done on the outside, figure five years in here.*

Latino Librarianship

Behind bars you stand
peering down into the cellblock landing
where porters mill,
leaning on mops and brooms.
You wear dark sunglasses
like your Indio ancestors
wore black war paint…

—Jimmy Santiago Baca, "Ese Chicano"

Library service to Spanish speakers has similarly faltered for much of the century, occasionally showing exciting signs of progress only to stumble for one reason or another. As in prison librarianship, momentum has not been sustained and as a consequence the need for basic measures to improve service to this established and growing community is rediscovered every few years. It was a century ago that California State Librarian James Gillis made the reasonable recommendation that professional library school programs include a Spanish-language requirement; in 1999, the Pío Pico branch of the Los Angeles Public

Library, to cite one example in a census tract that is about three-quarters Hispanic, employed but one Spanish-speaking staff librarian, who is not a native speaker.

The most promising activity in Latino librarianship coincided with the Chicano student movement of the late 1960s and early 1970s. At a time when activists were demanding a voice in their communities, reform-minded librarians saw obvious shortcomings in a public institution that served white America very well but somehow largely alienated minority groups even in their own neighborhoods. Community representatives spoke out, showing little reluctance to classify alienating practices and assumptions as anything short of oppressive discrimination.

Attempts at culturally sensitive library service were implemented, many of them very imaginative. Tricolor red-white-and-green bookmobiles ventured out to farm labor camps in the San Joaquin Valley, pumping Latino music out of roof-mounted speakers like an ice cream truck, staffed with bicultural librarians who charged no fines (Naismith 1982). Bilingual services and programs involving entire families were implemented; in addition to the language and literacy instructional focus that has long been part of libraries in immigrant communities, sites tried to shape programs that would involve the community in planning and execution. Needs assessment, one of the most notoriously underused tools in the kits of even those librarians who know its unquestionable value, was in its Golden Age.

No needs assessment study was more fascinating than Roberto Haro's now-forgotten "One-Man Survey" (1970). From 1967 to 1969 the young library crusader prowled the cracked sidewalks of Sacramento and East Los Angeles, talking to Hispanics about libraries. Some 600 people of all ages were interviewed, mostly in Spanish, and there was nothing clinical about Haro's technique. "The methodology of the survey," he writes, "was as unstructured as it could be. Although the recordkeeping was scrupulous, the interviewer sometimes had to resort to such devices as false moustaches and grubby street clothes to win the confidence of respondents encountered casually on the streets" (1970, 737).

The data Haro gathered are every bit as intriguing as his research methods. Although the presentation of statistics that do not necessarily add up undermines his assertion of "scrupulous" recordkeeping, somehow this study's quirks make it all the more compelling. Haro found that one-third of his informants had never set foot in a library of any kind; most of the others had done so only at school. When asked how satisfied they were with library service in the United States, more than three-quarters of Haro's sample told him plainly that they didn't care one way or the other!

What remains most important about the survey is the example Haro set for librarians in terms of community engagement. His regard for and active curiosity about the group under scrutiny stands as an admirable but neglected model. He writes, "As a professional, the librarian should be prepared to abandon the confines of the library, venture into the community, study and analyze its composition, determine its informational needs, and make appropriate plans to service those needs" (1970, 742). Such plans, furthermore, should be discussed and periodically reviewed in a forum that invites the active participation of the community.

What Haro accomplished with his one-man survey comes very close to anthropology. It stands in fascinating contrast to later, more conventional studies by researchers who seem to scorn Haro's sloppiness yet nonetheless fail to duplicate the richness of his findings.

It bears mentioning here that prison libraries, like public libraries, are statistics-driven institutions. Much of what typical correctional librarians and administrators know about their inmates comes from data gathered through an orientation more akin to what is described below than to Haro's approach.

Michael González, Bill Greeley, and Stephen Whitney (1980) used census tract surveying in 1977 and 1978 to try to understand the service needs of Hispanic residents of San Bernadino. It is revealing that their writeup makes frequent comparisons with Haro's findings, calling his quirky study into question without being nearly so critical of their own methods. They take pains to represent a more stable Hispanic population, noting, for example, that only 14 percent of their respondents had arrived within the past year, as opposed to the 41 percent reported by Haro. This is scarcely surprising, given that González et al. surveyed households instead of people on the streets. It would be unfair to suggest that their study is less legitimate than Haro's, but there can be little question which one arrived at a more profound understanding of its community. What is more, for all the self-consciously careful scientific control in the San Bernadino study, it would be problematic to assert that its snapshot of the community is any more accurate than that of the "One-Man Survey."

Vivian Pisano and Margaret Skidmore's (1978) experience illustrates why this is so, with a report whose refreshing frankness serves as an object lesson. The two librarians self-effacingly recount their ambition to apply sound social science research principles to a library needs assessment in a Spanish-speaking community in Richmond, California. This white-smock-and-clipboard approach was beset with problems from the beginning. The researchers found it impossible to obtain an acceptable sample; every type of list from auto registration to phone service would introduce economic bias. The labor-intensive fallback solution of visiting households was not much better; the hardest-working residents were also the hardest to find at home.

Survey instruments were standardized but inappropriate. A reading preference questionnaire included genres such as science fiction but omitted religious works, which turned out to be far more popular among the targeted respondents. Language problems further plagued the questionnaires; clumsily worded elements tended to confuse or even alienate respondents. Additionally, the researchers surmised that permitting and recording open-ended responses greatly enriched their data. They conclude, somewhat abashed, that "a less rigid, qualitative analysis may be a more effective and realistic method that will enable the library and the community to learn more about each other" (1978, 253).

It may be assumed that librarians in correctional institutions, populated as they are by closely monitored and carefully catalogued inmates, would find it easier to compile statistics on potential users. Certainly a great deal of personal information is potentially accessible to prison library staff, but its use varies from site to site. When I asked about the patterns and proportions of language use among the nearly 5,000 inmates in a facility which processes a good many immigration cases, the library director told me that she had not checked.

I will say more later about needs assessment and the effectiveness of a genuine approach like Haro's. The library profession's reluctance to embrace these "less rigid, qualitative" aspects of its work, racing instead to align itself somehow with the harder sciences, has allowed it to remain aloof from many of its users; the naively enthusiastic work of the 1970s did not gather momentum or serve to significantly reshape the role of the library in a diverse community. To be fair, the lessons of that era have not been entirely forgotten; Camila Alire and Orlando Archibeque, for example, point out in their guide to needs assessment in Hispanic communities that the "goal is not 100% accuracy" but rather simply finding useful information that can be used to improve services (1998, 69).

A recent editorial in *Library Journal* echoes a theme that has been sounding, in ever-changing contexts, for more than a century in U.S. libraries. The continuing failure of our libraries to reflect the groups they serve, writes John Berry, is an "awful professional oversight," and few in our overwhelmingly Caucasian profession would bother to dispute that.

> Librarians seldom learn the language, collect the literatures, or understand in any deep way the beliefs, traditions, morals and mores, lifestyles, or aspirations and expectations of the minority cultures in their midst. We reach out to hand them only our culture and heritage, rather than receiving and learning about theirs and respectfully adding them to our collections and personal service. (Berry 1999, 112)

Laments of this nature are nothing new in the library world.

Authority and Otherness

Oh, such a bunch of devils no one ever saw
Robbers, thieves and highwaymen, breakers
*   of the law*
They sang a song the whole night long,
The curses fell like hail
I'll bless the day that takes me away
From the Portland County Jail
                    —"Portland County Jail," American folk song

When Carl Sandburg put that tune in his *American Songbag*, he was likely unaware that there *is* no "Portland County Jail." Portland lies mostly in Multnomah County; thus the thousand-bed facility where I worked was officially called the Multnomah County Inverness Jail. I doubt I ever had an actual highwayman in my English as a Second Language classes, and as for singing a song the whole night long, I cannot say; I was part of the fortunate group that passed through the sally ports each afternoon toward the outdoors and a soft bed at home. The *pintos*—the word means "inmate" in jailhouse Spanish slang—and I occupied separate cultures, in more ways than one.

In considering library services to Spanish speakers on the outside and to prisoners on the inside, one crucial commonality is that the librarian almost certainly belongs to a different culture than the patron. Some service providers regard this as a doorway to discovery. Librarians, to be sure, are a racially homogenous group, but they also tend to see themselves as open-minded and interested in learning. Most acknowledge a responsibility to study the information needs and cultural norms of other ethnic groups and say that they *would* do so more thoroughly if they only had the time. In practice, librarians tend to assume a fallback position that, in situations of linguistic or cultural dissonance, allows them to save face by asserting their authority. The evident fear of having this authority usurped can lead librarians unwittingly into some absurd practices. This was illustrated brilliantly by Kary Shender, a "freelance linguist" who questioned working public librarians in two California systems about how they worked with Spanish-speaking patrons. Shender (1985) found that in many cases librarians go to great lengths to deny their ignorance of other cultures or to acknowledge that their own monolingualism may be a handicap. She writes that "one participant who is in constant contact with [Spanish-speaking] patrons but had limited Spanish skills responded that she didn't need Spanish. However, in another section of the questionnaire she explained that when necessary she calls in a translator!" (1985, 737).

Compare this to what happened when inmate José Bonilla, during a 1996 class-action lawsuit on behalf of nearly 200 Latino inmates, testified (through an interpreter, no less) that his monolingual infirmary doctors could not explain what type of medicine they were giving him or how to administer the dosage; a corrections official, instead of asserting that his infirmary was capable of serving its population, testified that Bonilla spoke "very fluent" English (Ly 1996).

The tendency in such a clearly delineated hierarchy is to hold subordinates responsible for misunderstandings or communication problems—blame the victim. My own conversations with non-Spanish-speaking librarians in heavily Latino areas have often hit precisely the same wall described by the linguist Shender, who found that, "Many librarians were confused about the nature of the Spanish spoken in their community, with comments such as, 'You know, they don't speak the *real* Spanish, so we have to do things a little differently'; and 'They speak mostly in phrases, so it doesn't matter if you've studied Spanish . . . you may still be in trouble' " (1985, 131).

Here the prevailing practice is clearly to deny that the community has anything to teach the librarian, a position diametrically opposed to that exemplified by Haro's "One-Man Study." Such an attitude leads the service provider toward a position not of needs assessment but of needs *assumption*. This is an insidious habit because it is so hard to recognize in one's self; it can, however, arise anywhere cultures are in contact.

Prescriptive Pulp Librarianship

Preso me encuentro tras de la reja
Tras de la reja de mi prisión
Cantar quisiera, cantar no puedo
Las tristes quejas del corazón

—*"La canción del prisionero,"*
Mexican folk song

Library books are free. Unless, that is, you are a librarian whose job includes ordering, inventorying, repairing, and replacing those books. A great deal of expense goes into running a library properly, and prison librarians as public servants must be conscious of budgetary concerns.

Foreign-language books are often considerably more expensive here than comparable editions in English. The constraints on a prison librarian's budget tend to put quality foreign-language editions in the category of luxury goods, particularly with the astonishingly high damage and loss rates reported in institutional libraries.

Still, most libraries would acknowledge their responsibility to make a healthy variety of recreational reading matter available to readers of Spanish, who make up the largest linguistic minority in almost every correctional facility in the United States.

What to do? Purchasing sufficient titles from a distributor of foreign-language materials would quickly eat up the acquisitions budget, restricting the library's ability to gather enough books to satisfy the English speakers who are, after all, its primary clientele. Any perceived imbalances in the collection could, perhaps, invite reprisals of vandalism and theft from inmates resentful of evident favoritism for the *pintos* who haven't even bothered to learn English.

Put yourself in the correctional librarian's place. Donations would be an instant remedy, but the problem is that very few Spanish books come in that way aside from Bibles, Books of Mormon, and other religious items. Occasionally the Mexican government frees up a few boxes of discarded textbooks, but somebody has to make contact with the consulate, and who has the time for that? Maybe if somebody got the word out in the Spanish-language media that the prison library is looking for books . . . but there again, you know, the *time.* . . .

Fortunately for prison librarians, savvy marketers have come to the rescue with a product known popularly as bolsilibros or Estefanías. These shirt-pocket-sized editions are truly pulp fiction, freely translated and abridged from mass-market U.S. paperbacks in the western and detective genres and set on newsprint with minimal quality control. I borrowed some from the Multnomah County Jail, which has boxes of undistributed Estefanías in storage. I found that the garish covers often did not match the always vaguely familiar stories inside (*Hábil con los naipes* contains not a single card-playing scene), that the spelling was unreliable and tended to deteriorate toward the end of a tale, and that now and then entire pages would be repeated side-by-side.

Still in all, the booklets were unfailingly entertaining. Were I in a Spanish-speaking prisoner's sandals I might consider the occasional Estefanía a worthwhile break from dominos, gin rummy, and the difficult-to-understand programs on TV. That is, if there were no other reading matter available in Spanish. And quite often in a correctional setting—for reasons noted above—there is not.

When the first electronic discussion list for correctional librarians convened, I joined soon after it began. The discussion on this PRISON-LIB list, whose membership is screened, is quite often frank and freewheeling. After I read some Estefanías, I floated a question to the list: Are librarians at all uncomfortable with those crudely thrown-together booklets, which they would probably consider substandard if they appeared in English?

The replies were revealing. Some suggested I was being judgmental, in violation of one of Ranganathan's Five Laws: *To every reader his book.* Almost every respondent emphasized that Estefanías are very popular with Hispanic readers, the most in-demand items in the library, in fact. Nobody acknowledged cost factors. No librarians described needs assessment efforts or preference surveys, either formal or informal. One did claim that he buys the work of, as he put it, all the best Spanish authors, yet the Estefanías are what fly off the shelves. He did not mention if he had ever tried shelving, say, magazines about soccer.

Although I suspect that participants on this electronic list are more sensitive than the average prison librarian, mistaken assertions and stereotypes occasionally surface, the same ones heard behind the desks of libraries on the outside: *Lending libraries do not exist in Mexico; anyone who can speak Spanish is automatically able to read it.*

It would be wrong for me to contradict the judgments of experienced prison librarians. Yet I am skeptical about the Estefanías. In the absence of principled investigation into what various groups of Spanish-speaking inmates *would* read if choices were available, it would seem some librarians are blindly accepting truisms and engaging in, without being entirely honest with themselves about it, budget-driven prescriptive librarianship, exactly the sort of practice that everyone from Ranganathan to Roberto Haro to they themselves reject, at least in principle.

Conversation with a Prison Librarian

Sad, sad and lonely,
Sitting in my cell
All alone, all alone
Thinking of days that's gone by me
And the days when I've done wrong

—"Seven Long Years in State Prison,"
American folk song

With her thirteen years' experience in school libraries and five years in the 6,000-volume facility at the Chuckawalla Valley State Prison in southeastern California, Betty Chávez is quick to say that she is "not a real librarian."

"I don't have *the degree,*" she explains, referring to the master's degree in library and information science that is the library world's equivalent of the diploma conferred on Scarecrow by the Wizard of Oz. Without it, Chávez works under the title of Library Technical Assistant, supervising her branch and the group of inmate clerks who assist with shelving, cataloging, and other essential library tasks. Her compensation is reflective of the level of professional repute that prison librarianship has achieved in California: She earns close to $2,500 monthly, doing work she says she thoroughly enjoys.

With the degree, she could expect to earn a good deal more. As an inmate, on the other hand, she would earn a great deal less. Her clerks are compensated at the rates of eight and thirteen cents an hour, depending on experience; alternatively, some opt for sentence reduction on a "day-for-day" basis, in which each seven-hour library work shift advances the prisoner's scheduled release by one day.

Chávez does receive extra pay for a valuable skill unusual among librarians: She speaks Spanish. I wondered if this, aside from other obvious occupational advantages, helps to guide her in materials selection. Her reply, although perhaps surprising to a non-librarian, was frank: "Oh, I don't read. I gave that up *years* ago. You know how you get burned out."

She pointed out that her staff of four clerks, by enlightened institutional mandate, represents the major ethnic groups of the inmate population: At any given time she works with one African American, one Hispanic, and one Caucasian; the fourth clerk "can be anything." She told me that the clerks help with material selection and, because book request slips are available, inmate input does receive consideration.

Chávez reported, in fact, that the day before I spoke with her a Spanish-speaking inmate had requested biographies of Villa, Zapata, and Joaquín Murrieta. One would suspect that this was not the first such request. But, rather than press this issue, I asked what Spanish-language materials were available, and with some enthusiasm she mentioned, among other items, the library's assortment of Estefanías.

Chávez exudes the same warmth that I have sensed in any number of dedicated career librarians—and yes, that is precisely what she is—who enjoy their work and care about their patrons. Some on the outside are surprised to learn that most prison librarians, as are most librarians in general, are female; few have ever reported security concerns. What with the assortment of cameras, heavy doors, and armed guards within, most people who work in correctional facilities will tell you they feel safer inside than out on the streets.

Terminal Island

Me aprehendieron los gendarmes
Al estilo americano:
Como era hombre de delito
Todos con pistola en mano
—"De Cananea," Mexican corrido

For the 600 inmates in custody at the United States Immigration and Naturalization Service Processing Center there, Terminal Island is aptly named. This mammoth grey industrial beachfront structure, surrounded by heavy fencing and coils of razor wire, is for most of its detainees the end of the line in the United States. Following a stay that averages seventeen days, most will be sent out of the country.

The facility's Assistant Officer in Charge, Anita Maker, told me that changing detainee demographics means that now, while most of the Center's population is Hispanic, "very few" are monolingual Spanish speakers. Skeptical as one might be that most occupants of an INS jail would be skilled speakers of English, the conditions of my visit to the facility's library allowed no contact with inmates to assess this claim.

The library—which until recently was called the Reading Room or Law Reading Room, indicating that its establishment was a product of *Bounds v. Smith*—is an enclosed, guarded area about thirty-five feet on a side with three large tables, some straight-backed chairs, two electric typewriters, a locked, refrigerator-sized metal cabinet containing law books, and a number of metal shelves and tubs filled with books and magazines. There is a shelf of romances, dozens of *Reader's Digest Condensed Books* anthologies, thirty-year-old college and high school textbooks on calculus, embryology, and Gregg shorthand, jumbled together with titles such as *The Effective Executive Interview*, most of them very worn, all apparent discards from libraries and personal collections.

The library's operations fall under the jurisdiction of Recreational Director Kevin Pauline, who told me the hardcover volumes cannot be removed to the "pods," that is, the common detention areas where the inmates sleep and spend most of their time, but that paperbacks do circulate. They are often lost; rapid inmate turnover ensures that nonessential personal effects like books are stolen or bequeathed to fellow inmates. Pauline is sanguine about such loss; most of his collection is donated or, in the case of the inevitable Estefanías, purchased at near-negligible cost.

Avid readers, Pauline told me, normally opt to have books sent into the facility. Friends and family can place orders with book retailers for delivery to detainees, though all such materials must of course be screened. In a multilingual environment like this, this usually presents problems—my introduction of Spanish-language newspapers to the Multnomah County Jail needed several months to finally be approved, and Marjorie LeDonne has gone so far as to suggest that "Spanish-language periodicals are virtually impossible to introduce because there is not the staff qualified to do the screening" (1974, 277).

Pauline finds that the most active library users are so-called jailhouse lawyers, prisoners whose avid legal research, sometimes self-interested, sometimes on behalf of fellow inmates, was the focus of *Bounds v. Smith,* and is often viewed by their keepers with a mixture of amusement and disdain. Mark Hamm et al. (1996) report that in-house disciplinary measures imposed by correctional institutions in the United States tend to target jailhouse lawyers disproportionately.

In any case, the uninviting library at this INS facility is used by only a small number of detainees, which Pauline puts at about 4 to 5 percent. I asked him how inmates are made aware of the library and its services, and they said that prisoners receive a handbook on intake. Asked if this guide to the nine-year-old facility has a Spanish version, Maker told me that one was being "finalized" even as we spoke.

Conclusions

En la celda donde estaba
Yo solo me divertía
Contando los eslabones
Que mi cadena tenía

—"Manuel Garza de León,"
Mexican folk song

It may be useful for prison librarians to think of their patrons in terms of the groups classically underserved by libraries in the public sector and to examine the needs assessment and outreach strategies that have targeted such groups on the outside. Understanding these communities seems particularly crucial in light of the fact that people of color constitute a disproportionately large segment of inmate population.

Correctional librarians must become researchers who recognize the panoply of cultures inside the walls. The differences and the complex interplay among Mexicans, Chicanos, urban and rural African-Americans, youth, indigenous groups from throughout the Americas—the list goes on—cannot be understood and accommodated by relying on pat stereotypes. Other nations, furthermore, have dealt with correctional policies in ways that U.S. professionals might find instructive. Kaytinka Reijnders, for example, explains that prison libraries in The Netherlands as a matter of policy keep materials in anywhere from eight to thirty-six languages (1996).

A return to the spirit of Haro—false mustache, grubby clothes, and all—is what is called for, with librarians who live in the communities they serve. These principles can apply in prison. Although I have not yet found a case of a prison library clerk who pursued the profession on the outside and returned to correctional library work, this would be an ideal, and interested inmate clerks should be encouraged to do so. Until that happens, outsiders will serve insiders, but there is no reason they cannot improve the way they serve by seeking to understand the cultures of their clientele. Daniel Suvak (1995) has written, within a librarianship context, about the folkways and behavior codes, the hierarchies and protocol, that define prison communities. Nancy Thomas and James Nyce (1998) have recently defended the application of principles of ethnographic research techniques in the information sciences. But such work is scarce and needs to be expanded.

Prisoners cannot be discounted as sources of useful information. When I asked journalist Paul Wright, editor of *Prison Legal News*, published author and an inmate journalist in the Washington State Penitentiary at Monroe, about library services to Spanish-speaking inmates, he mentioned a successful lawsuit that he had filed on behalf of some Hispanic inmates, but was also quick to write, "In general, they have a poor selection of *English* language materials!" (1999).

The reasons such conditions exist are complex indeed. Simple, quick solutions cannot be expected to solve these longstanding problems. But neither can librarians continue to overlook situations where their own good ideas and observations might be implemented—if only they were to formulate and present some. In learning to do so, librarians inside and out must turn to their anthropology shelves if they are to arrive at the kind of understanding and insight that will translate into credible, inclusive, and effective service.

References

Abu-Jamal, Mumia. 1998. Campaign of repression. In *The celling of America,* edited by Daniel Burton-Rose, Dan Pens, and Paul Wright. Monroe, ME: Common Courage Press.

Alire, Camila, and Orlando Archibeque. 1998. *Serving Latino communities: A how-to-do-it manual for librarians.* New York: Neal-Schuman.

Asch, Stephanie. 1998. Urban libraries confront linguistic minorities: Programs that work." In *Literacy, access, and libraries among the language minority community,* edited by Rebecca Constantino. Lanham, MD: Scarecrow Press.

Berry, John, III. 1999. Editorial: Culturally competent service: A new mandate to serve a new majority. *Library Journal* 124 (16) (September 1): 112.

California Department of Corrections. August 1999. *Library services supervisors' update.*

Chavez, Elizabeth. 1999. Personal interview, October 27.

Christianson, Scott. 1998. *With liberty for some: 500 years of imprisonment in America.* Boston: Northeastern University Press.

Coyle, William J. 1987. *Libraries in prisons: A blending of institutions.* Westport, CT: Greenwood Press.

Danky, James P., and Sanford Berman, eds. 1993. *Alternative library literature 92–93.* Jefferson, NC: McFarland.

Gallegos, Bee, and Lisa Kammerlocher. 1993. A history of library services to the Mexican-Americans and Native Americans in Arizona. In *Alternative library literature 92–93,* edited by James P. Danky and Sanford Berman. Jefferson, NC: McFarland.

González, Michael, Bill Greeley, and Stephen Whitney. 1980. Assessing the library needs of the Spanish-speaking. *Library Journal* 105 (6) (April 1): 786–89.

Hamm, Mark S., Corey Weinstein, Therese Coupez, and Francis Freidman. 1996. The prison discipline study: Exposing the myth of humane imprisonment in the United States. In *Criminal Injustice: Confronting the Prison Crisis,* edited by Eli Rosenblatt. Boston: South End Press.

Haro, Roberto. 1970. One-man survey: How Mexican-Americans view libraries. *Wilson Library Bulletin* 44 (7) (March): 736–42.

Harris, Marie, and Kathleen Aguero. 1989. *An ear to the ground: An anthology of contemporary American poetry.* Athens: University of Georgia Press.

Human Rights Watch. 1992. *Prison conditions in the United States.* New York: Human Rights Watch.

LeDonne, Marjorie. 1974. The role of the library in a correctional institution. In *Library and information services for special groups,* edited by Joshua I. Smith. New York: Science Associates/International Inc.

Lomax, Adrian. 1993. No more books behind bars. *Alternative library literature 92–93,* edited by James P. Danky and Sanford Berman. Jefferson, NC: McFarland.

Ly, Phuong. 1996. In D.C. civil trial, Latino inmates allege bias. *Washington Post,* June 24: B01.

MacCormick, Austin H. 1970. A brief history of libraries in American correctional institutions. In *Proceedings of the American Correctional Association centennial congress of correction.* Cincinnati, OH, October 12.

Maker, Anita. 1999. Personal interview, November 29.

Mendoza, Vicente T. 1954. *El corrido mexicano.* México, D.F.: Fondo de Cultura.

Naismith, Rachel. 1982. Field work: Outreach to migrants. *RQ* 22 (1) (Fall): 33–35.

Orland, Leonard. 1975. *Prisons: Houses of Darkness.* New York: The Free Press.

Paredes, Américo. 1976. *A Texas-Mexican cancionero: Folksongs of the lower border.* Urbana: University of Illinois Press.

Pauline, Kevin. 1999. Personal interview, November 29.

Pisano, Vivian M., and Margaret Skidmore. 1978. Community survey—Why not take an eclectic approach? *Wilson Library Bulletin* 53 (3) (November): 250–53.

Reijnders, Katinka. 1996. Library service for multicultural groups in Dutch prisons. *Journal of Correctional Education* 47 (3) (September): 127–32.

Reynolds, Mary. 1970. La Biblioteca Ambulante. *Wilson Library Bulletin* 44 (7) (March): 767.

Rubin, Rhea Joyce, and Daniel S. Suvak, eds. 1995. *Libraries inside: A practical guide for prison librarians.* Jefferson, NC: McFarland.

Sandburg, Carl. 1927. *The American songbag.* New York: Harcourt, Brace & World.

Shender, Kary Joseph. 1985. Language policies for libraries: A new perspective. *Lector.* 3 (4) (1985): 129-33.

Suvak, Daniel. 1995. The prison community. In *Libraries inside: A practical guide for prison librarians,* edited by Rhea Joyce Rubin and Daniel S. Suvak. Jefferson, NC: McFarland.

Thomas, Nancy P., and James M. Nyce. 1998. Qualitative research in LIS—Redux: A response to "A (re)turn to positivistic ethnography." *Library Quarterly* 68 (1) (January): 108–13.

Vogel, Brenda. 1977. Bailing out prison libraries. *Library Journal* 122 (19) (November 15): 35–37.

———. 1995. *Down for the count: A prison library handbook.* Metuchen, NJ: Scarecrow Press.

———. 1996. Supreme Court decision offers relief to prison librarians." *Corrections Professional* 1 (21) (July 22): 4–5.

Wright, Paul. 1999. Personal correspondence, October 21.

Partners in Success

Public Library Collection Development and the Role of Independent Spanish-Language Publishers and Distributors

Michael Shapiro

This chapter explores the role of independent Spanish-language book publishers and distributors and the support they give to public libraries. The author places emphasis on how libraries might best conceptualize the work of independent book distributors, how they define their work, and how their role differs from that of larger, usually corporate, book distributors. This important information can help libraries make more effective use of the services of independent book vendors.

In 1988 Michael Shapiro founded Libros Sin Fronteras, an independent importer-distributor of Spanish-language materials, and continues to direct the company as its president. He holds a B.A. from the University of California, Berkeley, a California state secondary school teaching credential, and an M.A. in Latin American studies (literature, poetry, and politics) from the University of New Mexico. He has been a visiting instructor at the University of Havana's Department of Communications, where he teaches "Aspects of Spanish Language Publishing and Distribution and the Needs of U.S. Libraries." He expects to continue his membership in REFORMA well into the twenty-first century.

$\mathbf{A}$ natural symbiosis occurs for public libraries when publishers and distributors successfully meld library objectives into their business practices. The dynamic interplay between public library Spanish-language collections and the "book vendors" (publishers and distributors) who serve them is the focus of this chapter.[1]

Families, public schools, and public libraries play an essential role in supporting and fomenting what many believe to be some of our country's greatest untapped resources: diverse, vibrant communities populated by multiple generations that maintain a unique cultural and linguistic heritage.[2] Thankfully, examples of these diverse communities representing numerous ethnic traditions abound, and public libraries continue to expand their services as national, state, and community demographics dictate.

Increasingly, public librarians throughout the country are finding themselves advocating, promoting, developing, and managing Spanish-language collections for fast-growing Spanish-speaking populations.[3] It is their responsibility to make and keep these collections prominent, visually attractive, long lasting, and appropriate to their patrons' needs. In addition, they must do so through the efficient use of library resources, financial, human, and other. Because the growth of Spanish-speaking populations is far outstripping the number of librarians experienced in the field of public library collection development and acquisitions, the role of the Spanish-language materials vendor is gaining importance to public (and other) libraries, and particularly in those areas where the arrival of a significant Spanish-speaking population is relatively recent.

Planning, developing, and managing public library Spanish-language adult, young adult, and children's collections is a complex and multifaceted enterprise; its execution can run the gamut from very thoughtful and efficient to quite ineffectual. As with any such endeavor, the definition of exactly what's needed and the assignment and delegation of tasks and resources are both the most important and the most challenging aspects of the job.

Creating and maintaining a Spanish-language public library collection is almost always a partnership and rarely the sole activity of any single individual, department, or organization. Within this partnership, Spanish-language book vendors are able to offer much more than a mere listing or catalog of titles. Public library collection development and acquisitions specialists will do much toward making the work of creating and maintaining Spanish-language collections more efficient and effective as they better understand and define how to make the most of Spanish-language vendors' skills, resources, and services.

One of the most important services Spanish-language materials vendors (both publishers and distributors) offer to public libraries is title recommendation. As the volume of Spanish-language materials for a growing Spanish-speaking domestic readership continues to mount, it becomes more and more difficult for public libraries to know just what to purchase and what not to pur-chase.[4] The effective marriage of a public library's Spanish-language collection development objectives with materials that fill that need requires a panoramic view of available materials. Spanish-language book distributors may at times have more expertise and experience in this work than the librarian or librarians responsible for collection building. The effective management of this resource through both oral and written dialogue, often in the form of a profile stating col-lection objectives, effective safeguards on quality and cost, and so forth, can go far in removing a major and very time-consuming burden from the shoulders of the librarian.

Many U.S.-based Spanish-language importer-distributors offer an exten-sive array of products and services to meet a public library's collection develop-ment needs. Some of these can include highly structured, risk-mitigated, and individually tailored standing orders, core and opening-day collections, ap-proval plans, annotated catalogs (print and electronic format) with excellent bib-liographic information, toll-free telephone numbers, and binding reinforcement services. Many vendors also regularly attend essential public library conferences and events: the summer and mid-winter American Library Association Confer-ence; the Guadalajara International Book Fair; the Public Library Association Conference; and the Texas, California, and other state library association confer-ences, to mention only a few.

In "Developing the Spanish Children's Collection," past REFORMA president Oralia Garza de Cortés comments on the role of book distributors:

> Distributors of books in Spanish for children play a critical role in developing the Spanish children's collection. They become the book selector in the absence of a librarian well versed in Spanish children's literature. The best of the distributors of children's materials in Spanish have acquired an expertise . . . that renders them competent to select material for a school or public library collection . . . finding a distributor that is knowledgeable of chil-dren's literature is crucial. . . . Increasingly, libraries, like most publicly-funded institutions, must adhere to the criteria for the selection of a vendor based on the lowest bid placed for that service within the city or county's public bidding process. Lamen-tably, such a one-dimensional process dismisses the qualitative aspect that a knowledgeable distributor may be able to provide. . . . Some distributors . . . offer selection services based on a profile of material requested by a particular institution. . . . Others . . . pro-vide approval plans where materials are shipped out, in an effort to allow selectors to view firsthand the materials considered for pur-chase. (2000, 75–90)

Rare abuses by unscrupulous vendors seeking to use standing orders and approval plans to "unload" dated or otherwise unwanted inventory into public library collections have in many ways sullied what most collection development specialists would agree is a very efficient, safe, and effective approach to Spanish-language collection development.

Spanish-language publishers themselves are not in a position to give unbiased selection advice, because they must sell those items they have chosen to publish. Large, non-specialized distributors, by their very nature, offer little in the way of careful selection. However, U.S.-based Spanish-language distributors do tend to meticulously pick and choose what they believe to be the best materials from a multiplicity of domestic and offshore sources. Many of these distributors, because of the nature of their client base, make their selection decisions very specifically to match the needs of public libraries. What's more, in most cases they do this work at no additional charge; it is part and parcel of their work as selection specialists. By gathering and making available selected works in a format amenable to their library clients, importer-distributors have accomplished what it would take anyone else innumerable hours to reproduce. For many of these vendors, the careful matching of Spanish-language titles to specific public library collection requirements forms the core and centerpiece of their work. Because they do it every day and their success as a business depends on it, they must keep well abreast of important developments in Spanish-language publishing worldwide. Clearly, no single vendor should ever pretend to make available all the materials relevant to public libraries. But by working with various U.S.-based importer-distributors, librarians both cover the broadest possible cross-section of available materials and limit the time spent ascertaining which publishers to work with or which titles warehoused by colossal, non-specialized Spanish-language distributors best meet their needs. Yet collection development and acquisitions librarians sometimes fail to take full advantage of the added value the Spanish book distributor offers.

The traditional large suppliers of English-language materials for public libraries put little or no emphasis on "evaluation and selection" as such, instead concentrating their attention and expertise on effective fulfillment of as broad and extensive a cross-section of material as possible. Large U.S.-based book distributors are unchallenged in their ability to make domestically published materials available to libraries quickly and efficiently. They nevertheless do not excel in the evaluation and selection of Spanish-language materials.

There is a very logical and sound business reason for this. Companies like those mentioned above grow their businesses through the high-volume turnover of an enormous and ever-expanding pool of titles. For this to be achieved, they purchase materials from largely domestic sources (publishers) in substantial quantities and enjoy generous payment terms (often 90 to 120 days) and the contractually guaranteed understanding that books (or "product") that do not perform (i.e., sell, or "turn") well enough will be returned to their producers.

For these large U.S.-based distributors, this mechanism for purchase and return of unsold merchandise does not coincide well with the world of Spanish-language publishing, a world still very much dominated by non-U.S.-based firms.[5] Even if offshore publishers were willing to accept returns, the cost of return shipping would be prohibitive. Here, the role of the small, independent Spanish-language book importer-distributor gains new meaning. Because returning merchandise overseas is generally not an acceptable option, the Spanish-language book importer-distributor's evaluation and selection skills must be well honed or it risks purchasing titles that no longer (or never did) meet its public library clients' needs and, by definition, the needs of their patrons.[6]

This U.S. Spanish materials distribution dilemma is exacerbated by something of a Spanish-language publishing crisis being felt by public libraries and their Spanish-speaking patrons.[7] Spanish-language publishers in the United States, like their English-language "big brothers," are subject to corporate globalization forces that often do not match up well with the diverse reading needs of U.S. Spanish-speaking communities. Publishing worldwide is increasingly falling under the domain of fewer and fewer participants, corporate media giants for whom profitability and return on investment is essential. Although "the growing Spanish-language market" has very much caught the eye of U.S. book publishers, they, their shareholders, and the volume-oriented distributors who sell their books seek profitability first, and profitability becomes synonymous with volume. Profit in book publishing is leveraged against the activities of other extensive investments (television and other media, insurance, construction, and health care).[8] The decisions to dedicate resources to publishing and whether to print any given title (be it English- or Spanish-language) are analyzed against a host of other profit-generating opportunities.

Publishing has thereby been recast into a diversified corporate structure that not only has to "hold its own" financially but has to compete with other potential investments. Publishing for smaller audiences all too often loses out to other investments. This is clearly reflected in the character of the Spanish-language titles most abundantly produced for the domestic market: an abundance of formula-driven titles;[9] materials by proven, well-known, and market-tested authors (writing in either original Spanish or translated from other languages into Spanish) rather than newer "riskier" ones; and "concept" or "packaged" books,[10] with movie and other product "tie-ins" and large, potential "cross-over" markets.[11]

Here the importance of independent publishers and importer-distributors of Spanish-language materials in the United States begins to come into sharper focus. Importer-distributors seek, find, and bring into the United States materials from Spanish-speaking countries that overlap with the educational needs and entertainment desires of U.S. Latinos. Nevertheless, the needs of U.S. Latinos seeking Spanish books are fully met by neither imported materials nor corporate, U.S.-based, Spanish-language publishers seeking mass-market successes.[12]

When materials do enter the purview of U.S.-based Spanish-language book importer-distributors, they become the focus of a complex and extensive internal dialogue about whether and to what extent a given title meets or doesn't meet the public library clients' needs and those of their patrons. These decisions are very complex ones, with many factors entering into the equation.

First and most obviously, the book has to be seen, or if not seen, at least some representation or reference to it must be discovered. Importer-distributors make use of numerous ways to bring books onto their radar screens. They keep in close contact (via e-mail, fax, telephone, etc.) with foreign publishers, scour print and online catalogs and other electronic resources, read Spanish-language reviews from Latin America and Spain (and the occasional review written in English),[13] and travel to domestic and international book exhibitions. It is only then that the real fun begins.

Issues that Spanish-language distributors must take into consideration when deciding to import a given title or a series of titles are innumerable. First, does the book and its subject matter fit clients' needs? Is the text well written? Does it effectively achieve its goal? Is it appropriate to Spanish-language readers (Hispanics; Anglos learning Spanish) in the United States? If the book is a translation, was it effectively translated into standard contemporary Spanish? Is the book's vocabulary overly regional, provincial, vulgar, or otherwise inappropriate or unfamiliar to a U.S. readership? (Or is its colloquial nature indeed its greatest asset?) Is the book well indexed? Does it include a table of contents, an ISBN number, and other essential bibliographic data? Is the book a first edition, or a first edition in Spanish? When did it (or will it) first make its appearance on the market? If it is a reprinting, has it been revised or corrected? Are its physical characteristics (especially paper and binding quality) acceptable, and will they allow for multiple circulations? Are the clarity of print and illustration, font size and selection, attractiveness of front cover and spine, and space of margins and gutters up to par? Might other existing titles offer a better treatment of a given subject? Does the publisher have a reputation for quality work, for timely and accurate order fulfillment?[14] Does the publisher own the rights to distribute the book in the United States? Who is responsible for the unexpected: mis-shipments, loss, damage, mis-billings, customs irregularities? How large was the book's initial print run, and how soon is it likely to go out of print? Will it be reprinted? Has the publisher released other books by this author or on this subject? What does the publisher understand to be the book's intended audience? Is the book priced fairly for the U.S. Spanish-language book market? Is the rate of exchange from a local currency a concern? Are the publisher's payment terms clear, fair, and well documented? What is the best means to ship the book to the United States? How costly and time intensive is that shipment likely to be?

As one might easily imagine, a barrage of questions like these (although thankfully not all questions need to be asked of all publishers about all titles) offers non-U.S.-based Spanish-language publishers new insights about the U.S.

market. Indeed, a major behind-the-scenes role of U.S. Spanish-language importer-distributors is to bring their clients' concerns (and by extension their "clients' clients' concerns") to the attention of publishers. If availability of appropriate titles is lacking today (and it certainly is) and as the U.S. market expands (as it certainly will), publishers will need more information about the specific needs of U.S. Spanish speakers. The small importer-distributor working closely with public libraries has a unique opportunity to keep a "finger on the pulse of the market" and create effective communication with foreign publishers.

If there's one key lesson to be learned, it's that public libraries need to be proactive and not reactive in building Spanish-language collections. Working effectively with vendors can often free librarians to do what they and only they can accomplish. Recruitment of qualified bilingual-bicultural librarians and staff is essential; it is difficult to imagine a sizable U.S. city today that doesn't need a knowledgeable and qualified Hispanic services librarian. The unfamiliarity with public libraries in Latin American countries—free, public access lending libraries are not a strong tradition in much of Latin America—increases the need for effective library outreach into Hispanic communities.[15] Success will be greatly hampered without strong, vocal advocacy for increased and proportionate funding for Spanish-language collections.

Diverse Spanish-language public library collections both acknowledge and empower Spanish-speaking communities and strengthen their role in our larger society. Investments made now will show enormous societal payoffs as public libraries and the Spanish-language publishers and distributors who serve them move together in partnership, building bridges, eroding borders, and supporting diverse communities.

Notes

1.   Although much of what is presented here may also be applicable to serials, audiovisual materials, and online resources, as well as to private, academic, correctional, and special libraries, the focus remains on books and public libraries.

2.   "If we see to it that immigrants and their children can speak only English and nothing more, then we will have missed one of the greatest opportunities of this new century. It's high time we begin to treat language skills as the assets they are. Unfortunately, too many teachers and administrators today treat a child's native language as a weakness if it is not English" (Education Secretary William Riley as quoted in McQueen 2000).

3.   "With more than 30 million Hispanics, the United States is already the fifth largest Spanish-speaking nation in the world. Within 10 years, only Mexico will have more Spanish-speakers" (Kiser 1999a).

4.   "Estimates from 1999 Department of Commerce data put the Spanish book market at a value of $368 million. It is larger than the U.S. market for Bibles and rivals that of the mail order English-language book business in the U.S." (Kiser 2000).

5.   "Mexico is the leading book importer with $69.2 million dollars of books, a figure that becomes $173 million when adjusted to reflect list price. Spain comes in second with $45.8 million, with Colombia, Ecuador and Argentina rounding out the top five. . . . Nearly 200 publishers in the U.S. and Puerto Rico reportedly publish books in Spanish and collectively account for $38 million dollars in annual sales" (Kiser 2000).

6.   There exists a continual competitive push and pull between large, high-volume book distributors with very efficient fulfillment mechanisms who wish to enter the Spanish book market and smaller importer-distributors who are experts in the field but lack the infrastructure of the larger distributors. The larger distributors seek access to the imported books desired by their customers but expect terms and conditions like those they enjoy from their U.S. suppliers.

7.   New technologies are indeed changing the character of this dilemma very quickly. Still, its continued effect on book publishers, distributors, and their clients is an interesting testament to the persistence of "old-school" book publication and distribution in the early twenty-first century.

8.   Although financial gain is clearly the raison d'être for corporate publishing, other gains are also considered and evaluated, including public relations opportunities and the social cachet attached to book publishing.

9.   Examples include such titles as *Sopa de pollo para el alma* (Chicken Soup for the Soul) and the *Para principiantes* (For Dummies) series.

10.   Publishers increasingly create "packaged" books. These are often very handsome, illustrated, nonfiction works developed and created by teaming various inhouse resources (writers, illustrators or photographers, offshore printing connections, etc.). This type of book publishing circumvents the payment of fees to authors outside the company.

11.   *Pokemon,* Disney, or other character-based titles (*Aladdin, The Lion King, Pocahontas)* are obvious examples.

12.

The following is a synthesis of what teachers and public librarians have repeatedly communicated to me as lacking for their Spanish-speaking students and patrons. Publishers, take heed: 1) High-interest/low-level adult and young adult reading. Large print editions of important fiction and non-fiction works both for low-level readers and the elderly or visually impaired. *Fotonovelas* with romantic (perhaps even uplifting and empowering), non-sexist, non-violent content.

2) Survival, "how-to" and illustrative testimonial materials written specifically for Spanish-speaking immigrants: information on employment assistance, basic health care, taxation, public and private schooling, financial aid, government bureaucracy, North American cultural norms. 3) Examinations of Hispanic, Chicano, Latino, African American and other minority and immigrant experiences. Folklore, traditions and holidays from world cultures and religions; examinations of parallels and interconnections between Latinos and other communities in the U.S. 4) Biographies of Latino and Latina role models, especially successful and accomplished "non-celebrities" of diverse ages and Latino/Hispanic cultural heritages. 5) Bilingual books for all age groups, professionally written (or translated) in standard Latin American Spanish. 6) Support and supplementary materials for elementary, middle, high school, and adult school curricula: U.S. and world history, geography, math, physical and natural sciences, vocational studies. 7) Original fiction and non-fiction in Spanish, at both popular and university levels—materials whose uniqueness, timeliness and import pose a challenge to the non-Spanish-speaking, monolingual majority. Fresh, intelligent Latino and Chicano voices and perspectives, written and published in the original Spanish. (Shapiro 1997)

13.   In spring 2001, the first volume of *Críticas: An English Speaker's Guide to the Latest Spanish-language Titles* was published by Cahner's, issuers of *Library Journal, School Library Journal,* and *Publishers Weekly.*

14.   For additional exploration of the cultural differences in the Latin American and U.S. book markets, see Kiser (1999b).

15.   For an excellent discussion of public library outreach to Latino and other diverse communities see Ocon (2000).

References

Garza de Cortés, Oralia. 2000. Developing the Spanish children's collection. In *Library services to Latinos: An anthology,* edited by Salvador Güereña. Jefferson, NC: McFarland.

Kiser, Karin N. 1999. Books across the border: Selling to the Spanish-language market in the U.S. *Publishers Weekly,* September 13.

———. 1999b. *Estrategias para vender libros en español en Estados Unidos. Mexico City: Editorial Pax.*

———. 2000. Spanish-language publishing in the U.S. nears critical mass. *Publishers Weekly,* September 18.

McQueen, Anjetta. 2000. Dual-language schools urged for immigrants. *Associated Press,* March 16.

Ocon, Ben. 2000. Effective outreach strategies to the Latino community: A paradigm for public libraries. In *Library services to Latinos: An anthology,* edited by Salvador Guereña. Jefferson, NC: McFarland.

Shapiro, Michael. 1997. What about the library market. *Publishers Weekly,* August 25.

Perspectives on
Public Libraries in Puerto Rico

Susan Freiband

This chapter is an overview of public libraries in Puerto Rico, including types, functions, support, users, collections, and services. Challenges are many, including the lack of adequately trained personnel, the low salary scale, limited outreach efforts, and a low community profile. The author offers strategies for strengthening connections between Puerto Rican public libraries and those in the United States, including exchange programs, visits, and field trips. Improved contact might expand perspectives on both sides and facilitate needed change.

Susan Freiband is currently a professor in the Graduate School of Information Sciences and Technologies, University of Puerto Rico, Río Piedras. Her interests are in the area of collection development, adult services, and multicultural librarianship. She is a former Peace Corps Volunteer and ALA Library Fellow, with library experience in Columbia and El Salvador.

113

Introduction

T his chapter presents a broad, general overview of public libraries in Puerto Rico today. Types of public libraries, their functions, support, users, collections, and services are described. Needs of, concerns of, and challenges facing Puerto Rican public libraries, as well as strategies for strengthening the interconnections between Puerto Rican and U.S. public libraries, are also discussed.

Types of Libraries in Puerto Rico

Public libraries in Puerto Rico today are in the process of transition. Since the early 1950s, most of the public libraries in Puerto Rico have been under the jurisdiction of the Puerto Rico Department of Education. They were administered centrally, part of a public library system developed within this large, bureaucratic government agency. However, in 1999 and 2000, as part of a general movement toward decentralization in education and in other aspects of Puerto Rican government, the sixty-one public libraries established and run by the Department of Education have been in the process of being turned over to the municipalities. As of 1999, there were sixteen area libraries among the sixty-one public libraries, some of them functioning as electronic public libraries, equipped with computers, FAX machines, and other electronic resources. The area libraries serve as resource centers for smaller, less well-equipped public libraries in their region.

In addition, there are sixteen municipal public libraries, originally not a part of the Department of Education's public library system but rather established and supported completely by the municipality. Besides these, there are four community libraries, which are public libraries founded as a result of local grassroots efforts by community groups or individuals functioning outside the jurisdiction of the municipality or the Department of Education. One of these community libraries is a children's library. The largest and most important of these libraries is the Dorado Community Library, founded by a group of U.S. women who created a public library based on what they were familiar with in the United States. This community library has influenced the development of the others on the Island, serving as a model in the provision of services and in obtaining community support.

Another type of public library in Puerto Rico is the "specialized public library." This category includes twenty-eight libraries in public housing projects, twenty-four in correctional institutions (jails and prisons), four mobile public libraries (bookmobiles, two of them electronic, under the aegis of the Department of Education), and the Library for the Blind and Physically Handicapped (part of the system supported by the Library of Congress).

Functions of Puerto Rican Libraries

From their inception the major role of the majority of public libraries has been to support the education of students, to help them with their studies. This is how most public libraries in Puerto Rico are viewed today, as places for students to go to do their homework.

At the same time, libraries have aimed to stimulate reading, listening, and viewing for pleasure, recreation, and personal growth. Some have functioned to combat adult illiteracy by offering reading classes for adults. Through the development of reference and circulating collections, they aim to provide information to satisfy user needs and interests. In addition, public libraries have offered a variety of exhibits, readings, recitals and other cultural activities, particularly during National Library Week. In this way, four traditional roles of public libraries (educational, cultural, informational, and recreational) have been addressed by public libraries in Puerto Rico and in that priority order.

Support for Public Libraries
in Puerto Rico

Until 1999, the majority of public libraries in Puerto Rico were supported by a mixture of national and federal funds, administered by the Department of Education, which had the responsibility of developing and controlling the budget. Unlike the situation in the United States, there are generally no public library boards except for the boards of the community public libraries. As previously mentioned, the movement is now toward municipal administration and support of public libraries. The municipalities are responsible for making decisions about how to best support their public libraries. Because there is no national or state library agency in Puerto Rico (as exists in the United States), the Department of Education administers and controls federal funding for public library development and maintains staff to work with and assist public libraries, including providing short training sessions for public library personnel. Staff of public libraries have been hired and trained by personnel from the Department of Education for years.

In the past, collections were centrally acquired, cataloged, processed by the Department, and then sent to the different public libraries throughout the Island. This centralized system had both disadvantages and advantages. In many cases individual local needs were not adequately met by the collections, which were developed by librarians from a central office in San Juan. On the positive side, because the books and other materials arrived at the local libraries already classified, cataloged, and processed, library personnel were not faced with this responsibility and could devote their efforts to helping patrons. The situation now demands that personnel take responsibility for developing their own collections, selecting, evaluating, and weeding them, as well as organizing and using them to provide services that their users need and want.

The sixteen municipal libraries receive all their support, including physical facilities, personnel, and collections, from the local municipality. In most cases, they were established in municipalities where there was no other public library. Their level of funding and support depends on the local political situation and on the attitude of local government officials, who may or may not be library oriented or familiar with libraries in general. There is a great variation in the level of support received at the municipal level.

The community libraries receive some funding from the Department of Education via the municipality. The municipality provides physical facilities, either space in a building or an entire building. However, the community libraries rely mainly on community support, member fees, and local fund-raising projects and activities, to which they devote much energy and effort in planning. They have been reasonably successful in these efforts and have been able to provide modern, up-to-date collections, computers, and other equipment. They have served as models for other public libraries in programming and in reaching out to other sectors of the community besides the students who are their primary users.

All types of public libraries have increasingly sought support from the private sector, from business and industry. They have written proposals and received funds from local, national, and international foundations and corporations for a variety of resources and services, programs, and activities. The Carnegie Public Community Library is a good example of this trend and serves as an excellent model for other public libraries on the Island. It has received funds from several local sources and has been able to provide a variety of dynamic, successful community programs as a result. (See also Chapter, "Carnegie Public Community Library as a Model Public Library in Puerto Rico.")

Users of Public Libraries in Puerto Rico

Traditionally, the majority of users of public libraries in Puerto Rico have been students at all levels, from elementary school to college and university. Because of the shortage of adequate school libraries, as well as the limitations on their hours of service, primary and secondary school students have turned to nearby public libraries to complete their schoolwork. In addition, parents and teachers have used public libraries for similar purposes, to help their children complete school assignments or to prepare them. To a lesser extent, business people, government workers, and other professionals use some public libraries. Retired persons, including the elderly, also use them, as do visitors to the Island and tourists. The unemployed, including school dropouts, are also public library users. Public libraries receiving federal funds are accessible to disabled users. Preschool children form another group of public library users; immigrants and newcomers to Puerto Rico constitute another small group.

Public Library Collections

On the whole, most public library collections consist primarily of print materials, particularly books. This includes both fiction and nonfiction circulating collections, as well as reference collections, principally dictionaries and encyclopedias. Textbooks are also part of book collections, particularly in small public libraries outside the major metropolitan areas, where students may not be able to afford to buy them. Most public libraries have a separate Puerto Rican collection, books written by Puerto Ricans or about Puerto Rico, which is heavily used by students and others. There are also small collections of magazines (with limited runs) and newspapers. Stacks are generally open, with direct access for all users.

In most cases, there has been little development of audiovisual collections such as videos, cassettes, and compact discs. In many public libraries there is limited or no equipment or space to use these materials, which are usually not circulated. There are few public access computers, except in the electronic libraries or in some area libraries. There is usually a vertical file, with pamphlets and clippings. There are some local government publications, which are generally not complete or up-to-date. There is no selective government depository public library in Puerto Rico.

Services Offered by
Puerto Rican Public Libraries

The service most frequently offered by Puerto Rican public libraries is circulation of materials, both internally and externally. Books can be checked out to take home. Although staff is available to answer reference questions, reference service is not well developed, nor is online searching or use of the Internet in reference work. When they can, staff members help users locate materials, use reference books, and find information. Reader assistance is given to individuals looking for particular books or books about particular subjects.

Most libraries prepare exhibits and displays. Some provide space for art exhibits. Cultural programs are planned and offered by most public libraries, particularly during National Library Week. These include arts and crafts activities, poetry and other readings, and storytelling. Authors and others give lectures and talks at the public library. Some libraries have book discussion groups. Book presentations are especially popular and important events in urban public libraries. Community libraries plan summer programs, including a variety of activities relating to reading and books for kids, especially aimed at primary school children. Community libraries are most like U.S. public libraries in terms of the types and varieties of cultural programs and activities offered. They are the most dynamic and active in programming, even though they face the same kinds of needs and challenges as other Puerto Rican public libraries.

Needs and Concerns of
Puerto Rican Public Libraries

The state of public library development in Puerto Rico is not comparable to that of the United States. Although there are some active, dynamic public libraries, such as the Carnegie Public Community Library, the Dorado Community Library, and the municipal libraries of Manati and Caguas, the majority of Puerto Rican public libraries face many problems and challenges and need much improvement.

They suffer from a lack of adequately trained personnel, because there are few professionals working in public libraries. The salary scale is low and working conditions difficult. Many public libraries, especially small rural ones, are not open on the weekends or evenings. Generally, there is not sufficient staff to provide the services needed. Because most staff members do not have formal training in librarianship, they have limited understanding and experience with the range of services, particularly outreach services, that modern public libraries can offer. For example, most public libraries do not provide specialized services to the elderly, young adults, the business community, or the unemployed. Most public library staff are not proactive, nor do they seek to identify, analyze, and then satisfy user needs and interests. Instead, they view their role as more traditional, as custodians and dispensers of books and other library materials, principally to students.

It is clear that the image of public libraries in the country needs to be changed, because they are viewed mostly as adjuncts to the school, as places for students or for children. Public libraries are generally under-used by adults. The public is generally not aware of the impact that a good public library can make in improving the quality of their lives, because most of them have never seen or used a good one. The exceptions are those Puerto Ricans who have lived in the United States or who travel between the Island and the Mainland. If they have developed the habit of using public libraries in the United States, then they are aware of the striking differences between Puerto Rican public libraries and those in the United States. Unfortunately, there is little information about their use of public libraries, either in the United States or in Puerto Rico.

The majority of Puerto Rican public libraries have not reached out to other community groups and organizations to cooperate or to promote their services. The public library generally has a low profile in the community. There is limited or no interlibrary cooperation. The concept of information or referral services is not clearly understood. On the whole, there is also limited use of the media for promotion of libraries and library activities, except during National Library Week.

Many public libraries do not have adequate, up-to-date collections, and lack a diversity of formats, particularly audiovisual resources. There is little knowledge of collection maintenance or preservation and little collection evaluation or weeding. Public libraries also lack space and physical facilities, as well as computers and other basic equipment, such as photocopiers.

Strategies for Strengthening Connections between Puerto Rican Public Libraries and Those in the United States

One of the strategies for addressing the challenges facing public libraries in Puerto Rico is to strengthen the connections between Puerto Rican and U.S. public libraries. In this way, libraries in Puerto Rico can benefit from what U.S. libraries have accomplished while U.S. librarians can learn more about Puerto Rico and Puerto Ricans to better serve the needs of this group of Hispanics in the United States. Establishing a formal exchange program for staff of Puerto Rican and U.S. public libraries is one important strategy to achieve this end. Through such an exchange Puerto Rican librarians could observe and experience first-hand the operations and activities of U.S. public libraries, which could serve as a model for them when they return to the Island. U.S. librarians could learn more about Puerto Rican culture, values, and lifestyles so that they could better serve Puerto Rican library users in the United States.

Visits to public libraries by both Puerto Rican and U.S. librarians could be used as a means to establish informal contacts between the libraries in the two countries, serving as a first step toward establishing more formal exchange programs. By visiting libraries and observing and talking with librarians on the job, much can be learned about types of collections and services that have been most successful, as well as needs and problems that exist. This can also be a first step toward determining ways to overcome or resolve them. Members of REFORMA, the National Association to Promote Library and Information Services to Latinos and the Spanish-Speaking, could be asked to facilitate the planning of these visits as well as the development of a more formal exchange program. Through communicating via e-mail, specific problems and issues could be explored and addressed on a one-to-one basis. Mentoring relationships can be developed in this way, benefiting both groups.

Inviting well-known U.S. public librarians to speak at conferences and continuing education activities in Puerto Rico is an important approach to strengthening the connection between Puerto Rican and U.S. public libraries. At the same time, these librarians could visit and consult at (either formally or informally) local Puerto Rican libraries. In this way, they could share their experience, knowledge, and expertise with colleagues and build important contacts and networks. This kind of networking is a critical step in improving the caliber of public library personnel in Puerto Rico, in stimulating interest among Puerto Rican library and information professionals, and in encouraging library science students to select public librarianship as a career. It has been difficult to persuade students to work in public libraries because of the salary and the working conditions. This kind of networking could stimulate a commitment on the part of these professionals and students to work toward the improvement of public libraries and assume strong, effective leadership and advocacy roles, both of which are for the most part currently lacking in Puerto Rico.

Planning field trips for library school students, faculty, and alumni (particularly those working in public libraries) to visit and observe, as a group, selected U.S. public libraries, especially those providing quality collections and services to Hispanics, is another important strategy to consider. The U.S. libraries could serve as models for developing better Puerto Rican public libraries. Those who have visited and observed the collections and services of the U.S. libraries can learn from what others have accomplished.

All of these strategies for strengthening connections between Puerto Rican and U.S. public libraries represent new approaches for many librarians on the Island, who have limited or no experience with public libraries or librarians outside the country. Most of them have not traveled or attended professional conferences in the United States. Even though they may have studied or read in the literature about U.S. librarianship and public library development, they lack firsthand, direct knowledge and understanding of what a good public library is and how to apply what these libraries do to their own local library situation. There is an urgent need to broaden their perspectives; to expand their horizons; and to stimulate innovation, creativity, and change. Public libraries in Puerto Rico, poised on the threshold of change, would benefit tremendously from the implementation of these kinds of strategies. They represent an opportunity to overcome some of the problems and challenges facing these libraries, as they seek new ways to improve their collections and services in an increasingly complex and changing technological environment.

The Effect of the Hispanic Demographic on Library Service to the Spanish Speaking

Denice Adkins

This chapter establishes a relationship between the Hispanic population proportion of a public library service area and the provision of library services recommended for Spanish-speaking or Latino users of the library. A brief review of literature is presented, illustrating the call for certain services to be provided by libraries for the Spanish-speaking and Latino communities. Among these services are the hiring of bilingual librarians, the provision of Spanish-language materials, and the provision of Spanish-language children's programs. Survey responses and population data were correlated, resulting in a positive correlation coefficient for each service, indicating that a relationship might exist. However, correlation coefficients were small, leading to speculation that other factors might also influence the provision of the recommended services for Latino patrons.

Denice Adkins is an assistant professor at the School of Information Science and Learning Technologies, University of Missouri, Columbia.

Introduction

In the thirty-one years since the release of Roberto Haro's "How Mexican-Americans View Libraries" (1970), a wealth of publications have been released that illustrate how libraries can improve their service to Spanish-speaking and Latino populations. The sheer number of these documents leads one to suspect that service to Latinos and the Spanish speaking is not improving. But is this the case? Are libraries failing these populations? This study attempted to answer that question for public libraries in the state of Arizona by analyzing whether libraries with a higher concentration of Hispanics in their service areas were more likely to provide services recommended by these publications than libraries with lower concentrations.

Literature Review

Thousands of words have been spilled on the subject of creating improved service to Latinos and the Spanish speaking. Fifteen works, published between 1970 and 1994, indicate some of the most pressing concerns in school and public libraries (Allen 1988, 1993; Ayala and Ayala 1994; Bareno et al. 1979; Cuesta 1990; Dyer and Robertson-Kozan 1983; Gonzalez, Greeley, and Whitney 1980; Haro 1970, 1981; Hispanic Services Committee 1990; Library Services to the Spanish-Speaking Committee 1988; Metoyer-Duran 1993; Tarin and Cuesta 1979; Thomas 1978; Zwick and Garza de Cortés 1989).

The employment of bilingual, bicultural library professionals was recommended in ten documents (Allen 1993, 452; Ayala and Ayala 1994, 29; Bareno et al. 1979, 11; Dyer and Robertson-Kozan 1983, 29; Gonzalez, Greeley, and Whitney 1980, 789; Haro 1970, 738; Hispanic Services Committee 1990, 65; Library Services to the Spanish-Speaking Committee 1988, 3; Tarin and Cuesta 1979, 33; Thomas 1978, 59). Providing larger and better collections of Spanish-language materials was recommended in nine documents (Allen 1993, 451–52; Bareno et al. 1979, 33; Cuesta 1990, 28; Dyer and Robertson-Kozan 1983, 29; Gonzalez, Greeley, and Whitney 1980, 789; Haro 1970, 738; Hispanic Services Committee 1990, 1; Library Services to the Spanish-Speaking Committee 1988, 2; Thomas 1978, 70). Five documents recommended providing programs in Spanish or bilingual formats (Allen 1993, 452–53; Ayala and Ayala 1994, 28; Hispanic Services Committee 1990, 52–53; Tarin and Cuesta 1979, 37; Zwick and Garza de Cortés 1989, 12).

Other recommendations included conducting community analyses (Allen 1988, 88; Ayala and Ayala 1994, 28; Bareno et al. 1979, 23; Haro 1970, 742, 1981, 22–23; Tarin and Cuesta 1979, 31), providing Spanish-language signage

(Hispanic Services Committee 1990, 15; Library Services to the Spanish-Speaking Committee 1988, 4; Tarin and Cuesta 1979, 32), and fostering collaboration between schools and public libraries (Ayala and Ayala 1994, 29; Dyer and Robertson-Kozan 1983, 29; Hispanic Services Committee 1990, 61; Tarin and Cuesta 1979, 33). However, this study focused on the presence of Spanish-fluent staff, Spanish-language materials for adults and children, and Spanish-language or bilingual children's programming.

In his survey of Mexican Americans in 1970, Roberto Haro observed that people who had grown up in the Mexican American culture "generally prefer to use libraries where Spanish is spoken and where Hispanic materials may be available to them" (1970, 739). The REFORMA Report Card echoed these sentiments: A majority of Latino users indicated that bilingual, bicultural staff, materials, and programs constituted indicators of successful service to Latino patrons (Ayala and Ayala 1994, Table III, 1–3, Table IV, 1–4). Latino library users suggested that "more current Spanish-language and bilingual books . . . more efforts at bringing the community into the library . . . more happy and courteous bilingual-bicultural staff" (1994, 16) would improve service. The literature strongly indicates that people of Hispanic heritage would like to see Spanish-speaking staff, Spanish-language materials, and Spanish-language programming. (In this chapter, the terms *Hispanic* and *Latino* have been used interchangeably. The demographic data used in this chapter refer to "Hispanics," whereas the library literature generally refers to "Latinos.)

Methodology

The hypothesis under investigation was that increased numbers of Hispanic residents in a library service area would produce an increase in public library services previously identified as essential to Spanish-speaking patrons. The null hypothesis was that there would be no increase in public library services offered, regardless of the level of Hispanic concentration. Demographic data were correlated with data provided by libraries on the services they offered to Spanish-speaking patrons to confirm a positive relationship between the variables.

Data were gathered using a cross-sectional, descriptive survey. The survey instrument was pretested by public library employees and modified slightly as a result of recommendations. The final instrument consisted of forty-six questions designed to elicit data about the number of librarians and paraprofessional staff who were Spanish-fluent, Spanish-language materials held by the library, and programs for children held in a bilingual or Spanish-language format. Recipients were also asked to indicate the zip code areas they served, in order to gather data about their service populations. The *Sourcebook of Zip Code Demographics* (CACI 1998) was used to determine population, Hispanic population proportion, and per capita income for each zip code area identified by respondents.

Surveys were mailed to 172 public library service outlets in the state of Arizona. For the purposes of this study, only central outlets and branch outlets received surveys (U.S. Department of Education 2000, ii). Usable surveys were returned by 62 percent of the recipients.

Of the recipients, forty (23 percent) public library service outlets were located in Metropolitan Statistical Areas. Metropolitan Statistical Areas are defined by the U.S. Office of Management and Budget as being "a core area containing a large population nucleus, together with adjacent communities having a high degree of economic and social integration with that core" (U.S. Bureau of the Census 2000). More than 52 percent of Arizona's population reside in a Metropolitan Statistical Area (U.S. Bureau of the Census 2001), and statewide library distribution tends to favor metropolitan areas as well (Department of Library, Archives, and Public Records 1998). Surveys were returned from twenty-four urban locations, a total of 22 percent of all returned surveys.

Hispanic populations in the survey areas vary from 1 percent in some towns to more than 70 percent in others, but counties in closer proximity to the Mexican border have greater proportions of Hispanic residents than those in the northern part of the state. Data from the most recent census show that more than a quarter of all Arizonans claim Hispanic ancestry, and in nine of fifteen counties the Hispanic population exceeds 15 percent (U.S. Bureau of the Census 2001). The mean Hispanic population for survey respondents was 25 percent. Some respondents had service populations that were less than 1 percent Hispanic; others had service populations that were more than 75 percent Hispanic.

To establish that there was a relationship between the Hispanic population variable and the variables indicating library services for Latinos and the Spanish speaking, the data were subjected to two-way correlation. The correlation coefficient, Pearson's r, measures the degree of association between two variables. A correlation coefficient of 0 would indicate no relationship; a correlation coefficient of 1 would indicate a perfect relationship. The square of the correlation coefficient indicates the proportion of variance of the dependent variable that can be accounted for by predicting from the independent variable, Hispanic population.

Two assumptions were made that limit the applicability of this research to other situations. First, it was assumed that library service areas could be represented with demographic data from zip code areas. Librarians know that in practice library boundaries are often established independently of zip code areas, and that patrons do not limit their library usage to one library.

It was further assumed that there is a relationship between Hispanic population and a Spanish-speaking community. The fact that someone self-identifies as Hispanic on a census form does not mean that he or she necessarily speaks Spanish or doesn't speak English well. In fact, only 8.2 percent of Arizonans report speaking a home language other than English and being unable to speak English "very well" (U.S. Bureau of the Census 2001). However, there is a strong correlation between Hispanic status and ability to speak a language other than English. In the 1990 Census, 600,537 Arizonans identified themselves as Hispanic. Of those, 72 percent indicated that they spoke a language other than English. In contrast, only 10 percent of people who were "not of Hispanic origin" spoke a language other than English. Spanish is the second most spoken language in the state of Arizona, spoken by 14 percent of Arizonans. Although the assumption seems logical that Hispanics are more likely to speak Spanish, no data were found that explicitly demonstrated the relationship between Hispanic status and language spoken.

Results

Hiring more Spanish-speaking, bicultural library staff is the single most highly recommended strategy for improving library service to the Spanish speaking, appearing in ten out of fifteen documents evaluated (Allen 1993, 452; Ayala and Ayala 1994, 29; Bareno et al. 1979, 11; Dyer and Robertson-Kozan 1983, 29; Gonzalez, Greeley, and Whitney 1980, 789; Haro 1970, 738; Hispanic Services Committee 1990, 65; Library Services to the Spanish-Speaking Committee 1988, 3; Tarin and Cuesta 1979, 33; Thomas 1978, 59). The Arizona survey found a weak but positive relationship between increased Hispanic population in a library service area ("Hispanic population") and Spanish-fluent librarians, with a correlation coefficient $r = 0.467$, $p < .05$. A stronger positive relationship was also found between Hispanic population and Spanish-fluent library clerks, $r = 0.649$, $p < .05$. The survey found that 17 percent of librarians were Spanish-fluent, as were 15 percent of library clerks and 16 percent of children's library staff. A weak positive relationship was found between Hispanic population and children's services staff, $r = 0.399$, p .05. (See Table 1, page 126.)

Haro (1970) found that his survey population preferred using materials oriented toward their culture. The REFORMA Report Card later lamented that, "In general, public library collections do not have the Spanish/bilingual and/or Latino materials to give the Latino community" (Ayala and Ayala 1994, 28). The Arizona survey found a positive relationship between Hispanic population and Spanish-language books, $r = 0.569$, $p < .05$. The mean number of Spanish-language books in the adult collection was 565, out of a total of 30,596. The average number of Spanish-language children's materials was 387, out of 13,694 total. A weak positive relationship was found between Hispanic population and Spanish-language children's books, $r = 0.361$, $p < .05$. Approximately one program in twenty-five was conducted bilingually or in the Spanish-language format. A weak positive relationship was found between Hispanic population and children's programming, $r = 0.355$, $p < .05$.

Table 1. Correlation Matrix

		Hispanic Population	Ratio of Spanish-Fluent Librarians	Ratio of Spanish-Fluent Clerks	Ratio of Spanish-Fluent Children's Services Staff	Ratio of Spanish-Language Adult Books	Ratio of Spanish-Language Children's Materials	Ratio of Spanish-Language Children's Programs
Hispanic Population	Pearson Correlation	1.000	.467**	.649**	.399**	.569**	.361**	.355**
	Sig. (2-tailed)		.000	.000	.001	.000	.001	.002
	N	89	82	63	71	80	77	77
Spanish-Fluent Librarians	Pearson-Correlation	.467**	1.000	.503**	.659**	.368**	.316**	.322**
	Sig. (2-tailed)	.000	.	.000	.000	.001	.006	.005
	N	82	86	61	70	77	75	75
Spanish-Fluent Clerks	Pearson Correlation	.649**	.503**	1.000	.573**	.245	.064	.405**
	Sig. (2-tailed)	.000	.000	.	.000	.059	.632	.001
	N	63	62	68	57	60	58	64
Spanish-Fluent Children's Services Staff	Pearson Correlation	.399**	.659**	.573**	1.000	.369**	.266*	.375**
	Sig. (2-tailed)	.001	.000	.000	.	.002	.029	.001
	N	71	70	57	77	70	68	70
Spanish-Language Adult Books	Pearson-Correlation	.569**	.368**	.245	.369**	1.000	.645**	.656**
	Sig. (2-tailed)	.000	.001	.059	.002	.	.000	.000
	N	80	77	60	70	87	83	78
Spanish-Language Children's Materials	Pearson-Correlation	.369**	.316**	.064	.266*	.645**	1.000	.353**
	Sig. (2-tailed)	.001	.006	.632	.029	.000	.	.002
	N	77	75	58	68	83	85	76
Spanish-Language Children's Programs	Pearson-Correlation	.355**	.322**	.405**	.375**	.656**	.353**	1.000
	Sig. (2-tailed)	.002	.005	.001	.001	.000	.002	.
	N	77	75	64	70	78	76	85

* Correlation is significant at the 0.05 level (2-tailed)
** Correlation is significant at the 0.01 level (2-tailed)

Discussion

Library literature recommends certain things for the library that wants to maximize service to its Latino and Spanish-speaking populations. The following recommendations have been made and seconded in library literature: Spanish-fluent library staff should be hired (Allen 1993, 452; Ayala and Ayala 1994, 29; Bareno et al. 1979, 11; Dyer and Robertson-Kozan 1983, 29; Gonzalez, Greeley, and Whitney 1980, 789; Haro 1970, 738; Hispanic Services Committee 1990, 65; Library Services to the Spanish-Speaking Committee 1988, 3; Tarin and Cuesta 1979, 33; Thomas 1978, 59), Spanish-language books should be stocked (Allen 1993, 451–52; Bareno et al. 1979, 33; Cuesta 1990, 28; Dyer and Robertson-Kozan 1983, 29; Gonzalez, Greeley, and Whitney 1980, 789; Haro 1970, 738; Hispanic Services Committee 1990, 1; Library Services to the Spanish-Speaking Committee 1988, 2; Thomas 1978, 70), and Spanish-format programming should be offered (Allen 1993, 452–53; Ayala and Ayala 1994, 28; Hispanic Services Committee 1990, 52–53; Tarin and Cuesta 1979, 37; Zwick and Garza de Cortés 1989, 12). Having developed an idea of what service to Latinos and the Spanish-speaking should consist of, the current study investigated whether public libraries were more likely to implement these changes if their service areas had high concentrations of Hispanics. The findings tend to reject the null hypothesis that libraries would not be more likely to implement these changes if their service areas did have high concentrations.

How much is enough? This question is particularly relevant when we look at providing library service to the Spanish speaking. How many Spanish-fluent librarians, clerks, or children's services staff must a library hire before it can say it is responsive to the community? "The best-case scenario for staffing is to have some bilingual Latino personnel," (Alire and Archibeque 1998, 142), but unfortunately, a more specific answer requires some knowledge of the community and the library.

How many books and programs are enough? "Without doing a community analysis that includes examination of census data, it is not possible to make successful, informed policy decisions," either about staffing or about book selection for Latino patrons (Developing collections for the Spanish speaking 1996, 331). In a school situation, the number of Spanish-language books in the library can be linked to the number of Spanish-dominant students enrolled (Allen 1993, 444; Thomas 1978, 59). The public library does not get reports of Spanish-dominant patrons as they move into the service area, so again, the public library must determine how much is enough based on knowledge of its own community.

A Florida newspaper estimated that "there are less than 1,000 Spanish-speaking librarians among the 152,000 librarians in the United States" (Lewis 2000); the Arizona survey found that 17 percent of Arizona's professional and paraprofessional librarians are Spanish-fluent. The positive correlations between Hispanic population and Spanish-fluent staff seem to indicate that Spanish-fluent staff—librarians, clerks, and children's services staff—are more likely to be found in areas having a higher concentration of Hispanics. However, as revealed by the relatively small values of the correlation coefficients, it becomes clear that Hispanic population has less of a relationship with Spanish-fluent librarians and Spanish-fluent children's staff than with Spanish-fluent clerks.

Again, positive correlations indicate that there is a relationship between Hispanic population and the library's stock of Spanish-language books for adults. There is a slight relationship between Hispanic population and Spanish-language children's materials. There is also a positive relationship between Hispanic population and Spanish-language library programming for children. In areas with a high concentration of Hispanics, libraries are more likely to stock Spanish-language materials for adults and children and more likely to offer Spanish-language programs for children.

Correlation does not imply causation, however. With the given results, we cannot determine whether libraries in areas with higher concentrations of Hispanics tend to hire Spanish-fluent library clerks, or whether Spanish-fluent library clerks tend to gravitate toward libraries in areas having higher concentrations of Hispanics. We cannot determine whether libraries in areas of high concentration have more Spanish-language books because they've made an effort to provide them to the community, or because the community has donated them to the library. Although common sense would seem to say that community needs and desires dictate the library's offerings, further research would have to be done to determine the validity of this claim.

More research should be done to determine the exact nature of the relationship between Hispanic population and a library's commitment to offering services of benefit to the Hispanic/Latino community. Avenues for future research include looking at other factors that influence a library's willingness to offer services to Latino patrons, including expectations of the Latino community, the roles of the library administration and trustees, the library's budget, and staff commitment to equal service for Latinos.

References

Alire, Camila, and Orlando Archibeque. 1998. *Serving Latino communities: A How-to-do-it manual for librarians.* New York: Neal-Schuman.

Allen, Adela Artola. 1988. Library services for Hispanic young adults. *Library Trends* 37 (1): 80–105.

———. 1993. The school library media center and the promotion of literature for Hispanic children. *Library Trends* 41 (3): 437–61.

Ayala, Reynaldo, and Marta S. Ayala. 1994. REFORMA report card. N.p.: Report Card Project Steering Committee.

Bareno, Laura A., Cheryl Metoyer-Duran, Hilda J. Prieto, and Robert G. Trujillo. 1979. *A guide for developing ethnic library services.* N.p.: California Ethnic Services Task Force.

CACI Marketing Systems. 1998. *The sourcebook of zip code demographics.* 13th ed. Arlington, VA: Author.

Cuesta, Yolanda. 1990. From survival to sophistication: Hispanic needs = library needs. *Library Journal* 115 (9): 26–29.

Department of Library, Archives, and Public Records. 1998. *Arizona library directory.* N.p.: Author.

Developing collections for the Spanish speaking. 1996. *RQ* 35 (3): 330–43.

Dyer, Esther R., and C. Robertson-Kozan. 1983. Hispanics in the U.S.: Implications for library service. *School Library Journal* 29 (8): 27–29.

Gonzalez, M., B. Greeley, and S. Whitney. 1980. Assessing the library needs of the Spanish-speaking. *Library Journal* 105 (7): 786–89.

Haro, Roberto P. 1970. How Mexican-Americans view libraries. *Wilson Library Bulletin* 44 (7): 736–42.

———. 1981. *Developing library services and information services for Americans of Hispanic origin.* Metuchen, NJ: Scarecrow Press.

Hispanic Services Committee, The Chicago Public Library. 1990. *Hispanic services: A practical manual for the public librarian.* Chicago: Author.

Lewis, Charles. 2000, August 18. USF's library science program honored for diversity. *The Business Journal of Tampa Bay* [Online]. Available: http://tampabay.bcentral.com/tampabay/stories/2000/08/21/focus6.html. (Accessed June 11, 2001).

Library Services to the Spanish-Speaking Committee, Reference and Adult Services Division, American Library Association. 1988. *Guidelines for library services to Hispanics.* Chicago: American Library Association.

Metoyer-Duran, Cheryl. 1993. The information and referral process in culturally diverse communities. *RQ* 32 (3): 359–71.

Tarin, Patricia, and Yolanda Cuesta. 1979. Guidelines for library service to Spanish-speaking Americans. In *Latino materials: A multimedia guide for children and young adults*, edited by Daniel Duran. New York: Neal Schuman.

Thomas, R. A. 1978. The role of media centers in bilingual education. In *Cultural pluralism and children's media*, edited by Esther R. Dyer. Chicago: American Association of School Librarians and American Library Association.

U.S. Bureau of the Census. 2001. *American Fact Finder* [Online]. Available: http://factfinder.census.gov/servlet/BasicFactsServlet. (Accessed April 6, 2001).

U.S. Bureau of the Census, Population Division, Population Distribution Branch. 2000, January 10. *About metropolitan areas* [Online]. Available: http://www.census.gov/population/www/estimates/aboutmetro.html. (Accessed April 4, 2001).

U.S. Bureau of the Census, Population Division, Population Estimates Program. 1999. *Population estimates for counties by race and Hispanic origin: July 1, 1998.* [Online]. Available: http://www.census.gov/population/estimates /county/crh. (Accessed March 28, 2000).

U.S. Department of Education, National Center for Educational Statistics. 2000. *Public libraries in the United States: FY 1997* [Online]. NCES 2000-316, by Adrienne Chute and Elaine Kroe. Available: http://nces.ed.gov/pubs2000 /2000316.pdf. (Accessed April 4, 2001).

Zwick, Louise Yarian, and Oralia Garza de Cortés. 1989. Library programs for Hispanic children. *Texas Libraries* 50: 12–16.

A New Vocabulary for Inclusive Librarianship

Applying Whiteness Theory to Our Profession

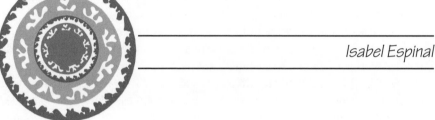

Isabel Espinal

Discussions on ethnicity in the library profession tend to focus only on ethnic minorities. This chapter proposes a new way to talk about inclusiveness, by bringing in whiteness theory, a concept from anthropology and cultural studies.

Isabel Espinal is past president of the Northeast Chapter of REFORMA and works as a bilingual outreach specialist and reference librarian at the W.E.B. Du Bois Library of the University of Massachusetts at Amherst. Born in Brooklyn to parents who had recently emigrated from the Dominican Republic, she holds a B.A. in Latin American literature and civilization from Princeton University and an M.L.I.S. from the University of California at Berkeley. In 1999, American Library Association President Sarah Long appointed Ms. Espinal to the Library Education Task Force #4 on Library Education and Personnel Stratification, which will continue its work until early 2002.

T his chapter introduces a new conceptual framework, from the fields of anthropology and cultural studies, into ethnic librarianship: whiteness studies. I use the term "ethnic librarianship" to mean the work and issues of people of color vis-à-vis libraries and librarians. Approximately thirty years ago, librarians of color started forming ethnic caucuses within, as supplements to, or as protests against, the American Library Association. Among these were REFORMA: The National Association to Promote Library Services to Latinos and the Spanish Speaking; the Black Caucus of the American Library Association; the Asian Pacific American Library Association; the American Indian Library Association; and the Chinese American Library Association. These caucuses have done an incredible amount of work with very few resources. They have provided scholarships for people of color to enter the profession, mentoring to incoming and continuing librarians, a *space* within librarianship for librarians of color, training and development for librarians of color, training and development concerning issues of library services to communities of color, literary and professional awards that recognize writers of color and librarians of color, and so forth. Yet the North American library scene continues to have enormous gaps in numbers of librarians of color as well as in services to communities of color. The latest large-scale attempt to address these issues was initiated under the leadership of Elizabeth Martínez when she was executive director of the American Library Association. She instituted the Spectrum Initiative, a nationwide $1.5 million project that provides scholarships to fifty students of color each year for the three-year period that funding is available. Another recent nationwide effort culminated in 1997 with the institution of a diversity officer, a first in the history of the American Library Association.

Spectrum. Diversity. Ethnic. People of color. Latinos. Spanish Speaking. Black. Chinese. Indian. These are some of the words we are currently using to address the cultural inequities in librarianship. But what's missing from our vocabulary list? Notice that there is no mention of whites or whiteness. It is assumed, for example, that people of color means people of non-white color. White is taken not to be a color. Also, white is assumed not to be ethnic. Please don't get me wrong; I'm not here to accuse the library ethnic caucuses or the Spectrum Initiative or any other group that I have mentioned of reverse racism or of denying whites their rights, as some have done. Quite the contrary! I hope to show in this introduction to the concept of whiteness in librarianship that alleging reverse racism is a typical white cultural practice that is fundamentally racist. What I do want to say by bringing up the topic of whiteness in librarianship is that unless we address whiteness, unless we identify and name it, many of the problems that plague us collectively and as individual librarians of color will continue. The theme of REFORMA's second national conference is The Power of Language. I hope to show how powerful the language of whiteness studies can be in furthering our work as Latina/o librarians.

It is imperative for those of us in the field of librarianship who are working to overturn the racial domination of whites in the profession to apply whiteness theory anthropologically to the profession of librarianship. Indeed, it is time for those of us who are active in the ethnic caucuses of the profession to admit that overturning racial domination is what we are doing. We need to make explicit how this profession in the United States, and perhaps worldwide, has been defined by whiteness. We also need to examine whiteness in librarianship vis-à-vis other professions. Currently there are crises and problems in librarianship that have been articulated in terms of the profession's response to diversity. The most significant problems are often expressed as librarianship's inadequate response to the changing cultural and racial demographics of its clientele and its very low numbers of people of color in its ranks and seeming inability to attract them to the profession. These crises and problems stem from the field's very constitution as a white profession and cannot be solved or even tackled until the facts of whiteness in librarianship and libraries have been exposed in a systematic way.

Conversely, applying whiteness theory to librarianship can make a contribution to whiteness studies and anthropology in that it allows for an examination of how whiteness is played out specifically, by uncovering behaviors of individuals, practices of institutions, and histories of groups. There are particularities to librarianship and libraries that help to highlight specific aspects of whiteness. One example is the predominance of women in the profession, which can help us examine how sex and gender operate in relation to whiteness and what impact affirmative action has had in libraries, both on people of color and on whites.

This suggests a new anthropological approach: "Ethnographers" of whiteness, who are living in situations where whiteness manifests itself, in cultures of whiteness, can provide a unique perspective on the discipline of anthropology. Although these ethnographers may not be professionally trained as anthropologists, they, as are traditional anthropologists, are living in a culture different from their home cultures and need to uncover the principles of the "foreign," in this case white, culture.

The approach to whiteness used in this chapter is elaborated by Dr. H. Enoch Page, a professor of anthropology at the University of Massachusetts, in a seminar called "The Anthropology of Whiteness." It is also supported by both the readings assigned in the seminar and many found through library research. I took this seminar in the hopes of answering some of the questions and doubts I had about the way we talk about and even think about cultural and racial differences in librarianship. I found that there is much that we can apply from the ideas presented in the seminar and the readings, and I am happy to be able to share my insights with others in my profession. I will identify the various elements of study we followed in the seminar and discuss their application to the profession of librarianship.

Defining Whiteness, Whiteness Theory, Sensate Theory, White Cultural Practices, and White Public Space

Because many people in the field of librarianship as well as in the field of anthropology may not be familiar with some of the terms used in this paper, I will start off with some definitions. For Latina/os these definitions may be particularly useful because our cultures do not recognize the same definitions. Angel Oquendo writes, "The particular system of race-consciousness that prevails in the United States is foreign to the Latino community in the United States and so is the conceptual apparatus that corresponds to that system, including the peculiar notions of blackness and whiteness" (1995. Accessed June 12, 2001 from Lexis-Nexis Academic Universe on the World Wide Web: http://lexis-nexis .com/universe).[1] However, I would argue that as Latinos in this country, who have lived an alternative racial experience from the dualistic black-white divide, we are in a good position to help point out these definitions and indeed have been pointing out the contradictions of this system for some time.

I'd like to elaborate on what is meant by *whiteness* and the importance of this word. North American mainstream—white—culture is not accustomed to looking at whiteness or recognizing its very existence. In contemporary everyday speech and written white discourse it is indeed considered impolite and racist to discuss such a concept. Writers and scholars of whiteness studies[2] make an important contribution to the discourse on race by showing us how and why we can talk about whiteness, race, and racism. Writers such as Charles Mills, Ruth Frankenberg, Angel Oquendo, and H. Enoch Page explain that race is not a biological fact but a social fact, a social construction. Not long ago, mainstream white discourse *did* posit that race was a biological fact, a view that scholars of color such as W.E.B. Du Bois were critical of and that activists of color, such as Martin Luther King Jr., fought politically. This white discourse has been called *essentialist racism* because it constructed and promoted the view that there was an essential difference between whites and non-whites, a difference they were born with. Essentialist racism has been repudiated in white public discourse, but it has not completely disappeared. Indeed, writes one whiteness scholar:

> Essentialist racism has left a legacy that continues to mark discourses on race difference in a range of ways. First, precisely because it proposed race as a significant axis of difference,

essentialist racism remains the benchmark against which other discourses on race are articulated. In other words, the articulation and deployment of essentialist racism approximately five hundred years ago marks the moment when, so to speak, race was made into a difference and simultaneously into a rationale for racial inequality. It is in ongoing response to that moment that movements and individuals—for or against the empowerment of people of color—continue to articulate analyses of difference and sameness with respect to race. Thus for example, when the women I interviewed insisted that 'we are all the same under the skin,' within what I have described as a color-evasive and power-evasive discursive repertoire, they did so partly in response to essentialist racism . . . essentialist racism—particularly intentional, explicit racial discrimination—remains for most white people . . . paradigmatic of racism. This, as I have argued renders structural and institutional dimensions of racism less easily conceptualized and apparently less noteworthy. (Frankenberg 1993,139)

Kamala Visweswaran puts it this way: "In other words, to say that race has no biological meaning is not to say that race lacks meaning" (1998, 77). Du Bois has been one of the most eloquent writers on this point:

[S]ince the 15th century these ancestors of mine and their other descendents have had a common history; have suffered a common disaster and have one long memory. . . . The physical bond is least and the badge of color relatively unimportant save as a badge; the real essence of this kinship is its social heritage of slavery; the discrimination and insult; and this discrimination binds together not simply the children of Africa, but extends through yellow Asia and into the South Seas. It is this unity that draws me to Africa. (quoted in Visweswaran 1998, 78)

Likewise, whiteness as used in this study is not a biological reality or construct but rather a social and ideological one. Dr. Page, in his detailed definition of racism, presents this definition of whiteness:

As a generative principle of racism, "ideological whiteness" refers to a dual behavioral process entailing enactments of identity formation and resource access legitimation, both of which were practices once overtly recognized as aspects of "white supremacy," but which now may be more subtly and covertly reproduced as an observable and routine set of implicitly prescriptive, but explicitly disavowed, white supremacist beliefs and practices to which all who identify as "white" (or who behave as "whitened") are expected to adhere—especially white males—if they wish to maintain their own racial standing as members of these two privileged white groups and assert their negotiable right to privileged resource access.[3]

Whiteness may become a biological reality only insofar as the embodiment of whiteness as a social category leads to biological responses. Whiteness, however, is not an abstract concept; we infer it through people's behaviors, not by what may or may not be inside their heads. In lectures, Dr. Page defines it as a "behavioral repertoire," the behaviors he calls "white cultural practices." Sensate theory of whiteness, a complete elaboration of which is beyond the scope of this chapter, delineates how whiteness becomes embodied. Sensate theory, as explained by Dr. Page, maintains that the only way we can know reality is through our sensory apparatus. The combination of our behaviors and our sensations leads to the sensate basis of self-embodiment and racial identity, affecting each one of us who live in this racialized society on an *individual feeling* level.

Whiteness, however, is also very much about how *collective* actions are defined and in many ways *disguised*. The concept of "white public space" helps us understand this:

> White public space exists where controlled access to material and immaterial resources is managed by those who attempt to govern mass perception and the social construction of reality. . . . It is a highly politicized and shifting symbolic material dimension in which the dominant racial group routinely benefits from the governmental or corporate control that it exercises over information. . . . It entails an array of managed symbolic and material spaces that may be conquered, acquired, deployed, extended or retained, partly through coercion and partly through deception, but it more often endures through the routine bureaucratic production and dissemination of mass produced information. . . . In white public space, things of racial significance are made to seem fair, just, legitimate, and simplistically obvious when the embodied experiences of racial targets scream that they clearly are not.[4]

Not only can I, as a librarian of color, relate the definition of whiteness and white public space to my profession, but I also notice the use of library "buzzwords" in both of these definitions, words such as *access, information, bureaucratic, routine,* and *public.* Although it is not likely Dr. Page was thinking of libraries specifically when writing these definitions, I do not think the overlap with library terminology is coincidental. I would like to posit that the traditional

North American library institution is an example of a white institution and white public space.

Dr. Page has stated in his lectures and writings that it is important to study whiteness from a black perspective. He has also noted that the majority of writings on whiteness that have received critical attention in mainstream academic venues have been written by whites. I do not know what definition of "black" Dr. Page was using in this statement, but I will assume a broad one and take as "black" any perspective that is non-white. By this I do not mean to oversimplify the issues, nor to negate or obliterate Latino, Asian, Native American, or other non-white perspectives. On the contrary, I wish to state openly and clearly that my non-white perspective is a Latina perspective, one of many Latina perspectives. As Dr. Page's statements suggest, the concept of whiteness, although seemingly new in the mainstream culture and especially in academia, is not so new in the academic writings of people of color nor in the popular cultures of people of color.

David Roediger elaborates on this point:

> But few Americans have even considered the idea that African Americans are extremely knowledgeable about whites and whiteness. In the mainstream American culture, and certainly in intellectual circles, a rough and unproductive division of labor exists where the claiming of expert knowledge and commonsense wisdom on race are concerned. White writers have long been positioned as the leading and most dispassionate investigators of the lives, values, and abilities of people of color. White writing about whiteness is rarer, with discussions of what it means to be human standing in for consideration of how racial identity influences white lives. Writers of color, and most notably African American writers, are cast as providing insight, often presumed to be highly subjective, of what it is like to be a "minority." Lost in this destructive shuffle is the fact that from folktales onward African Americans have been among the nation's keenest students of white consciousness and white behavior. (1998, 4)

Similarly, I would like to suggest that the concept of whiteness is not new in the cultures and discourses of librarians of color. I expect that much of what I am saying is not new to librarians of color. What probably is new is the framing of these issues in this theoretical apparatus. I also suspect that there are many instances and patterns of whiteness that I have not covered or even alluded to here but that other librarians of color have either exposed in writings or have experienced. This brings me to an exciting possibility for this line of study in terms of anthropological and ethnographic methods. My suggestion is for those readers who are either librarians of color or library patrons of color (or race cognizant/race traitor whites)[5] to add to this ethnography of whiteness in librarianship by contributing their own examples and experiences. This method may very well subvert the power of the (traditionally white) anthropologist, as well as the very notion of the professional anthropologist.

Conducting a Literature Search for the Term "Whiteness" as a Subject or Keyword in the Professional Library Literature

That whiteness has not been addressed as a topic in librarianship and library studies is borne out in a review of the library literature. In December 1999 I conducted a search in the library literature section of the online database Firstsearch, which produced no hits on either "whiteness" or "white privilege" as keywords in the article title, subject, or content fields. However, a search in *Sociological Abstracts* (in February 2001) yielded 92 records with the word *whiteness* in the title and 214 with *whiteness* in at least one field in the record.

Examining Areas of Librarianship Where Whiteness and White Cultural Practices Are Factors

Racial Make-up of Staff

Evan St. Lifer and Corinne Nelson (1997) report that, according to American Library Association data, Latinos represented 1.8 percent of the profession in 1985 and 1.8 percent in 1991; blacks, 6.1 percent in 1985 and 6.28 percent in 1991; Asians 3.4 percent in 1985 and 3.85 percent in 1991; and whites, 88.5 percent in 1985 and 87.7 percent in 1991. Deborah R. Hollis (1996) has compared the percentage of people of color in librarianship to other professions where women predominate—nursing and teaching—and found that the percentage in the library field was the lowest, 14.4 percent, compared to 16.2 percent in nursing and 16.2 percent in teaching.

Management of Libraries

When we look at the managerial level, more striking underrepresentation figures are found for African American, Latina/o, Asian American, and Native American managers. For example, at present there is only one Latina who is the director of an elite ARL (Association of Research Libraries) library, a group of more than 120 libraries. Also, Al Milo, moderator of the

REFORMANET electronic list, has compiled lists of public library directors who are Latinos and has commented on REFORMANET on how few there are.

Services to and Attitudes Toward Non-Whites and Defining Library Service as a Service for Whites

Non-librarian members of REFORMA are sometimes in a good position to elicit information about the behaviors and opinions of mainstream librarians regarding Latinos, whereas REFORMA librarians may not be privy to such behaviors and opinions. At a recent library conference in the South, a white librarian told a Spanish-language book vendor: "It's useless. Those people don't read." Another non-librarian REFORMA member, who works as a library advocacy director for a nonprofit organization, heard a similar comment from a librarian about Latinos in Northern California. The advocacy director, a light-skinned Puerto Rican, had not made her non-white status known to the librarian prior to this comment. When she told the librarian that she was Puerto Rican and that the librarian should stop making racist comments, the librarian exhibited extreme shock and surprise. The librarian obviously had been trying to engage in the white cultural practice that Christine Sleeter calls "white racial bonding," defined as

> interactions that have the purpose of affirming a common stance on race-related issues, legitimating particular interpretations of oppressed groups, and drawing we-they boundaries. These communication patterns may consist of inserts into conversations, race-related "asides" in conversations, strategic eye-contact, and jokes. Often they are so short and subtle that they may seem harmless. (1994, 261)

When asked if libraries are in the service of whiteness, Dr. Page answers in the affirmative and offers libraries' classification and subject headings as the first example:

> My question: "Do you think that libraries are in the service of whiteness?"

> Dr. Page's answer: "Oh I don't think there's any question about it. The Dewey Decimal system is in the service of whiteness and I don't think that the Library of Congress system changes the pattern too much. . . . For example: most of the stuff pertaining to my area of study, especially as it regards Black people, is going to be under *Black*, is going to be under *Afro American*, is going to be

under *Negro*, is going to be under *Black Americans*, is going to be under all these different, diverse subject headings. There is no way in which the Dewey Decimal system or the Library of Congress system puts all of those things in the same place. So you're going to find it under American Studies, some of it under sociology, some of it somewhere else, and somewhere else. . . . If the Library were working to serve the interest of overcoming whiteness, it would have to say, "We are using the Dewey decimal system or the Library of Congress system, but in addition to that we're also going to systematize stuff that has not been accessible in the past." And that would help me a lot. (1999)

Collections

REFORMA, the Black Caucus of ALA, and other groups have focused a lot of their attention through the years on looking at library collections to see how well the collections included materials by non-whites. In the beginning years of these organizations, especially those of the ethnic library caucuses, they too often found that library collections across the country did not include enough materials by non-white authors. Lillian Castillo Speed, head librarian of the Ethnic Studies Library at the University of California, Berkeley, writes that

at the beginning of the Chicano movement, mainstream libraries either discarded or did not collect materials from the Chicano perspective. They were considered too political, too ephemeral or too specialized. Chicano libraries in the Southwest were established by students who foresaw the need to document and preserve this information. The same was true for Puerto Rican, Dominican, and other ethnic collections. (REFORMA 2000)

Digital Initiatives

Digital initiatives are all the rage in libraries. Digital libraries are seen as the future of librarianship. Yet many libraries and librarians who have jumped wholeheartedly into digital initiatives are paradoxically quite bound by tradition in their approach and the patterns of the past: the tradition and patterns of whiteness. Many of the studies on the "Digital Divide" are really a continuation of the age-old racial information divide. REFORMA's Information Technology Committee (ITC) has begun to address this point in a major way with a series of position papers called "REFORMA's Information Technology Agenda":

A number of recent studies reveal that there are disparities in access to telephones, personal computers, and the Internet. These disparities are marked by race, ethnicity, income, education and place of residence. These inequalities signal not only lack of access to technologies but, more fundamentally, access to resources which are becoming critical in today's society. It is in this larger sense that we refer to a "digital divide" between the haves and the have-nots. The use of high technologies among Latino communities is only now beginning to be investigated. Currently we do not have a demographic profile of Latinos that includes key technology and communication variables. At the national level the "Falling through the Net" series published by the National Telecommunications and Information Administration (NTIA) has provided the most useful information. This influential series has noted that there is not only a persistent but an increasing gap in computer and on-line use among Latinos and African Americans. The Tomás Rivera Policy Institute has also made important contributions to our understanding of these issues, especially in the areas of computer ownership and school use. Regional trends are beginning to be tracked by research organizations like the Center for Virtual Research at the University of California, Riverside. (REFORMA 2000)

Definition of Competencies

What makes a good librarian? We need to look at the established definitions closely to see to what extent a definition is culturally or racially bound.

Measurement of Good Library Service and Good Libraries

A white cultural practice identified in Dr. Page's seminar is the practice of maintaining that white reality is the norm. Related to this are the practices of using universalism—allegedly treating everyone the same—to defend whiteness, and perpetuating and applying "pseudo-universalistic notions of standards" (Gabriel 1998, 88). That is, in a white-dominated society, standards are applied and are described as neutral, universal, and true for all people. But in fact the criteria are not universal. They come from a white perspective. In librarianship, an example of this is over-reliance on statistics in the management and funding of libraries. One of the most commonly used statistics in libraries is to count the circulation of materials. Most often this is a count of how many books, videos, CDs, and other materials are checked out of a library in a certain period, usually by month and then by year. These circulation figures are used for many kinds of comparisons. One of the most common ways in which circulation statistics are used is to compare circulation among different libraries as a measure of a library's value or importance to a particular community. I would maintain that this type of analysis is indicative of a white cultural practice; it is unfair if not racist. Communities whose libraries have high circulation figures are seen as placing a high value on their libraries, whereas those whose libraries have low circulation figures are seen as not caring about their libraries. Similarly, those libraries with high circulation figures are seen as doing a good job, and those with low circulation figures are seen as doing a poor job. Those of us who have worked in libraries serving non-white communities know that there are reasons for the low or non-use. We also know that what may be considered low use in other communities may not be considered low in our communities because of different lifestyles, leisure time available for reading books, and literacy levels, among other factors. The introduction and use of circulation statistics are attempts to standardize the management of library service, to use a "neutral" measure by which libraries can be compared. But using the ethnographic lens from whiteness studies reveals that this practice is not neutral.

There are likely to be other cases throughout the country in which library circulation figures are used in what ultimately turns out to be a racist way, regardless of intentions to be just. A research survey of how libraries use circulation statistics would make a great contribution to the study of librarianship but is beyond the scope of this paper. I will discuss three cases with which I am familiar to demonstrate why this is an important question and to show whiteness at work in librarianship. In 1997 and 1998, I was the manager of a branch library of a small library system in a small, racially mixed city in southwestern Connecticut, within commuting distance of New York City. The branch was in a neighborhood that had high concentrations of African Americans and Latinos and growing numbers of Asians in addition to whites. Many of the residents had low incomes. I took the job of manager knowing that that particular branch library had more than once been slated to be closed down by the majority white city council, the majority white library board, and the all-white library system administration. I had read in the local newspaper and heard from librarians and politicians that the major reason for wanting to close down the library was low usage and that the low usage was demonstrated in the library's low circulation figures vis-à-vis the other branch in the system and other branch libraries in Connecticut. One day, in a meeting of library managers, I criticized the use of circulation statistics as a way to judge how well my library was doing. I talked about how my previous job of managing a library in an almost all-white, middle-class neighborhood in a nearby town showed me that circulation numbers were culturally and socially relative, not a universal or neutral measure. I said that from my experiences in the two branches I might have a person from one neighborhood who checks out ten books per week, whereas in the other neighborhood a person might check out one book per week; yet, in both cases, as a librarian, I could feel equally successful. A white male manager in the meeting took issue with my comparison. Insisting that what I was proposing was pure nonsense and illogical, he said, "Don't tell me that one equals ten. One does not equal ten!" Others in the room either defended his point of view or were silent. I felt discredited, as if I were negating the "truth" of the statistics. But I know I was experiencing the rigidity of a white perspective; there was no room for discussion of who makes these rules (white people),[6] whose standards are used (white standards), and whose interests are served by those rules and standards (the interests of whites and whiteness). Yet, from my own experience of having worked in these two neighborhoods that were culturally very different, I saw that the circulation numbers were not a product of how well I was doing or how effective I was in my job as a library manager. Nor can these numbers alone be relied on to give a complete analysis of the library's effectiveness.

Existence, Role, and Funding of Libraries in Geographic Areas Where Non-Whites Predominate

The misuse and abuse of statistical measures too often lead to decisions not to fund services for communities of color, and this is a phenomenon not limited to libraries. As Paul Wachtel writes,

> From a quite different vantage point, the low scores of students in poorly funded inner city schools, rather than being viewed by middle class whites as a compelling indication that greater funding is needed, often serve as a rationale for maintaining the very inequities that generate them.
> The white attitude frequently is: "These kids can't learn; the reading scores show it again and again. So what's the point of pouring good money after bad in a futile effort to bring them up to standard? Better to spend the money on kids who can learn!" The result of course is that once again the scores in the inner city schools are low and the rationale for not investing in them is maintained. (1999)

Similarly, the attitude too often seems to be "Those people don't read. Why spend money on libraries in those neighborhoods?" A faculty member of color who was interviewed for this chapter spoke about how the community he grew up in had to fight to even have a library in the neighborhood, that libraries were reserved for white neighborhoods. Greg Reese, 1999 president of the Black Caucus of the American Library Association, writes about his early experiences as a library school student and how he was moved to pursue a Ph.D. in the field to research and write about the disparities in funding of libraries in black communities versus those in white communities. He was dissuaded from doing so because this was not considered an appropriate subject of study in librarianship (Reese and Hawkins, 1999). The fact is, however, that the situation undeniably exists and deserves legitimate study. Recently, as president of the Black Caucus and as a library director, Greg Reese was able to use his position to halt the planned closure of libraries in predominantly Black neighborhoods in Savannah, Georgia (*Black Caucus Newsletter* 1999). Lack of funding in public library budgets for libraries in non-white communities has prompted communities of color to start their own libraries using outside sources of funding. Such is the case with the César Chávez Library in Oakland, California.

Access to Technology

Now that more and more of the functions of libraries have been transferred to high-technology arenas, a new white public space—the Internet—has been created that poses additional threats to information access for non-whites. It is interesting to note that, when the Internet was introduced in libraries, the standard of service and the audience to whom it was marketed was white. I was a librarian in the first library in Connecticut to offer Internet access, and it was not until I introduced workshops and marketing in Spanish that any thought was given to providing this new library service to the Spanish speakers of that city. Likewise, the first effort to market the new service to that city's African American community came much later than the introduction of the technology and was initiated by an African American librarian. Thus whiteness theory offers another way to look at the "Digital Divide."

Everyday Culture and Behavior of Librarians

Many librarians of color have commented that they are more accepted if and when they look and act white. For example, Deborah Hollis states,

> To be brutally honest, in the academic setting they will look for the non-threatening minority who looks 'safe.' I can shoot my mouth off because I'm a light-skinned African American. Those colleagues of mine who have more of an 'ethnic' look have more difficulty; they are not taken as seriously because the administration doesn't think they will 'fit.' Hollis works 'on the front lines,' she said, because she looks 'ethnically ambiguous' or 'okay' to students. People of color on a campus will be the housekeeping and maintenance detail primarily, and if it's a predominantly white school, the students might not think that a minority can be in a position of authority. (quoted in St. Lifer and Nelson 1997, 42)

Explaining How Principles of
Sensate Theory
Clarify These Practices in Librarianship

Sensate theory, a theory elaborated in seminars by Dr. Enoch Page in relation to whiteness, posits that the only way we can know reality is through our sensory apparatus; the theory places an emphasis on sensations and emotions. There are many examples in librarianship of how racial knowledge is embodied knowledge. One area I would like to point out is the physical reaction that many librarians of color have to whiteness, which often results in either a very angry or very tearful reaction or both. For example, Khafre Abif, an African American male children's librarian, has been told he is "not exactly the type one would expect to find splayed on the canary-colored rug of a public library reading *Goodnight Moon* to a gaggle of three- and four-year-olds." Abif recounts his experience:

> One week after I celebrated my first anniversary at the District of Columbia Public Library, I found myself in tears. . . . I realized I was crying because I felt so many disappointments despite the progress that had been made. I cried because I felt the library administrators were not functioning as I thought they should. I cried because the bureaucratic politics made me feel powerless. . . . Thus, I cried because of the frustration of dealing with children's librarians and managers who did not have the same cultural orientation as me. . . . I felt that new approaches, focuses, and directions needed to be channeled into our schools and our public libraries. I wanted change and the power to make things happen. (quoted in St. Lifer and Nelson 1997, 42)

For Abif, the experience of encountering whiteness in the library setting is one that is felt in the body; it is more than an intellectual abstraction. Likewise, my experiences of whiteness in my work as a librarian have often led me to tears. The reaction I have received from my white colleagues has been very different from that of colleagues of color.

Conducting an Ethnographical Study of White Cultural Practices Evident in a Large Academic Library

The library staff is mostly a bunch of "white women in sensible shoes." This comment is the closest the librarians at one academic library have come to admitting their whiteness. It was made by a member of the Library's Diversity Committee—a committee that in 1999 was composed of six white female library employees and two non-white female employees, of which I was a member—and has been repeated often by others. This humorous statement gets to the heart of the problem, in essence stating that, on the surface, there is nothing threatening about librarianship's whiteness. The white woman who told the joke should be given credit for having sensibility. But before you can do anything about whiteness, you have to go further than this. You have to identify whiteness and describe it in detail, which is what traditional anthropological ethnography has done about all kinds of cultural practices. This is not a safe academic type of study for either whites or non-whites. As a new student of anthropology who is also a librarian of color, I'm in a special position to do an ethnography of this profession. It is exciting for me to do this type of "reverse ethnography" and to practice "reverse applied anthropology" in this way. However, it is also an enterprise that can be risky due to the lack of understanding about the very concept of whiteness and the emotions involved.

I hope that this chapter can be a beginning by introducing the concept of whiteness into our professional vocabulary. I also hope it offers a venue for anthropologists to do original fieldwork that can help update the discipline of anthropology. Most anthropology has been carried out from the point of view of whiteness without mentioning its own whiteness, traditionally toward the cultures of people of color who are seen dualistically as the Other. Instead of examining the cultures of people of color as the "target" cultures, a whiteness study will take the culture of whiteness as its object. Additionally, a whiteness study by a librarian of color avoids the dualism found in most traditional anthropology in that the librarian of color/anthropologist must address her or his own whiteness and the white cultural practices she or he partakes of. Although whiteness can and has been shown to have its own definition and identifiable set of practices and principles, the sensate theory of whiteness posits that whiteness can be embodied by anyone, regardless of color. Finally, whereas much of applied anthropology has had a "development" focus of trying to "fix" the target cultures (of people of color) or preserve them, applying a theory of whiteness to the very real problems of librarianship reverses the approach by suggesting that it is the whiteness that needs fixing—or, rather, eliminating. In our professions as well as in ourselves.

Notes

1.   Among the Latino writers, Caribbean ones have been especially vocal on points of race vis-à-vis whiteness and blackness. See, for example, Jesús Colón (1982) and Piri Thomas (1973).

2.   Not everything that falls under whiteness studies follows the same approach. Indeed, Dr. H. Enoch Page criticizes most whiteness scholarship for its overemphasis on identity and lack of attention to behavior, among other things.

3.   This quote comes from a handout Dr. Page gave us in the seminar.

4.   Ibid.

5.   The term "race cognizant white" is one that appears in the literature of whiteness to denote white people who are aware of their whiteness, whereas "race traitor whites" denotes those who go beyond that to denounce whiteness as a concept, an ideology, and a political system. See, for example, Alison Bailey (1998).

6.   Although we must be very careful not to confuse the issue and ascribe whiteness only to white people, because of the demographics of the library profession, it is most likely whites who are making these rules, but it need not always be so. There are many cases where people of color become the agents of whiteness. Ward Connerly in California is but one example. In the particular cases under discussion here, it just so happens that it is whites who are making the rules.

References

Babb, Valerie. 1998. *Whiteness visible: The meaning of whiteness in American literature and culture*. New York: New York University Press.

Bailey, Alison. 1998. Locating traitorous identities—Toward a view of privilege-cognizant white character. *Hypatia-A Journal of Feminist Philosophy*13 (3): 27.

Behar, Ruth. 1996. *The vulnerable observer: Anthropology that breaks your heart*. Boston: Beacon Press.

Black Caucus Newsletter, Spring 1999.

Chambers, John. 1983. *Black English: Educational equity and the law*. Ann Arbor, MI: Karoma.

Colón, Jesús. 1982. *A Puerto Rican in New York and other sketches*. New York : International Publishers.

Corvin, Sue Ann, and Fred Wiggins, 1989. An antiracism training model for white professionals. *Journal of Multicultural Counseling and Development*17 (3) (July 1): 1105.

Flagg, Gordon. 1999. Early sit-in reenacted at library 60 years later. *American Libraries* (October): 18.

Frankenberg, Ruth. 1993. *White women, race matters: The social construction of whiteness*. Minneapolis: University of Minnesota Press.

Gabriel, John. 1998. *Whitewash: Racialized politics and the media*. London, New York: Routledge.

Hartigan, John, Jr. 1997. Establishing the fact of whiteness. *American Anthropologist* 99 (3) (September 1): 495.

Hill, Michael, ed. 1997. *Whiteness: A critical reader*. New York: New York University Press.

Holder, Judith C., and Alan Vaux. 1998. African American professionals: Coping with occupational stress in predominantly white work environments. *Journal of Vocational Behavior* 53 (3) (December 1): 315.

Hollis, Deborah R. 1996. On the ambiguous side: Experiences in a predominantly white and female profession. In *In our own voices: The changing face of librarianship*, edited by Teresa Y. Neely and Khafre K. Abif (139, 142–43). Lanham, MD: Scarecrow.

Latour, Bruno. 1979. *Laboratory life: The social construction of scientific facts*. Beverly Hills: Sage.

Lévi-Strauss, Claude. 1958. *Race and history*. Paris: UNESCO.

Marcus, George, ed. 1992. *Rereading cultural anthropology*. Durham, NC: Duke University Press.

Marcus, George E., and Michael M. J. Fischer. 1986. *Anthropology as cultural critique: An experimental moment in the human sciences*. Chicago: University of Chicago Press.

Martin, Rebecca. 1994. *Libraries and the changing face of academia: Responses to growing multicultural populations*. Metuchen, NJ: Scarecrow Press.

McCook, Kathleen de la Peña, ed. 1998. *Women of color in librarianship: An oral history*. Chicago: American Library Association.

Morin, Richard. 1997. Unconventional wisdom: The new facts and hot stats from the social sciences. *Washington Post* (January 12): C5 (Outlook section).

Morrison, Toni. 1992. *Playing in the dark: Whiteness and the literary imagination*. Cambridge, MA: Harvard University Press.

Mufwene, Alikokos, et al. 1998. *African-American English: Structure, history, and use*. New York: Routledge.

Oquendo, Angel R. 1995. Reimagining the Latino/a race. *Harvard BlackLetter Law Journal* 12 (Spring): 93–129.

Page, Helán [Enoch]. 1988. Dialogic principles of interactive learning in the ethnographic relationship. *Journal of Anthropological Research* 44: 163–81.

———. 1999, December. Personal interview.

Page, Helán E[noch], and R. Brooke Thomas. 1994. White space and the construction of white privilege in U.S. health care: Fresh concepts and a new model for analysis. *Medical Anthropology Quarterly* 8: 109–16.

Reese, Gregory L., and Ernestine L. Hawkins. 1999. *Stop talking, start doing! Attracting people of color to the library profession*. Chicago: American Library Association.

REFORMA: The National Association to Promote Library and Information Services to Latinos and the Spanish Speaking. 2000, July. *Information technology agenda*. Available: http://www.reforma.org/ITC/itcita.html. (Accessed June 11, 2001).

Roediger , David R., ed. 1998. *Black on white: Black writers on what it means to be white*. New York: Schocken Books.

Scott, Nancy E. 1989. Differences in mentor relationships of non-white and white female professionals and organizational mobility: A review of the literature. *Psychology* 26 (2/3): 23.

Sleeter, Christine. 1994. White racism. *Multicultural Education* 1 (4) (Spring): 5–8, 39.

St. Lifer, Evan, and Corinne Nelson. 1997. Unequal opportunities: Race does matter. *Library Journal* (November 1): 42–46.

Thomas, Piri. 1973. *Down These Mean Streets*. New York: Alfred A. Knopf.

Visweswaran, Kamala. 1998. Race and the culture of anthropology. *American Anthropologist* 100 (1): 70–83.

Wachtel, Paul. 1999, November 11. E-mail posting re: "Race in the Mind of America." Available: http://www.blackradicalcongress.org.

Watt, Sherry K. 1998. The story between the lines: A thematic discussion of the experiences of racism. *Journal of Counseling and Development* 77 (1) (Winter): 54. (Special Issue: Racism: Healing Its Effects).

Wilson, Matthew. 1999. Who has the right to say? Charles W. Chestnutt, whiteness, and the public sphere. *College Literature* 26 (2) (Spring): 18–35.

Wise, Tim. 1998. Is sisterhood conditional? White women and the rollback of affirmative action. *NWSA Journal* 10 (3): 1.

Part 4

Latino Programs and Models of Service

Bilingual Formats for Story Times and Storytelling Presentations

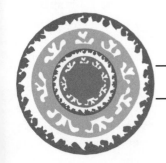

Diana Borrego ◆ Lorena Flores

Bilingual presentations enrich story time and storytelling programs by adding flavor, color, and ambiance to our tales. Code-switching (alternating between Spanish and English) during storytelling presentations introduces the Spanish language to non-Spanish speakers and validates the native speaker's use of the language. This chapter covers three formats the authors have successfully used during bilingual story time and storytelling sessions. The formats selected depended on the audience and the Spanish-language skills or comfort level of the presenter.

The authors wish to acknowledge María Kramer and Armando Ramírez for their assistance and expertise in both the presentation and the writing of this paper; and also to thank Ana-Elba Pavón for her invaluable input and knowledge.

Diana Borrego was born in Ciudad Juárez, Chihuahua, and migrated to the United States during the 1960s. Ms Borrego obtained her M.L.S. from San Jose State University and has been a children's librarian for twelve of her fourteen years as a librarian. She is currently employed by San Jose Public Library in San Jose, California.

Lorena Flores, a native of San Jose, California, is currently working on her M.L.I.S. at San Jose State University. She is an ALA 2000 Spectrum Scholar and a REFORMA Scholarship recipient. She currently works for San Jose Public Library in Technical Services, Collection Development Unit.

As our communities become culturally and linguistically diverse, there is a yearning to experience the various traditions of the world through language, food, music, media, dance, and literature. The more cultures an individual experiences, the more he or she is able to break down existing barriers. Experiencing diverse traditions through literature and storytelling is one way communities can familiarize themselves with all facets of a culture. Public libraries are unique institutions in that they have the resources to introduce bilingual story times and storytelling to their communities. Bilingual presentations enrich our programs by adding flavor, color, and ambiance to our tales. In addition, bilingual presentations introduce the Spanish language to non-Spanish speakers while validating the native speaker's use of it in a positive and effective way. The use of Spanish in a public setting with a mixed audience creates acceptance and community. While the non-Spanish speaker is being educated and immersed in another culture, a welcoming atmosphere is being created for the native speaker, who is in the process of assimilating into a new culture while at the same time trying to maintain ties to Latino culture. Language and culture are closely linked, and studies have shown that alternating between two languages (also known as code-switching) in general "indicate[s] the dual affiliation with two cultures" (Poplack 1980). This contradicts the traditional stereotype that code-switching is due to language deficiency and that it is harmful in the acquisition of language (Legenhausen 1991).

This presentation consists of three formats we have successfully used during our bilingual story time and storytelling sessions in public library settings. We based them on the needs of the community and the Spanish-language skills and/or comfort level of the presenters. The first and second formats are recommended for presenters who do not have command of a second language (Spanish) but are ready to include words in other languages in their story times. The third format is for presenters who are fluent in both Spanish and English and who can code-switch without hesitation at specific points in the story. This more enriching format offers a more colorful, effective, and concise way of conveying a cultural image.

Two Presenters:
Alternating English and Spanish

In the first format the story is read by alternating from English to Spanish, page by page. This format works best with "two presenters, one reading the English text on the first page, the other reading that same page in Spanish, etc." (Agosto 1997). Juanita Alba's *Calor: A Story of Warmth for All Ages* (1995), is one of many bilingual books that lend themselves to this format. This format is best suited for monolingual audiences of either English or Spanish. An additional source of material for bilingual presentations is found in translations of popular titles, such as *The Napping House*, by Audrey Wood (1984). When selecting translated titles the following criteria were considered: reader appeal, literary and artistic quality, and overall presentation.

Bilingual books are the perfect source to use with this format because the material is already in two languages, and many bilingual books convey images of Latino culture. A people's cultural portrayal and their history have the power to build bridges across cultural boundaries and empower youth with a positive sense of self-identity and self-confidence (Smolen and Ortiz-Castro 2000).

Reading the story from beginning to end in one language and then in the other language is a variation of the first format. This format works best with short stories and popular themes; for example, *I Hear a Noise* by Diane Goode (1988) serves as a good model for this variation. The most important criterion to follow for this variation is the selection of the books. In this case, there is a minimal amount of text and a popular theme. Titles with minimal text can be easily translated from one language into the other and can be told or read twice (once in English and once in Spanish) without losing the audience. If translations are not available for your favorite story time titles, we recommend that you translate them yourself or have a colleague or volunteer translate them for you. Keep in mind that you may encounter an interested listener who requests a copy of the translated title.

One Presenter:
Sprinkling English with Spanish

In the second format the story is read predominantly in one language (English) with key words and/or phrases repeated throughout the text in the other language (Spanish). *Delicious Hullabaloo = Pachanga Deliciosa* by Pat Mora (1998) is an excellent choice for this format, particularly for the monolingual audience. The use of semi-bilingual books familiarizes the non-Spanish speakers with the Spanish language, allowing them to adapt some of the words and phrases into their English vocabulary. Semi-bilingual books can also "give children who are insecure about their English skills the confidence to tackle a book written primarily in their second language" (Agosto 1997). This format is recommended for librarians who do not speak Spanish but are willing to test the rhythm of the language to flavor their story times with a Latin *ambiente* (ambiance). This presentation is suitable for a monolingual and a beginning bilingual audience.

One Presenter:
Bilingual Spanish and English

The third format is a bilingual presentation, which code-switches from one language to another while still maintaining the grammatical consistency of both languages (Becker 1997). This is the most challenging of the formats mentioned in this chapter because it requires the storyteller to be proficient in both languages (Spanish and English) as well as in code-switching. The code-switching format is powerful and it has the magical capability of transporting both the teller and audience into the two worlds or languages from which they derive. This format works best with a bilingual audience. We recommend that the storyteller maximize the use of tones, gestures, and selection of words and phrases so that the stories capture the essence of the culture. For example, in the telling of *Borreguita and the Coyote* by Verna Aardema (1991), a storyteller emphasized the Latino culture in one scene where Borreguita gestures to indicate how her master savors his delicious tacos. The intonation of the Spanish words selected transported the listener and storyteller to the culture, and most important, held the audience's attention.

There is no single *right way* to do a bilingual presentation. The formats presented here have been used and been found to be effective in doing story times at the San Jose Public Library. The aim is to create an exciting atmosphere so that your audience can have a meaningful and enjoyable cultural experience. For best results in maintaining the interest of younger audiences, we highly recommend using books with little text. Longer stories can also be used but work better with older audiences who can appreciate them and reminisce about their heritage. The most rewarding of all formats is the code-switching storytelling technique, because it offers the best of both worlds for everyone.

Offering glimpses of other cultures through literature helps children understand values and ideas other than those of their native culture. As seen here, one way in which monolingual audiences can experience culture through literature is by introducing words and phrases from another language. Although this presentation concentrates on reading and telling stories, formats such as music, rhymes, and poetry can also be introduced. In recent years, bilingual publishing has flourished. The result is an increase in the number of well-written, Spanish-English picture books that capture the rhythm of the language, provide cultural insight, and reflect the Latino experience. We can only hope that this trend continues.

References

Aardema, Verna. 1991. *Borreguita and the coyote.* New York: Alfred A. Knopf.

Agosto, D. 1997. Bilingual picture books: Libros para todos. *School Library Journal* 43 (8): 38–39.

Alba, Juanita. 1995. *Calor: A story of warmth for all ages.* New York: Lectorum Publications.

Becker, K. R. 1997. Spanish/English bilingual codeswitching: A syncretic model. *Bilingual Review* 22 (1): 3–31.

de Mejía, A. 1998. Bilingual storytelling: Code switching, discourse control, and learning opportunities. *TESOL Journal* 7 (6): 4–10.

de Ramirez, S. B. B. 1998. Storytellers and their listener-readers in Silko's "storytelling" and "storyteller." *American Indian Quarterly* 21 (3): 333–58.

Goode, Diane. 1988. *I hear a noise.* New York: Dutton.

Legenhausen, Lienhard. 1991. Code-switching in learners' discourse. *International Review of Applied Linguistics in Language Teaching* 29 (1): 61–74.

Mora, Pat. 1998. *Delicious hullabaloo = Pachanga deliciosa.* Houston: Piñata Books.

Patterson, I. M. 1998. Charlotte Public Library speaks español: Approaching the Hispanic community through storytelling. *North Carolina Libraries* 56 (4): 145–47.

Poplack, S. 1980. Sometimes I'll start a sentence in Spanish y termino en español: Toward a typology of code-switching. *Linguistics* 18: 581–618.

Reed, B. 1995. Storytelling: What it can teach. *School Library Journal* 34: 35–39.

Smolen, L. A., and V. Ortiz-Castro. 2000. Dissolving borders and broadening perspectives through Latino traditional literature. *Reading Teacher* 53 (7): 566–79.

Wood, Audrey. 1984. *The napping house.* San Diego: Harcourt Brace Jovanovich.

Entendidos

Library Services to Hispanic Gay Teens and Their Families

Ina Rimpau

A reference referral for a Hispanic family with a gay teenager prompted the author to review her library's Spanish-language books on sexuality to find out what they had to offer gay, lesbian, and bisexual teens and their families. The following annotated bibliography of twelve books is presented in the format of a booktalk.

Ina Rimpau has her M.L.S. from McGill University in Montreal, Canada. She has been working in La Sala Hispanoamericana at Newark Public Library since 1995.

Introduction

La Sala Hispanoamericana is Newark Public Library's Spanish-language collection and also the largest Spanish-language public library collection in New Jersey. We provide Spanish-speaking patrons with a level of service in reference and in collection development that is comparable to that received by English-speaking patrons. Our bilingual staff does outreach and programming and develops computer classes in Spanish. I also work for MultiMAC, a multilingual interlibrary loan program operating out of Newark Public Library that provides collections in the eleven languages most widely spoken by recent immigrants to New Jersey, library signage and translation services for those languages, workshops on customer service in a multicultural environment for library staff, and consultations. This makes us a clearinghouse for questions regarding library services to speakers of languages other than English, and we frequently get calls from other libraries, mainly from New Jersey but also from around the country.

Several months ago, I was called by a librarian who had been approached by a patron bringing in a Hispanic family, consisting of a mother, a father, and a fifteen-year-old son. The parents were distraught because the son had just come out to them as gay and they were afraid he was going to burn in hell. The family friend, translating for the family, was asking for materials in Spanish to help everyone adjust to this new development, and asked if the library had books on adolescent sexuality that would be supportive of the gay teen and might help his parents come to terms with his being gay. I knew that our collection contained several sexuality books, but I checked specifically for materials about gay, lesbian, and bisexual teens.

What I'll be doing here is booktalking. I'll start off describing the titles I *don't* recommend. I'm saving the best for last. Although the original reference question pertained to male gay teens, I'll also be discussing books that address girls.

📖 *Yo, adolescente* was published in Mexico in 1990 (Pick de Weiss and Varga-Trujillo 1990). The only mention of homosexuality is under the heading "Las desviaciones sexuales"—sexual deviations, under which we find "sexual orientations." By inference, then, any sexual orientation is a deviation. We find listed in this book homosexuality and bisexuality, exhibitionism, transvestism, and hermaphrodism. So we have a misdemeanor, a fetish, and a medical condition incorrectly labeled as "orientations." There is no acknowledgment that the reader might actually be gay.

📖 *Hablemos de sexo* (Eyre and Eyre 1999) is a translation of *How to Talk to Your Child about Sex,* which was published in the United States (Eyre and Eyre 1998). It does not mention homosexuality at all and has an explicit anti-safe sex message, claiming that condoms are not reliable and shouldn't be used because their purpose is to "prevent something bad, not attain something good." Condoms save lives; it verges on criminal irresponsibility for anyone to discourage the use of them. I also want to say here that advocating abstinence outside of marriage leaves gays and lesbians completely out in the cold. Gays and lesbians cannot legally marry. It is cruel to offer no alternative to celibacy. A life of celibacy can be rewarding providing that it is freely chosen. The fact that the vast majority of adults do not choose celibacy speaks for itself. Heterosexuals have no business demanding a way of life for gays and lesbians that they themselves cannot maintain.

📖 Scott Talley's *Como hablarles a sus hijos sobre el sexo* (1993) discusses the "causes" of homosexuality, listing incest and lack of appropriate role models, and tells parents to do everything in their power to prevent their children from being gay, for example, by "promoting" the differences between women and men.

📖 *Conozcamos a nuestros hijos del nacimiento a la pubertad* is a 1999 Mexican publication (Uribe de Alanís 1999). It has a Dear Abby format, where people write in their problems and the author gives advice; I use the term "advice" loosely. One mother writes to say that her twelve-year-old son is worrying her because he has always been different from other boys and likes things that girls like. The advice this mother gets is to discourage "feminine behavior." She is also advised to take him to a psychologist because it is vital that this "problem" be resolved before the boy reaches puberty. So behavior is dealt with only at its most superficial level, not addressing the underlying issues of the boy's probable sexual orientation or the parents' reaction to it.

📖 *¿Qué le pasa a mi cuerpo?* (Madaras 1987a) is a translation of *The What's Happening to My Body? Book for Girls* (Madaras 1987b). Only one and one-half pages, out of 240—wedged between the chapters covering STDs and rape—cover homosexuality. Most of that space is devoted to reassuring the reader that having homosexual fantasies or experiences doesn't mean a person is gay, but for those who are pretty sure they are, "this, too is natural and you're not alone." That's it. That's the extent of this book's information and support for queer teens.

📖 *La sexualidad en la adolescencia* (Westheimer, Kravetz, and Karola 1987) is a translation of *First Love: A Young People's Guide to Sexual Information*, co-authored by Dr. Ruth (Westheimer, Kravetz, and Karola 1985). Homosexuality is segregated in a chapter of its own, never integrated into discussions of dating and friendship. We find the claim that psychologists have changed their opinion regarding the "causes" of homosexuality because of the "political power" gays have nowadays. Scientists changed their opinions of homosexuality based on research and education. The far right regularly brings up the "political clout" of gay people. The vast majority of queer[1] people in this country live without any protections against discrimination. So much for our clout. Although generally tolerant, the chapter finishes with the suggestion that a teen struggling with his or her sexuality should consult, among others, a priest. I believe this is one issue for which the Catholic Church will not provide useful answers.

📖 *Guía sexual para la adolescente* (Voss and Gale 1987), a translation of *A Young Woman's Guide to Sex* (Voss and Gale 1986), was the first book I encountered that mentioned gay organizations as a source of information and support and discussed the advantages along with the possible repercussions of coming out, factual information that is crucial to teens. Teens run the risk of losing their housing, not to mention their chances of an education, when they come out, so they need to be very pragmatic about when to come out and to whom. The boys' version, *Guía sexual para el adolescente*, does not go into that detail, opting instead for the "these feelings are normal and it doesn't mean you're gay" line. It is very interesting that boys are given much less support in "their" edition of this book.

📖 *El libro de los chicos* (Schneider 1995), a sex education book for boys, first published in German, is supportive, characterizing homosexuality as a normal sexual identity and encouraging boys to seek support from gay organizations, while warning them about being taken advantage of. Safe sex information is lacking, implying that oral sex between men is not a risk factor for contracting AIDS. The book also discusses how to deal with people who attack gays.

📖 *Acéptate, acéptalo: como explicar y comprender las distintas orientaciones sexuales* (Powers and Ellis 1999), is a translation of *A Family and Friend's Guide to Sexual Orientation* (Powers and Ellis 1996). It contains many personal histories, none of them written by teens. Of particular relevance to Hispanics is the discussion of the spirituality of queer people and religious sanctions against homosexuality. We are told that Leviticus in the Old Testament considers homosexuality an abomination; Leviticus also considers the eating of shellfish an abomination and yet there is no grassroots effort to put seafood restaurants out of business. People select which prohibitions and rules are relevant and useful for the lives we lead today.

📖 *Claves para una saludable sexualidad de tus hijos* (De Freitas 1999) is a translation of *Keys to Your Child's Healthy Sexuality* (De Freitas 1998). The copy I examined was published in 1992. It reassures parents that same-sex attractions between growing children are "normal" and don't necessarily mean that their child is gay. Sound familiar? On a positive note, it says that sexuality is not chosen, is not "caused" by anything, and cannot be changed. This is not exactly a gay pride parade, but I feel it is vital that parents and families, along with queer teens themselves, not be misled as to the possibility that sexual orientation can be changed. It cannot. A person may find his or her sexuality evolving, but nobody can by sheer force of will change his or her orientation. Additionally, this book mentions gay and lesbian couples outside the "gay" chapter, in the chapter on marriage and divorce.

📖 *Sexo . . . ¿Qué es?* (Harris and Emberley 1997), a translation of *Let's Talk about Sex* (Harris and Emberley 1994b), is really geared toward pre-teens, but I'm including it because it's one of a very few books that, in addition to providing information about homosexuality, integrates gays and lesbians into its general discussion of families and relationships. I also really like this sexuality book because it is explicit and has a sense of humor. I've observed teens being completely engrossed in it and parents somewhat taken aback.

📖 *Puentes de respeto: creación de apoyo para la juventud lesbiana y homosexual* (Whitlock and Kamel 1992), a translation of *Bridges of Respect: Creating Support for Lesbian and Gay Youth* (Whitlock 1989), was published by the American Friends Services Committee and a Chilean Quaker group. It is a guide for youth social workers in the United States and includes testimonials by gays and lesbians and an extensive list of organizations.

Returning to the reference question at the beginning of this chapter, the books I decided to send for the Hispanic family were *Puentes, Sexo, . . . ¿Qué es?, El libro de los chicos,* and *Guía sexual para el adolescente. Acéptate* and *Claves* were not yet part of my collection. Almost as soon as they were acquired, processed, and put on the shelf, my copies of *Acéptate*, along with my copies of *Puentes*, disappeared and had to be replaced. You'll find that books with queer themes are frequently lost to the library.

After several weeks, I heard from the librarian who had originally asked me for help. She was profusely grateful. She said that she had been revisited by the family and their friend, and that the family had undergone a transformation. The parents asked for an extension of the loan period of the book *Puentes de respeto*, saying they had found it most helpful and that they were urging a local Spanish bookstore to carry it. I was happy to hear that they had found the material helpful, and it intrigued me that they were so enthusiastic about a book written for social workers by American and Chilean Quakers. Upon reflection, I realized that it was the one book that brought a spiritual dimension to the issue of homosexuality. Spirituality and religion are important parts of Hispanic culture, and they are tools we can avail ourselves of in our educational work.

This experience is very compelling to me because it brings together so many aspects of my work as a public librarian:

- There is the outreach to an isolated, underserved group, in this case, triply so, by virtue of being young, queer, and Hispanic

- There is providing the information to the entire family, with its varying information needs

- There is the understanding that an approach that works for me— scientific and political—is not the one that is going to work with everyone.

As queers, we are so used to being rejected and oppressed by most religions that we tend to forget religion's transformative, radical potential to change and educate people. I am now personally appealing to writers, publishers, and distributors to publish books in Spanish that come from a religious perspective and that affirm lesbian, gay, bisexual, and transgendered people. I urge our allies to protest blatantly homophobic, incorrect, and misleading texts regarding sexuality in general.

There is a wonderful tradition in Hispanic families of cohesiveness and mutual love and support. In her book about raising kids with Hispanic values,

Raising Nuestros Niños, Gloria Rodriguez (1999) missed the opportunity to exhort Hispanic parents to give the same love and support to their queer children that they give to their straight children. It is my hope that in a future edition lesbian, gay, bisexual, and transgendered people will be explicitly included, for we already know that we are parts of our families.

Notes

1. Note on the use of the word *queer*: It has been reclaimed by lesbians, gays, bisexuals, and transgendered people, especially younger ones, because it encompasses all of the aforementioned categories and all the variations in between. It is particularly useful when talking about those teens who are unsure of their orientation and feel outside of the heterosexual, strictly gendered paradigm.

References

De Freitas, Chrystal. 1999. *Claves para una saludable sexualidad de tus hijos.* Buenos Aires: Errepar.

———. 1998. *Keys to your child's healthy sexuality.* Hauppauge, NY: Barron's Educational Series.

Eyre, Linda, and Richard Eyre. 1998. *How to talk to your child about sex: It's best to start early, but it's never too late: A step-by-step guide for every age.* New York: Golden Books.

———. 1999. *Hablemos de sexo.* Miami: Downtown Book Center.

Gale, Jay. 1984. *A young man's guide to sex.* New York: Holt, Rinehart & Winston.

———. 1989. *Guía sexual para el adolescente.* Translation by Ariel Bignami. Buenos Aires: J. Vergara Editor.

Harris, Robie H., and Michael Emberley, illus. 1994a. *It's perfectly normal: A book about changing bodies, growing up, sex, and sexual health.* Cambridge, MA: Candlewick Press.

———. 1994b. *Let's talk about sex: Growing up, changing bodies, sex and sexual health.* London: Walker.

———. 1997. *Sexo . . . ¿Qué es?: Desarrollo, cambios corporales, sexo y salud sexual.* Barcelona: Ediciones Serres.

Madaras, Lynda. 1987a. *¿Qué le pasa a mi cuerpo? Cómo ayudar a su hija a convertirse en mujer.* Mexico City: Editorial Diana.

———. 1987b. *The what's happening to my body? book for girls : A growing up guide for parents and daughters.* New York: Newmarket Press.

Pick de Weiss, Susan, and Elvia Vargas-Trujillo. 1990. *Yo, adolescente.* Mexico City: Manuales Planeta.

Powers, Bob Alan Ellis. 1996. *A family and friend's guide to sexual orientation.* New York: Routledge.

———. 1999. *Acéptate, acéptalo: Cómo explicar y comprender las distintas orientaciones sexuales.* Barcelona: Paidos.

Rodriguez, Gloria. 1999. *Raising nuestros niños.* New York: Simon & Schuster.

Schneider, Sylvia. 1995. *El libro de los chicos.* Madrid: Loguez Ediciones.

Talley, Scott. 1990. *Talking with your kids about the birds and the bees : A guide for parents and counselors to help kids from 4 to 18 develop healthy sexual attitudes.* Ventura, CA: Regal Books.

———. 1993. *Cómo hablarles a sus hijos sobre el sexo.* Bogotá, Colombia: Grupo Editorial Norma.

Uribe de Alanís, Esperanza. 1999. *Conozcamos a nuestros hijos del nacimiento a la pubertad.* Mexico City: Editorial Trillas.

Voss, Jacqueline, and Jay A. Gale. 1986. *A young woman's guide to sex.* New York: Holt, Rinehart & Winston.

———. 1987. *Guía sexual para la adolescente.* Buenos Aires: J. Vergara.

Westheimer, Ruth, and Nathan Kravetz. 1985. *First love: A young people's guide to sexual information.* New York: Warner Books.

———. 1987. *La sexualidad en la adolescencia.* Buenos Aires: Emecé.

Whitlock, Katherine. 1989. *Bridges of respect : Creating support for lesbian and gay youth.* 2d ed. Written for the American Friends Service Committee. Rachael Kamel, editor. Philadelphia: American Friends Service Committee.

Whitlock, Katherine, and Rachael Kamel. 1992. *Puentes de respeto: Creación de apoyo para la juventud lesbiana y homosexual.* Santiago, Chile: Comité de Servicio Chileno Cuáquero.

Carnegie Public Community Library as a Model Public Library in Puerto Rico

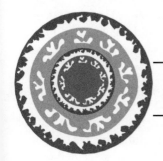

Josefina Gómez de Hillyer
Marie Flores Ortiz

In this chapter the authors give an overview of the Carnegie Public Community Library of the Department of Education as a model public library in Puerto Rico. They include a history and general description of the library and its programs. Justifiably proud of their library, they give us an idea of the innovative and creative strategies they have instituted to reach the Puerto Rican community. The library has had a great impact on the quality of life of Puerto Rican children, young adults, and adults.

Josefina Gómez de Hillyer obtained a B.A., cum laude, from Bryn Mawr College, an M.A. from the University of Chicago, and an M.L.S. from the University of Puerto Rico, Río Piedras Campus. She has been director of the Carnegie Public Community Library since 1995. She is a former president of REFORMA—Puerto Rico Chapter. A member of Beta Phi Mu, she is currently president of the Puerto Rico Librarians Association.

Marie Flores Ortiz obtained a B.A., summa cum laude, and an M.L.S. from the University of Puerto Rico, Río Piedras Campus. She has been the coordinator of the Young Adult Project at the Carnegie Public Community Library since its inception in June 1999. She is a member of Beta Phi Mu and is secretary of REFORMA—Puerto Rico Chapter.

Introduction

T he Carnegie Public Community Library of the Department of Education is a model public library in Puerto Rico. It has occupied a unique place among the cultural institutions on the Island. This chapter describes the functions of this library, specifically in relation to the development and promotion of reading programs. These programs are organized for children, young adults, and adults using a variety of strategies.

History and Description of the Library

The Carnegie Public Community Library was established in 1916 in San Juan and quickly became an institution that had a great cultural impact in Puerto Rico. It was the first library building built in Puerto Rico. It scheduled conferences, concerts, story hours, and many other activities. It also expanded services to the whole Island, taking book boxes and later bookmobiles to the countryside and other places where library services had never been offered.

In September 1989 Hurricane Hugo struck the Island and devastated the library. Most of the collection was lost, and what was saved was donated to other libraries. The building lost its roof and windows and was flooded. The library closed and reopened in May 1995 in the historically remodeled building. The information resources are all new.

The library's mission is to fulfill the informational, educational, cultural, and recreational needs and interests of the municipality of San Juan through the development of a collection of printed, audiovisual, and electronic materials and an aggressive information and reference program. Since the re-inauguration of the library it has attracted users from communities beyond San Juan.

The library is divided into seven areas:

1. Information and Referral houses a vertical file containing information on community agencies, services, foundations, and activities. This area also offers information on library activities and handles registration of new adult users.

2. Audiovisual Materials includes a large collection of videos, music CDs, including the "Música para todos" [see page 174] collection donated by REFORMA in 1996, and cassettes. Viewing and listening equipment is available for patrons to use in the library. The majority of the material in this collection circulates.

3. The Ramón Mellado Parsons Children's Room, with materials for infants through twelve years old in all formats, was named for the late secretary of education, who was widely respected for his interest and efforts on behalf of Puerto Rican children.

4. The Young Adult Room, made possible by a grant from the Carnegie Corporation of New York, includes books and other materials for users twelve to eighteen years old.

5. The reference area for adults has an extensive bilingual collection and is a census and government documents depository.

6. The circulation room for adults is divided into general, biography, Puerto Rico, and fiction collections. It also offers computer and Internet services for the blind.

7. The Harold Lidin Magazine and Newspaper Room, named for a well-known journalist, has an extensive and varied collection due to the fact that it is made up primarily of undeliverable periodicals donated by the U.S. Postal Service. It also includes local newspapers on microfilm that can be read and printed.

In addition, the library has two community meeting rooms, the Luis O'Neill de Milán Multiple Use Room and the smaller Audiovisual Room. Other resources are two electronic bookmobiles, each with eight computers and a small reference collection. These visit disadvantaged communities, schools without electronic libraries, and special institutions, such as those serving young adults and children.

The library's collection consists of printed, audiovisual, and electronic formats in Spanish and English. There were 21,436 items recorded in the public catalog as of June 30, 2000, not including audiovisual and electronic materials.

The library is administered by a board of directors named by the governor of Puerto Rico and is presided over by the secretary of education. The library staff of the Department of Education serves in a consulting capacity. The library also has an active Friends of the Library group that helps to manage funds received through grant proposals written by the library director.

Reading Programs for Children

The reading programs for children have been organized with the following goals in mind:

1. *To promote Puerto Rican children's literature by introducing to the children the work of local writers and illustrators.* This has been accomplished through "Lee Conmigo," a story hour sponsored by The Procter & Gamble Company. It began in 1997 and has been renewed yearly. Once a month, local authors and illustrators are invited to read their work. This has been a trendsetting activity, recognized by the Instituto Puertorriqueño del Libro Infantil. For many authors, it has been the first time that they have received honoraria to read to children. Following the readings, activities such as writing and arts and crafts based on the story take place. Major Puerto Rican children's authors and illustrators have participated in the program. In addition, book presentations are given periodically as the opportunity arises. Authors and publishers see the children's room as a desirable place to present their literary creations.

2. *To improve reading skills of kindergarten to third grade children who are below reading level for their grade and belong to low-income communities.* This is accomplished through the "Lee con Carnegie" program, part of the America Reads–Puerto Rico Lee initiative of the federal Corporation for National Service Ameri-Corps*VISTA program. This tutorial program is in its third year. It was developed to address the needs of the communities of La Perla and Puerta de Tierra. More than 90 percent of the residents of these communities live below the poverty line. The children's reading and comprehension skills are well below their grade level. In addition to addressing these needs, the program's long-term goals are to keep the children in school, encourage them to become life-long learners, help them become productive citizens in the future, and keep them away from social problems, such as substance abuse.

3. *To promote reading in general and make it FUN.* This is accomplished through reading festivals organized in conjunction with other institutions. For example, the library annually sponsors "Festival del Cuento en Familia," "Festival del Cuento Puertorriqueño," and "Festival de Verano en la Carnegie" with the co-sponsorship of other institutions such as the University of Puerto Rico Graduate School of Library and Information Sciences and Headstart.

4. *To promote the use of different types of reading materials by school children, providing activities to develop search skills.* Special activities are organized according to the needs and interests of the schools and also groups such as Headstart and Scouts. Since 1995, the library has been assisted in this goal by a Title VI grant for the Electronic Information Center for the Young Researcher at the Carnegie Library, which benefits schools in the San Juan area. This is a structured program in which the students are taught search skills, not only in the use of materials in different formats but also in the creation of conceptual maps used to organize the searches. The specific aim is to help the children with their science projects. In the program each group visits the library three times.

5. *To promote reading interests through outreach programs using two electronic bookmobiles.* Each bookmobile has eight computers with Internet access and a basic reference book collection. Acquired in 1999, they visit low-income communities, schools without electronic libraries, and juvenile institutions.

6. *To develop reading readiness in disabled children while integrating them into a mainstream children's environment.* This is accomplished through the Toy Library for Children with Disabilities, an innovative new service. This joint project was made possible in conjunction with the Puerto Rico Technology Assistance Project, College of Health Related Professions, University of Puerto Rico Medical Sciences Campus (*Proyecto de Asistencia Tecnológica, Colegio de Profesiones Relacionadas con la Salud, Recinto de Ciencias Médicas, Universidad de Puerto Rico*). The Department of Education is encouraging other public libraries to develop similar programs. The toys help develop reading readiness, eye-hand coordination, and other skills needed for reading and writing.

7. *To develop reading skills and promote reading enjoyment by offering a summer program in June and July.* This program is organized by AmeriCorps*VISTA members at the library. Because it is free, it provides needy children with an opportunity they would not otherwise have. It emphasizes reading, the use of different library materials, workshops on creativity, language learning such as English and French, and arts and crafts.

Reading Programs for Young Adults

The Carnegie Public Community Library was the first library in Puerto Rico to focus on the establishment of a program and space for young adults. The program includes an electronic bookmobile unit, which provides services to teenagers who do not have access to the main library. Most Puerto Rican public libraries have few resources in their collections for young adults. They offer mostly information services for children and adults and usually do not have a specific place in the library for teens.

The Carnegie Public Community Library has a young adult room with full services. In this area, teens twelve to eighteen years old can read, do their homework, watch movies, play games, listen to music, and participate in workshops and activities. It is a place where they can spend time either having fun or fulfilling their educational needs. The electronic bookmobile unit of the Carnegie Public Community Library serves as a library branch for the Young Adult Project. It offers services to teens in public schools and juvenile detention institutions and also outreach services to economically disadvantaged communities. This project was created as a result of a competitive proposal to the Carnegie Corporation of New York. The Young Adult project received $500,000, which has allowed the library to hire personnel to manage and run the project and to acquire a young adult collection. At the same time, support activities in the electronic bookmobile have been developed.

Puerto Rican young adults have special needs and interests that distinguish them from other members of society. Young Puerto Ricans are very active and full of energy. They use this energy listening to music, dancing, going to the beach, going to the movies, watching TV, listening to radio, visiting malls, surfing, roller blading, and so forth. There is a sector of the young adult population between the ages of twelve and eighteen that does not adjust to the educational system in Puerto Rico. Some drop out of school. There are different factors that lead teens to become dropouts, including low academic performance, discipline problems, and unplanned pregnancy. Many high-risk students have parents who never finished high school. For them this is not a priority. If the socioeconomic status of a family is low, the student will probably have to go to work to support the family or at least put food on the table. Teachers with a lack of interest in motivating their students to acquire knowledge and to learn are another factor. Other problems facing teenagers in Puerto Rico are violence, lack of clear moral values, use and abuse of drugs and alcohol, crime, and disorders such as anorexia and bulimia.

To help young adults overcome the problems mentioned, information professionals need to establish special services for this sector of the population. The Carnegie Public Community Library has taken the first step with its Young Adult Project.

The Carnegie Public Community Library has acquired a collection that satisfies the needs and interests of young adults in the community. The collection areas were identified through focus groups. At present, the library provides print material, including books and magazines, in reference, Puerto Rico reference, professional careers, art, movies, literature, music, religion, self-help, and reading interest (mystery, drama, adventure, horror, suspense, romance, fiction, and science fiction). The library also has other resources covering the topics mentioned above: CD-ROMs, videos, DVDs, databases, and the Internet.

In the Young Adult Room, professionals trained to work with teenagers offer workshops and conferences geared to their needs and interests. Writers are invited to share their experiences with young adults and to encourage them to read and to expand their knowledge. Among the workshops offered are "Self-Esteem and Motivation," "Sexuality and Its Consequences," "Drug and Alcohol Prevention," "Responsible Fatherhood and Motherhood," "How to Select a Career," "How to Prepare for a Job Interview," and "Juvenile Delinquency Prevention."

The objectives of the workshops are to help young adults become aware of better opportunities for them in society. Most teenagers fail to recognize the consequences of an early pregnancy; others don't know what career to choose or what work opportunities are available to them. In addition to the educational and personal workshops, there are acting classes and art classes to stimulate the cultural and artistic interests of youth.

The electronic bookmobile unit also gives the library the opportunity to offer workshops to young adults who do not visit the main library. Using the bookmobile's information resources, teens prepare presentations using computers and their software programs. The experience has been enriching because it provides an opportunity to develop creativity skills. Teens are motivated to learn about new and exciting areas of knowledge that they may have previously ignored.

The project intends to reach beyond the San Juan metropolitan area. This will be accomplished through the creation of a Web page and a CD-ROM. The project's resources are useful for librarians in other public and school libraries who would like to develop information projects for young adults. Through this project, young adults will receive positive encouragement to help them believe in themselves and contribute to society. The library feels very proud to have the opportunity provided by the Carnegie Corporation of New York to develop this project for young adults. It will have a great impact on Puerto Rican society, and many teenagers have enjoyed the wide range of services the library can offer because of it.

Reading Programs for Adults

Reading promotion programs for adults are organized with specific goals in mind:

1. *To promote the creation and knowledge of Puerto Rican litera-ture.* This is accomplished by working with authors and publishers. Starting in 1996 and continuing through 1998, the library was selected by the Miller Brewing Company to participate in the na-tional Read About Me–Aprende de Mí program. The Carnegie was only one of a few selected libraries whose program was re-newed, not once but twice. The list of authors is a "Who's Who" of contemporary Puerto Rican literature. Their books were acquired and exhibits of their work were presented in the lobby. The pres-entations were recorded and are available in the Audiovisual Room, and the written presentations are available as reference materials. This program was especially effective because most authors present their work either in an academic environment or in bookstores. The general public felt very comfortable hearing them in a library environment. The authors appreciated the oppor-tunity to think about their work, put it in perspective, examine their literary development, and receive feedback from the general reading audience. The question-and-answer sessions following the talks were very rewarding, delving into the process of literary creation and author-reader relationships.

   Another way to promote reading for adults is through book presentations. Often authors come to the library to present their books, but publishers call as well, because they recognize the value of promoting their books in a library environment. The library has worked with large and small publishers.

2. *To promote reading in general through lectures and "conversato-rios" (talks) on different subjects, mostly sponsored by the Funda-ción Puertorriqueña de las Humanidades from 1996 to the present.* The first lecture series focused on the "Música para todos" record collection donated by REFORMA. Lectures on the sociology of salsa were presented. Later these lectures were incorporated into a best-selling book on salsa. The library was chosen by the Fundación to host its annual Humanist of the Year Award. Occasions such as these can stimulate lecture series. For example, when Luis Rafael Sánchez was awarded the prize, there were talks on his journalistic

output, his novels, his dramas, and his essays. Lately, various subjects deemed to be of general interest have been selected, such as "*Memoria y cultura*" (Memory and culture) and "*Periodismo e historia*" (Journalism and history). As always, the books discussed and others on the subject are bought for the circulating collection.

3. *To promote literary creation by library users.* The library offers the free use of computers and writing programs in the different areas of the library. This service is widely used by the general public. For example, a homeless gentleman has used these facilities to write a book. Since 1995, the community poetry group HONTANAL has met at the library every month. One poet is highlighted each time, but all poets attending can read one of their poems. Later the poets discuss their work. Attendance has increased exponentially, and many published works have been born here. The poets come from all over the Island, and the library is their home.

    Another project is "El Poder de Escribir–The Power of Writing" workshop on short story writing sponsored by the Harold Lidin Foundation. This has previously been done in an academic or school setting but is a new program in a library setting. Many people come because they want to write but do not know how to approach such an undertaking. They feel free in the library and their creativity flourishes.

4. *To promote the use of materials through exhibits.* Exhibits are located in each room of the library and in the lobby. These exhibits include author of the month (related to lectures or book presentations), new acquisitions, thematic displays in relation to holidays, and community organizations with a particular interest (such as recycling).

5. *To promote the use of the Library by community organizations for research and reading.* The first partnership to further this goal was established with the Puerto Rico Genealogical Society. They have deposited their books in the Reference Room, together with library holdings on the subject. The materials constitute a collection widely used, not only by the Society's members but also by the community in general.

Innovative and Creative Strategies within the Puerto Rican Reality

For our library to function effectively and for its goals to become a reality, coordination with the community is the first essential step. Innovative activities are organized with the cooperation of Island institutions, as has been described. Creativity is also important; the library director writes proposals for specific projects and looks beyond the Island, reaching out to national organizations such as the Carnegie Corporation of New York. In the writing of the Young Adult Proposal, for example, where branch libraries were a must, the library proposed the electronic bookmobile as a branch library because the Carnegie does not have a branch.

The library also benefits when its facilities are used as a practice library for educational programs. The Graduate School of Library and Information Science of the University of Puerto Rico, Río Piedras Campus, has sent students for practice courses. The library has also been the subject of several master's thesis studies. These analyses help the institution grow. The School of Public Communications at the same university and at Sacred Heart University have also arranged for these practice courses for their students.

University students majoring in public communications have handled public relations at the library since 1999. The library depends on community time slots in the media because it does not have a budget for this purpose. Community relations are very important in spreading the word about library services and activities.

The Friends of the Library group has been most helpful as a fiscal agent for the administration of grants written by the director. The members are active in the library's activities and very supportive of its programs. The small but dedicated group of volunteers helps in special activities. With further creativity and innovative strategies, this area could be strengthened and developed.

Honors, Recognitions, and Awards

The library was named Public Library of the Year 1995 by the Puerto Rico Librarians Association. This was a very important recognition because it was the year in which the library reopened after the destruction caused by Hurricane Hugo. It also helped publicize the services offered. In 1997, the 1st International Puerto Rico Book Fair awarded the library second prize for Excellence in Marketing and Public Relations.

Recognition of the library by ACURIL (Association of Caribbean University, Research, and Institutional Libraries) in June 2000 spotlighted the development of library programs since 1997. These awards include the President's Award for Outreach Services to Communities with Special Information Needs and the Award for Creativity in Programs to Promote Reading in Children. The fact that librarians in the Caribbean look to the Carnegie Public Community Library as an example makes the staff proud. It is an incentive to continue developing the services offered and to seek out new program opportunities with flexibility and vision.

Conclusion

It is clear that the Carnegie Public Community Library has developed a range of important services and programs for children, young adults, and adults. It has been a pioneer and a dynamic force in stimulating the promotion of reading among users at all three levels, through both public and privately funded projects. These projects have had a positive impact on the quality of life for Puerto Rican children, young adults, and adults. They have made the Carnegie Public Community Library a model Puerto Rican public library.

Part 5

Documenting
Latino Lives and Creativity

Queer Community History and the Evidence of Desire

The Archivo Rodrigo Reyes, A Gay and Lesbian Latino Archive

Luis Alberto de la Garza
Horacio N. Roque Ramírez

To create an archive of a time, a place, and a community is no small achievement. This chapter documents the history and the significance of the Archivo Rodrigo Reyes, which in turn documents the gay and lesbian Latino community in the San Francisco Bay Area since the mid-1970s.

Originally from Eagle Pass, Texas ("El Águila"), Luis Alberto de la Garza is currently a Ph.D. student in comparative ethnic studies at the University of California at Berkeley. His interests lie in archives, library special collections, museum collections management, and Chicano/Mexicano visual culture. In summer 2000, he assisted in processing the collection pertaining to Mexican printmaker José Guadalupe Posadas (1852–1913) at the Library of Congress. He has also been a curator assistant at The Mexican Museum, San Francisco, California.

Inmigrante santaneco from El Salvador, Horacio N. Roque Ramírez earned his Ph.D in comparative ethnic studies at the University of California, Berkeley (2001). He is completing an oral history study of queer Latina/Latino community formations in the San Francisco Bay Area, has taught creative writing workshops in Spanish for Proyecto ContraSIDA Por Vida, a sex-positive queer Latina/o HIV agency in San Francisco, and has contributed to the anthology *Virgins, Guerrillas & Locas*. He is currently a University of California President's Postdoctoral Fellow at UCLA.

Introduction

Because we have imbibed some of the public images that we were given, because we have absorbed the silences of others and made them our own, it is no easy task nor trivial undertaking to move from silence into visibility and voice. It is a challenge that cannot be taken lightly, but must be met with boldness, responsibility, and scrutiny. (Omosupe 1991)

The Archivo Rodrigo Reyes (ARR)[1] was born from the life and creative efforts of Chicano/Tejano gay activist and artist Rodrigo Reyes (1945–1992). Reyes moved to San Francisco in 1970 and co-founded the Gay Latino Alliance (GALA) in 1975. Before passing away from AIDS complications, Rodrigo Reyes made sure that his collection of slides, photographs, video and audio recordings, periodicals, flyers, books, posters, manuscripts, and other ephemera remained a part of local San Francisco community history. Located in Berkeley, California, the collection has contributed to community-based artistic and historical projects and exhibitions that have continued the legacy of lesbian and gay Latino work and activism in the Bay Area.

"Self-portrait, Rodrigo Reyes." Courtesy of Luis Alberto de la Garza and Archivo Rodrigo Reyes.

Rodrigo Reyes took himself from silence into visibility. Along the way he also took others for whom visibility meant remaining within their community and grounding their work in their national and local histories. To do so, San Francisco Bay Area writers, artists, and activists such as Rodrigo Reyes built organizations, funded community-based galleries and cultural centers, and made important connections between desire and racial ethnic struggles. Moving deep into the cultural and political voids in the 1970s and 1980s, these individuals gave their lives for the visibility of Latinas and Latinos in the Bay Area. In this discussion of a local Latino archive, we must begin with the body of Rodrigo himself. Just as the self-portrait of his life/body begins to reveal Rodrigo, it also offers us the opportunity to consider the process of creating and preserving community archives and history.

Friends and Grassroots:
The History of the Archive

Rodrigo was the close friend of one of the co-authors of this chapter for more than fifteen years.[2] Meeting in Washington, D.C., at the first National March for Lesbian and Gay Rights in 1979, they and other lesbian Latina/Chicana and gay Chicano/Latino activists marched with the Third World contingent that met at Howard University separately from the white mainstream. This contingent proceeded to crash the march by moving in front of it until it reached the Washington Monument. Rodrigo Reyes was representing the San Francisco Gay Latino Alliance (GALA), an organization he had helped build four years earlier with other Latinos and Latinas.[3]

Rodrigo cared about defining himself within his Chicano/Latino community as a gay man who challenged the sexual barriers that exist within it. He believed that "the task of establishing and maintaining communication with non-gay Latinos is very important because the pain of isolation from family and community is probably one of the worst aspects of gay oppression" (Reyes 1981). Rodrigo was a visible leader within the Latino community in the Mission District of San Francisco. He was the executive director of the Mission Cultural Center (MCC) and participated in several local boards, including the one for the Mission Neighborhood Health Center. His accomplishments in the artistic sphere and among service delivery organizations make for a litany of contributions. This individual, with a Texas migrant farm working background, was able to contribute to the Latino community, the lesbian and gay community, and the Bay Area in general.

After Luis Alberto de la Garza moved to the Bay Area in 1987, there were many occasions on which he and Rodrigo talked about the need for a Chicano/Latino gay and lesbian archive to highlight this community's own history, culture, and art. Rodrigo recognized a potential in Luis and encouraged him to pursue his interest in specialized library collections and archives. Together, they envisioned a collection that would gather, chronicle, preserve, and make accessible materials that reflected the actions, dreams, and lives of this community. Like others active in that period—Virginia Benavidez, María Cora, Diane Felix, Juan Pablo Gutiérrez, Hank Tavera, for example—they were concerned with the preservation of community history. Shortly after Rodrigo's death, the "Archivo Rodrigo Reyes: A Chicano and Latino Gay and Lesbian Archive" was formed. Several interested people met for about two to three months after his death, but when his possessions were turned over to Luis (as stipulated by his last will and testament), interest in the group waned and was soon lost. Still, the initial intent of those efforts was to establish a historical archive in the Bay Area with Rodrigo's materials as its base.

The Public Record of Desire

Saw him last night. Got to know him a little more. . . . He lives in a totally heterosexual world. . . . Thinks of himself as a "thief," stealing from his straight world moments here and there where he can express his gay side. He tells me he would like to incorporate me into his world. Everything under the table. Me, well, I am a public man. A lot of people know I am gay. It would be difficult. And then again he may never call me again. (Reyes various)

"1970s San Francisco." Courtesy of Luis Alberto de la Garza and Archivo Rodrigo Reyes.

Rodrigo Reyes *was* a public man. In negotiating his erotic, romantic life with fellow men in San Francisco, his public persona could hardly remain behind. As an activist and organizer, he brokered and dealt in information. This was his business: to create, process, and collect evidence of the lives and labors of women and men that put "gay Latino" on the historical map of the Bay Area. The materials that have become the Archivo Rodrigo Reyes are by no means exhaustive of all the organizations, events, battles and internal struggles, failures, and successes of gay Latinos in the Bay Area since the mid-1970s. But the collection is an important base, a foundation for the public, for students and researchers, and for librarians to consider what it means to connect racial and sexual politics and communities in history.

"Gay Latino Alliance (GALA), San Francisco, 1970s." Courtesy of Luis de la Garza and Archivo Rodrigo Reyes.

The ARR is an extension of the community that has helped build Latino San Francisco, and queer Latino San Francisco in particular. In its collection of hundreds of slides, photographs, and posters, for example, the ARR proves that gay Latinos and lesbian Latinas have been central in making San Francisco cultural and political institutions count. The collection provides evidence that whereas gay Latinos primarily conducted work at the local level, they were in close contact with national and transnational struggles for de-colonization, anti-imperialism, and community empowerment. An image from the collection demonstrates that the international movement against U.S. intervention in

Central America had loud, public support among gay Latinos in San Francisco. The question of gay Latino "pride" in that case went beyond erotic/sexual parameters and made connections between local queer bodies and Latin American nations as territories to be rid of foreign control.

Rodrigo Reyes was a man, a gay man, whose desires moved him across and along other bodies in his community. Rodrigo's erotic life, of course, shaped the content and context of his world and gave him sensibilities and tastes reflected in the ARR. Whereas the collection contains materials in which women are visible, the vast majority of visual culture in the ARR frames men and their bodies. In the photography documenting gay pride parades and festivals, for example, it is the sensual posing of the prototypic masculine man that we see. This is the body desired by men such as Rodrigo. This is also the public, erotic Latino

"Gay Freedom Parade, San Francisco, 1970s." Courtesy of Luis de la Garza and Archivo Rodrigo Reyes.

man dancing and sexualizing in 1970s San Francisco, only a few years before the onslaught of the AIDS epidemic in the 1980s and 1990s. In addition to this emphasis on masculinity and this historical record of desire, the ARR also contains the images of some women activists and cross-dressing artists, but the core remains stereotypically male. Still, the existence of the ARR has prompted others in the community to think of their own roles in making history. The ARR has also allowed researchers not only to use the collection for local community history projects but also to expand it.[4]

The Uses and the Making of Public History

The regenerative life of any archive depends on its use. That is, for the materials in the collection to become living documents of generations past, they must become visible and usable. In this regard, the Archivo Rodrigo Reyes, despite not yet having a permanent home, has already benefited the growing cultural, intellectual, and social landscape that has been queer Latino San Francisco for the last three decades. Students, Bay Area community members, and grassroots activists have utilized the Archivo's materials to support numerous artistic, educational, cultural, and political projects in the San Francisco Bay Area. Given the collection's wide array of holdings, the materials have lent themselves to multiple uses and goals.

The Archivo's collections fit within and expand the knowledge base about the rich cultural traditions and struggles Latino San Francisco has waged since the 1960s. The Centro Cultural de la Misión (MCC), for example, was born in 1977 and since then has remained a critical anchor point for Latino arts, politics, and resistance in the Mission District and the larger city.[5] As part of this tradition, some of the Archivo's holdings have occasionally found their way into this renamed Mission Cultural Center for Latino Arts (MCCLA). One such occasion occurred in 1994 with "El Arte Sana: Fourth Annual Lesbian, Gay, and Bisexual Latina/o Pride Festival," which included an archive exhibit featuring the ARR holdings.[6]

Additionally, given the lasting legacy of gentrification, class antagonisms, and police repression in the Mission District, the MCCLA marks a community's determination not to be removed, not to be made invisible in the city's race to entertain, house, and cater to its growing affluent residents.[7] Amid these transformations and struggles for permanence, the Archivo's contributions to the MCCLA and other community-based cultural and art centers becomes that much more important in their role both *to race* the city's increasingly white landscape and simultaneously *to sex* its heteronormative Latino histories, past and present.[8]

In recent years, the Archivo Rodrigo Reyes has also contributed to the artistic work of Galería de la Raza, a long-standing community-based arts gallery and space in the heart of the Mission District. For the Galería's "Queer Raza:

El Corazón Me Dio un Salto" exhibit, the ARR provided material that once again spoke to the tradition of queer Latino activism within Latino San Francisco.[9]

Like any good archive, the Archivo Rodrigo Reyes has been effective not only for what it already embodies and exhibits through its collection but also for where these contents lead or point. Hardly an exhaustive collection of all the materials and visions necessary to reconstruct and imagine "queer Latino San Francisco" in all its complexity and contradiction, the Archivo does provide critical clues for the dedicated, committed researcher to follow and build upon.

"San Francisco, 1970s." Courtesy of Luis de la Garza and Archivo Rodrigo Reyes.

Given the ARR's strategic location in Berkeley, California, it has served as a base for class presentations for several courses at the University of California, Berkeley campus. In Chicana and Chicano studies, for example, slides and photographs from the collection have introduced gender and sexual politics to courses addressing the Chicano Movement, typically silent about the patriarchal and homophobic ethos of much Latino/Chicano ideology and politics in the last four decades.[10] By making visible the genders and sexualities of gay men and lesbian women in 1970s San Francisco and the struggles to make sexual education less rigid and less closeted about queer positions and sensibilities in the context of AIDS, and racism, the ARR has indeed allowed students to pose broad challenges about what constitutes "politics" for Latinas and Latinos. In 1997, among over 350 attendees and six panel presentations, the Archivo Rodrigo Reyes once again came alive at the University of California, Berkeley campus. Entitled "¡Con la Boca Abierta! Voicing Struggle and Resistance in Queer Raza

Communities," this student-initiated two-day long gathering at the university made connections between the earlier periods the ARR documents and late 1990s queer Latina and Latino organizing in California. Two years later, in collaboration with the Northern California Gay and Lesbian Historical Society, the ARR made its collection available, along with the materials still in personal archives, to create "Making a Case for Community History," an exhibit produced by the Gay, Lesbian, Bisexual, and Transgender Historical Society of Northern California and the Center for History of Sexual Diversity, which took place June 18–25, 1999 at the Castro Theatre and July 10–25, 1999 at Galería de la Raza. On both of these occasions, the ARR was a key source of materials that refuse to separate gender and sexuality from the history of Latino community struggles in the San Francisco Bay Area.

"San Francisco, 1970s." Courtesy of Luis de la Garza and
Archivo Rodrigo Reyes.

Making the Archivo Rodrigo Reyes
a Permanent Body

The use of archives takes us to a critical juncture. There almost always appears to be an inverse relationship between access and preservation. But access cannot be measured similarly for all communities. Given the invisibility of queer Latina and Latino communities, a queer Latino archive holds that much

A BENEFIT FOR
CURAS AT
THE MIDNITE SUN

CURAS
(Community United in Response to AIDS)

Is a Non-
munity Or-
dedicated to
Latino Gay/
Community
epidemic.
port will
sands of
Lives, and

profit Com-
ganization
Educate the
Lesbian
on the AIDS
Your Sup-
save thou-
Latino

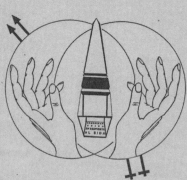

will bring love and
support to Latinos living
with AIDS.

DECEMBER 25, 1991
7 pm to Closing
MIDNITE SUN
4067 - 18 Street.

For Information Call :
CURAS, (415) 255-2732
347 Dolores Street
Nos. 113, 117, and 128

Or ask Viva at the Bar
for more information

"CURAS (Comunidad Unida en Respuesta al AIDS/SIDA—Community United in Response to AIDS/SIDA) benefit." Courtesy of Luis de la Garza and Archivo Rodrigo Reyes.

ore importance. Laying the groundwork for what eventually becomes a neatly ·ganized archive is no easy task. To begin with, the collecting usually begins ith an individual's unwavering belief that his or her community history is wor- .y of preservation and that without his or her constant, daily efforts at preserva- ɔn, such history may be lost. Such a task is labor-intensive, and it is frustrating. rganizing an archive itself is often thankless work, but it is also an exciting iterprise.

Where do queer archives begin or end for Latinas and Latinos? Perhaps a hite-controlled, mainstream public library or queer archive wants to focus only ı those institutions and histories "obviously" queer: annual gay parades or iarches, film festivals and art exhibits, and so forth. But what about the materi- s of community-based agencies in which queer women and men first witnessed ɔmophobia and drugphobia? Most Latino HIV agencies in the 1980s, for exam- .e, refused to recognize queer men on their own sexual terms. In San Francisco, ɔmmunity-based health agencies and clinics did not easily nor willingly face up ▸ the sexuality of queer men and women and their particular health needs. But ie work such women and men did to challenge the sexism and homophobia in ·cal health policies and decisions *is* part of queer Latino history, and indeed part f the evidence in the Archivo Rodrigo Reyes.

Twenty-five years ago, de la Garza believed the task at hand was a matter f collecting "everything" that was Chicano/Latino queer material. But nowa- ιys, because of all the interest in archives and technological advances, it seems iore a matter of locating the resources, materials, and archival collections elec- ·onically because this format seems to be the most accessible to the majority of ιe public. And yet, this move to electronic access does not necessarily work out ι practice. Too few of the existing queer Latino materials become visible irough online reference means. Lack of online links between mainstream data- ιses and sites and queer Latina/o materials makes for this disconnection. Most :ferences that can be made to those sources embedded in mainstream lesbian, isexual, transgender, and gay collections in larger libraries, universities, or ar- uives remain invisible.[11] Even when archives and libraries with large budgets ioose to place queer collections online, materials from communities of color ·e usually an afterthought, if remembered at all. Thus, the idea of collecting for ɔsterity and making materials accessible to a larger community remains a key iission of this project, invariably with the idea of making visible our own Chi- ιno(a)/Latino(a) chronicles and desires to history. Physically, the Archivo may :side at a leading Bay Area academic institution in the near future. However, ɔpies and duplicates of some materials will be made available to various grass- ɔots archives scattered throughout the Bay Area.

"San Francisco, 1970s." Courtesy of Luis de la Garza and
Archivo Rodrigo Reyes.

Conclusion: The Historical Body
and Memory of a Community

*Last night the homage given to Rodrigo convinced
me how rare it is to be colored and queer and live to
speak about it. In honoring Rodrigo, one young man
said, "Rodrigo devoted his entire life to the community." And, I would like to add, he devoted his entire
passion to his own brown brothers. He delighted in
their beauty, their desire, their hope. He wanted
them to be free, and righteously. I believe that in
Rodrigo's final months and in his final words, he saw
a much clearer road toward that freedom, and that
it had something to do with the freedom of women,
too. I believe he started to understand this not in
his head, but in his gut, when he looked upon so
much death and drugs and despair within his own
community. (Moraga 1993b)*

The Archivo Rodrigo Reyes is about the making of a body. This is a body that begins with Rodrigo Reyes—an erotic body, a desiring body, a political body—but becomes a communal one. Upon the death of Rodrigo Reyes, his archives entered a different life. The ARR is Chicano and Latino history in the form of a queer body. It is not a queer body solely because of the Archivo's contents on queer sexualities from the Latino Bay Area; the holdings in fact contain much more, as has been discussed above. But the Archivo is indeed queer and colored through the collector's agency and interest to keep whole some of the fragments of a multi-gender, multiracial community facing multiple disappearances, gentrification, police brutality, breast cancer, AIDS, and a racist and segregationist educational system. In this historical context, the body that was and is the life and work of Rodrigo Reyes expands the visions and the efforts we should maintain to ensure that our histories and those of our own bodies remain behind us, however fragmented. The desires he put into practice through his community organizing and collection efforts chronicled many of these struggles, individual and collective.

The wealth of queer Latina and Latino materials, visions, and histories that have been generated since Rodrigo's death in 1992 has expanded our sense of local community archives significantly. Still, under the threats of class oppression, racism, sexism, AIDS, and sexual and gender phobias, Latina/o women, men, and transgenders in the San Francisco Bay Area continue to claim identity, space, and rights. Cultural production and visibility in the hands of artists, writers, health workers, club promoters, and performers still challenge static conceptions of collective membership. The work for such queer Latina/o visibility has been plentiful and varied, and a brief overview should include the late gay Chicano health worker and *teatrista* Hank Tavera's annual queer Latina/o performance art shows at the MCCLA; the community-based *talleres* of the sex-positive, multi-gender queer Latina/o HIV agency Proyecto ContraSIDA Por Vida; the queer Latina women's club scene with long-time Chicana lesbian activist Diane Felix at the controls of the rhythms; the literary anthologies strongly based in the Bay Area, Carla Trujillo's *Chicana Lesbians* and Jaime Cortez's *Virgins, Guerrillas, and Locas*, following the classic *This Bridge Called My Back* and the less known *Ya Vas, Carnal*; the comedic performances by Latin Hustle (Al Luján, Jaime Cortez, Adriana Gordon, and Lito Sandoval); the playwriting and theatrical productions of Cherríe L. Moraga, Ricardo A. Bracho, and Jorge Ignacio Cortiñas; the photographic records of Silvia Ledezma, Patrick "Pato" Hebert, and Virginia Benavídez; the video and film productions by Janelle Rodríguez, Ana Berta Campa, Veronica Majano, Osa Hidalgo de la Riva, Gustavo Cravioto, Mario Callitzin Huerta, Valentín Aguirre, Augie Robles, and Mary Guzman; and, of course, the labor and art from transgender performers like Adela Holyday, Carla Gay, and Teresita la Campesina, still working with gender at community agencies, bars, restaurants, and homes. In these bodies and minds, *cultura* and desire still thrive with great pulse among queer Latinas y Latinos de la Bahía.

Notes

1.   Two small grants in 1998–1999 from the University of California, Berkeley's Graduate Assembly (Education Improvement Grant) and the Chancellor's Activities Funds supported the student-based project "Archivo Yerba Buena," which initially organized the collection in the Archivo Rodrigo Reyes. The authors acknowledge the collaborative, joint effort in conceptualizing and writing the present article. (The listing of authors' names is alphabetical.) The authors acknowledge the invitation from Kathryn Blackmer Reyes to present this discussion at the Second REFORMA Conference in Tucson, and thank her for her support. This chapter is an abridged version of that presentation. Financial support from the University of California, Berkeley's Graduate Opportunity Program made travel possible for the authors. All images appear courtesy of the Archivo Rodrigo Reyes (ARR) and Luis Alberto de la Garza. The authors acknowledge the editorial assistance of Lily Castillo-Speed and Michael Shapiro and the technical support of Kathryn Blackmer Reyes in the production of the images.

2.   Luis Alberto de la Garza.

3.   Luis Alberto de la Garza was representing the Vanguardia Irma Serrano of Austin, Texas, along with Jesse Johnson and Juan Pablo Gutiérrez, both of whom also currently live in San Francisco. The Vanguardia derived its name from that of the scandalous Mexican actress (dubbed *encueratriz* by Juan Pablo Gutiérrez) and was used because the group could not agree on a common name. To gain funding for travel to Washington, D.C., for the 1979 march, the group hurriedly accepted this name.

4.   One of the authors of this chapter, Horacio N. Roque Ramírez, has used the ARR to come into contact with women and men to conduct an extensive oral history project of queer Latino community formations in the Bay Area. As part of his dissertation project, the interviews and transcriptions will in turn enlarge the collection that made the project possible in the first place. See Roque Ramírez (1995, 2001a).

5.   For a discussion of some of the cultural and political struggles leading to the Centro Cultural de la Misión, see Herrera (1998).

6.   The dates of the exhibit were June 4–30, 1994. Individuals concerned with the preservation and visibility of an independent queer Latino/a archive in the Bay Area recently thought the MCCLA to be the location for this archive. However, because of lack of resources and institutional backing as well as general mistrust among organizations and individuals, no serious efforts have ever taken root. Generally, individuals wanting their personal archives to go public and to stay in the Bay Area consider depositing them at larger university library collections in the area (UC Berkeley and Stanford University, for example), the San Francisco Public Library, or the Gay, Lesbian, Bisexual, and Transgender Historical Society of Northern California—all of which remove control of such materials from grassroots queer Latina/o hands. Given these dynamics of power among individuals and/or institutions, few personal collections have been organized. This essay attests to the co-authors' efforts to preserve but one of these collections, that belonging to the late Rodrigo Reyes. The co-authors are

also in the process of organizing the materials of the late Hank Tavera (January 19, 1944–February 27, 2000). For a critique of the collecting practices in the San Francisco Public Library, see Baker (1998).

7. For a closer look at a high-profile political struggle surrounding Latino youth and police repression in the Mission District, see Heins (1972). For a historical summary of immigrant communities and politics in the San Francisco Bay Area, see Roque Ramírez (2001b).

8. For a provocative analysis of the importance of examining "the place of race in our lived realities as gendered sexual subjects" see Yarbro-Bejarano (1994).

9. This exhibit was organized by Galería de la Raza from June 24 through July 29, 1995. The exhibit was one of three in which emerging Latina/o artists were showcased. This series of exhibits and salons (discussions) were planned and conducted under the name of the Regeneration Project.

10. See Gutiérrez (1993) and Gutiérrez (1994); Moraga (1993); Curry Rodríguez, Pendleton-Jiménez, and Roque Ramírez (1999); and Romo-Carmona (1994). Bisexual and transgender politics of visibility and identity emerged strongly in the late 1980s, and especially in the 1990s. For useful discussions on bisexual and transgender visibility and rights, see, respectively, Pérez (1995); and Pasillas (in progress). Three additional studies examine various dimensions of visibility and identity among queer Latinas and Latinos in the San Francisco Bay Area. They are Cora (2000); Rodríguez (forthcoming); and Rosales (in progress).

11. Two useful guides to identifying these materials are de la Garza (1994) and De la Tierra (2000).

References

Aguirre, Valentín, and Augie Robles. 1994. *¡Viva 16!* Produced, written, and directed by Valentín Aguirre and Augie Robles. Video. 23 min. 21st Century Aztlán.

Baker, Nicholson. 1998. Weeds: A talk at the library. In *Reclaiming San Francisco: History, politics, culture*, edited by James Brook, Chris Carlsson, and Nancy J. Peters. San Francisco: City Lights Books.

Benavídez, Virginia. 2001. Moments in time from the 20th century: The photographs of Virginia Benavídez. Photo and art exhibit at the Gay, Lesbian, Bisexual, and Transgender Historical Society of Northern California, June 8–August 31, in San Francisco.

Bracho, Ricardo A. 1997. *The sweetest hangover (& other STDs)*. Directed by Roberto Varega. Dramaturgy by Cherríe Moraga. Produced by Brava! for Women in the Arts. San Francisco, April 20–27.

————. 1999. *Fed up! A cannibal's own story*. Directed by Reginald McDonald. Dramaturgy by Reginald McDonald, with Jorge Ignacio Cortiñas. Produced by Theatre Rhinoceros. San Francisco, May 6–June 5.

Cora, María. 2000. Nuestras auto-definiciones/Our self-definitions: Management of stigma and identity by Puerto Rican lesbians." Master's field study report, San Francisco State University, Ethnic Studies.

Cortez, Jaime, ed. 1999. *Virgins, guerrillas & locas. Gay Latinos writing about love*. San Francisco: Cleis Press.

Cravioto, Gustavo, and Mario Callitzin. 1998. *Del otro lado*. 1998. Film. Directed by C. A. Griffith. Produced by Fred Foley, Mario Callitzin, Gustavo Cravioto, and C. A. Griffith.

Curry Rodríguez, Julia, Karleen Pendleton-Jiménez, and Horacio N. Roque Ramírez. 1999. Without women, feminists, and queers, are we ethnic studies? *ColorLines* 2 (2) (Summer): 24–25.

De la Garza, Luis A. 1994. *Preliminary Chicano and Latino lesbian and gay bibliography*. San Francisco: El Arte Sana.

De la Riva, Teresa "Osa" Hidalgo. 1992. *Mujeria: Primitive and proud*. Written, directed, produced, and animated by Teresa "Osa" Hidalgo de la Riva. Video. Royal Eagle Bear Productions.

De la Tierra, Tatiana. 2000. Latin@ lesbian, gay & bisexual bibliography, June 27. State University of New York, Undergraduate Library, Buffalo.

Gutiérrez, Ramón A. 1993. Community, patriarchy, and individualism: The politics of Chicano history and the dream of equality. *American Quarterly* 45 (1) (March): 44–72.

————. 1994. Decolonizing the body: Kinship and the nation. *American Archivist* 57 (Winter): 86–99.

Guzman, Mary. 2000. *Desi's looking for a new girl*. Written and directed by Mary Guzman. Film. Produced by Fontana Butterfield.

Hebert, Patrick. "Pato." 1996. *Yo soy lo prohibido*. Photograph series. San Francisco.

Heins, Marjorie. 1972. *Strictly ghetto property: The story of los siete de la raza*. Berkeley, CA: Ramparts Press.

Herrera, Juan Felipe. 1998. Riffs on Mission District raza writers. In *Reclaiming San Francisco: History, politics, culture*, edited by James Brook, Chris Carlsson, and Nancy J. Peters. San Francisco: City Lights Books.

Ledezma, Silvia. Various dates. *La India series*. Photograph series. Albany, California.

Majano, Veronica. 1998. *Calle Chula*. Written, directed, and produced by Veronica Majano. Film. Video Data Bank, Chicago.

Moraga, Cherríe. 1993a. Queer Aztlán. In *The last generation: Prose and poetry*, 145–74. Boston: South End Press.

———. 1993b. Tribute. In *The last generation: Prose and poetry*, 175–78. Boston: South End Press.

Moraga, Cherríe, and Gloria Anzaldúa, eds. 1983. *This bridge called my back: Writings by radical women of color*. New York: Kitchen Table: Women of Color Press. [1981. Persephone Press].

Ochoa, Marcia. In progress. Club moves: Migrating identities and social space in Latina lesbian San Francisco. Unpublished manuscript, Social and Cultural Anthropology Department, Stanford University.

Omosupe, Ekua. 1991. Black/Lesbian/Bulldagger. *differences: A Journal of Feminist Cultural Studies* 3 (2): 101–11.

Pasillas, Andrea M. In progress. A transsexual cultural perspective. Unpublished manuscript, San Francisco.

Pérez, Laura M. 1995. Go ahead: Make my movement. In *Bisexual politics: Theories, queries, & visions*, edited by Naomi Tucker. New York: Harrington Park Press.

Reyes, Rodrigo. Various dates. Green and gold diary. Archivo Rodrigo Reyes.

———. 1981. Latino gays: Coming out and coming home. *Nuestro Magazine* (April): 42–45, 64.

Reyes, Rodrigo, Francisco X. Alarcón, and Juan Pablo Gutiérrez. 1995. *Ya vas, carnal*. San Francisco: Humanizarte Publications.

Rodríguez, Janelle. 1995. *Public service announcement: Proyecto ContraSIDA Por Vida*. Directed by Janelle Rodríguez. Produced by Janelle Rodríguez and Ricardo A. Bracho. Video. Sabrosura Productions.

Rodríguez, Juana María. Forthcoming. *Coraje y corazón: Rhizomatic readings of queer Latinidad*. New York: New York University Press.

Romo-Carmona, Mariana. 1994. Introduction. In *Compañeras: Latina lesbians*, edited by Juanita Ramos. New York: Routledge.

Roque Ramírez, Horacio. 2001a. Communities of desire: Queer Latina/o history and memory, San Francisco Bay Area, 1960s-1990s. Ph.D. Dissertation, University of California, Berkeley.

———. 2001b. San Francisco. In *Encyclopedia of American Immigration*, edited by James Ciment. Armonk, NY: M. E. Sharpe.

———. 1995. El poder de la boca: Power and play in "doing" oral histories. *Ripples Magazine* 1. (1) (Fall): 20–22.

Rosales, Karla. In progress. Los papis chulos: A study of the self-identification process of Chicana/Latina butch dykes. Master's field study report, San Francisco State University, Ethnic Studies.

Trujillo, Carla, ed. 1991. *Chicana lesbians: The girls our mothers warned us about.* Berkeley, CA: Third Woman Press.

Yarbro-Bejarano, Yvonne. 1994. Expanding the categories of race and sexuality in gay and lesbian studies. In *Professions of desire: Lesbian and gay studies in literature*, edited by George E. Haggarty and Bonnie Zimmerman. New York: Modern Language Association.

Latina Lesbian Literary Herstory

From Sor Juana to *Days of Awe*

Tatiana De la Tierra

This chapter provides an overview of Latina lesbian publishing herstory, including texts from the United States, Spain, Latin America, and the Caribbean. The herstory presented begins with the work of Sor Juana Inés de la Cruz and covers Latina lesbian literary representation from the 1980s to the present. Among the main points established are that visible Latina lesbian literature began to be published in the United States in the 1980s and has evolved since, that lesbians have also been visibly publishing in Latin America since the 1970s, and that there is a noticeable increase of Latin@ lesbian and gay academic publishing from the mid-1990s to the present. The chapter illuminates some of the difficulties in identifying and collecting Latina lesbian literature, offers political perspectives on publishing, and presents practical suggestions for librarians who want to bring greater visibility and validity to Latina lesbian and gay library materials. The Selected Bibliography includes bibliographic information for all the titles directly mentioned in the text as well as a contemporary selection of Latino lesbian and gay titles published from 1998 to 2000.

Tatiana De la Tierra has an M.F.A. in creative writing from the University of Texas at El Paso and a M.L.S. from University at Buffalo, where she is a reference and instruction librarian. She has conducted original research on subject headings, information storage and retrieval, and cataloguing. Her writings have been published in periodicals and anthologies since 1987. She was one of the founders and editors of the Latina lesbian magazines, *esto no tiene nombre* and *conmoción*.

*lesbian literature is the unwritten bestseller
that all lesbians are reading, all the time: it
consists of our every moment.*[1]

I was a new player from the Greek isle of Lesbos, a twenty-two-year-old enthusiastic lover of women. Hairy women, radical women, feminist women, witchy women—women were my home. The moment I came up for air, when the love haze floated to the surface like oil on water, I hit the bookstores, the libraries, the music shops. I went in search of *me*, or rather, a reflection of me, a Colombian immigrant and proud maricona.[2] I knew exactly what I was looking for: a Latina Monique Wittig, a Latina Virginia Woolf, a Latina Sappho, a Latina Amazon. But it was 1982 and Latina lesbian *literatura* and culture was happening everywhere in the world except in the card catalogs. The white lesbian-feminist publishing revolution of the 1970s that had birthed feminist publishers and bookstores coddled white lesbian feminist culture. Latinas and other women of color—we had to fend for ourselves.

By the turn of the millennium, however, I could name un montón of Latina lesbian writers and artists. How can this be? Did I step through a magical-realist wall into a room packed with literary jotas who reside on another planet? Hardly. Latina lesbian *literatura* has been around for as long as Latinas and literature have existed. There has always been a problem however, in being able to identify, collect, store, and retrieve this body of work.

*lesbian texts are passed from hand to hand and
mouth to mouth between lesbians. they are
located on the skin, in the look, in the geography of
the palms of the hands.*

Any library whose mission includes providing service to Latin patrons should have a decent collection of Latin@[3] lesbian and gay literature. Homosexuality is not a North American invention. South Americans, Mexicans, Caribeñ@s, Latin@s, "Hispanics," and Chican@s are also gay. We are immigrants from el sur, we were born on U.S. soil, we hail from Aztlán, we are "Americans" with Latin roots. We speak Spanish, English, Spanglish, and Caló. We are U.S. citizens and resident "aliens" and "illegals." Latin@ lesbians and gays do not fit into a neat category, we do not have a singular voice. However, we *do* exist, we *do* have a body of literature, and our books *should* be on bookshelves in libraries everywhere. Homosexuals, queers, dykes, maricones, jotas, patos, areperas, tortilleras, manfloras—whatever the term may be—have the well-documented tradition of going to the library and looking ourselves up in the catalog as part of the "coming out" process. We *need* to see ourselves reflected in literature. To not see yourself in print is the equivalent of not existing.

lesbian literature exists in pieces: in flyers, newsletters, magazines, chapbooks, bathroom stalls, notes, novels, e-mails, love letters, on tiny scraps of paper.

The following is a selected herstorical overview of Latina lesbian publishing. The discussion focuses on works authored by Latinas in the United States as well as texts from Latin America, Mexico, and Spain. Books in Spanish, regardless of their origin, belong in this discussion, as these are scarce. The scope will be limited to books in Spanish, English, and Spanglish. Brazilian works and authors are not included because I am not fluent in Portuguese or sufficiently knowledgeable in this literature. This overview is a reflection of my own experiences as a writer, researcher, publisher, and librarian. And it is shaped, in part, by the inherent complexity of the "Latina lesbian" identity— language, culture, politics, geography, and lesbofobia—that has contributed to the difficulty of pinpointing what exactly constitutes Latina lesbian literature.

I want to acknowledge the connection between Latina lesbians who reside in the United States and lesbians from Latin America and the Caribbean. Latinas in the United States have been visible (and sometimes unwelcome) participants in the Latin American Lesbian Feminist Encuentros that have taken place since the first gathering in Cuernavaca, México in 1987. The Encuentros, which have been hosted in Argentina, Costa Rica, Puerto Rico, and Brasil, have provided an opportunity for the informal sharing of lesbian publications. Periodicals, hand-made poetry books, pamphlets, zines, and one-print-run novels have been passed from hand to hand, from Latin America to the United States and back, for some time.

lesbian literature also exists in texts that don't seem to have anything at all to do with lesbians or literature: a customer copy of an American Express receipt; dinner for two at Café Aroma; a torn pack of Trojans that once housed bright red lubricated condoms; a box of Celestial Seasoning's Raspberry Zinger; a matchbook cover with "Le Metro" on the outside and "call me" on the inside.

The herstory of published Latina lesbian literature begins in the seventeenth century with Sor Juana Inés de la Cruz (1648–1695), a Mexican nun and brilliant poet reputed to have been enamored of Leonor Carreto, the Marquise of Mancera, object of some of Sor Juana's ardent love poems. Prominent and homophobic scholars such as Octavio Paz passionately refute the possibility that Sor Juana was una jota cloistered among nuns. But Sor Juana has also been revisited by feminist and queer-friendly scholars and translators who interpret her life and her work through a lesbian lens. Sor Juana is a Latina lesbian icon whose legend has inspired notable creative productions, such as the film *Yo, la peor de todas* (1990), made by the Argentine director Maria Luisa Bemberg; the compact disc *Sor Juana Hoy* (1995), a musicalized recording of Sor Juana's texts by the Mexican performer Ofelia Medina; and the historical fiction novel, *Sor Juana's Second Dream* (1999), written by Chicana lesbian scholar Alicia Gaspar de Alba. Sor Juana was una chingona who opted for the convent's women-only space, a feminist who challenged the patriarchy at its intellectual core, a heretic who communed with God, a poet of the highest category. She is the great-great-great literary grandmother of nosotras, "the worst of all," the Muse who penned the infamous words herself: "Yo, la peor de todas. I, the worst of all."

We have other literary ancestors, but we don't know all of their names, or we don't yet have the "proof" or literary scholarship that will allow us to name them. Chilean Nobel poet Gabriela Mistral (1889–1957) is also considered to have been a lesbian by some scholars. Like Sor Juana, she did not leave lesbian (or bisexual) declaratory statements behind, yet if you read between the lines of her work and piece her life together within the context of the times, you think that yes, it's likely that Gabriela Mistral was a lesbian.

There are also writers whose names we *do* know as Latina lesbians who consciously avoid or deny these identifiers; these writers will remain unnamed here. Homophobia, whether it is self-imposed and internalized or whether it exists as a social construct, does affect literary production and distribution. Also, the separatism under which lesbianism often exists contributes to the "disappearance" of lesbian texts. The herstory of our literature is incomplete.

> *lesbians live in houses with writings on the wall that indicate the way to lesbianism. these texts abound but they are offered only to lesbians; this is why lesbian literature seems scarce.*

In 1971, Uruguayan lesbian Cristina Peri Rossi published *Evohé,* a collection of erotic poetry (translated into English in 1994). The first poem, "Definiciones/Definitions" sets the tone:

PALINSESTO.—Escrito debajo de una mujer.

PALIMPSEST. — Text written underneath a woman.
(Peri Rossi 1994, 10–11)

Other poets and writers were published in the 1970s and 1980s, such as Magaly Alabau and Lourdes Casal (Cuban); Bessy Reyna (Cuban/Panamanian); Alicia Gaspar de Alba (Chicana); Sabina Berman, Nancy Cárdenas, Amparo Jiménez, and Rosamaría Roffiel (Mexican); Nemir Matos, Coqui Santaliz, and Luz María Umpierre (Puerto Rican); and Diana Bellesi, Alejandra Pizarnik, Reina Roffé, Ilse Fuskova, and Mercedes Roffé (Argentinian).

In the 1980s, easily identifiable Latina lesbian texts began to flourish. This is when a number of significant books were published, the first (known) of their kind, books that left their mark in contemporary herstory. *This Bridge Called My Back: Writings by Radical Women of Color* (1981), although not exclusively a Latina lesbian publication, involved Latinas in a collective voice of resistance that continues to resonate. *This Bridge* was also translated into Spanish as *Esta puente, mi espalda*, and a new version, *This Bridge We Call Home*, is to be published in 2002. Argentine lesbian Sylvia Molloy published her novel, *En breve cárcel*, in 1981 (translated into English as *Certificate of Absence* in 1989). Chicana writer Sheila Ortiz Taylor published *Faultlines* in 1982 (translated into Spanish as *Terremoto* in 1991). Cherríe Moraga, who successfully conceptualized her Chicana and lesbian identity using a mezcolanza of literary techniques, published her classic *Loving in the War Years* in 1983 (a revised edition was published in 2000). Lesbian-edited *Cuentos: Stories by Latinas* was also published in 1983. My favorite book, *Las andariegas*, by Colombian writer Albalucía Angel, was published in 1984. A band of gypsy women travel together in this book of poetic prose, all written in lower case, with text that meanders on the page like a dream sequence:

estaban en un claro de la selva, rodeadas por
criaturas que parecían también encandiladas,
como si vieran sílfides o gnomos y sólo el vuelo de
mariposas con las alas azules cruzaba ese dulzor.

(Angel 1984, 130)

Another outstanding book, published in 1987, is Gloria Anzaldúa's *Borderlands/La Frontera*, a landmark work of poetry and prose that brings consciousness to being (a lesbian) on the border of the United States and México. *Compañeras: Latina Lesbians, an Anthology* was also published in 1987; this book's value lies in its herstorical documentation. Rosamaría Roffiel's autobiographical novel *Amora* (1989) intimately exposes the lesbian-feminist discourse and drama of the author's home in Mexico City. And Carmen de Monteflores's novel *Singing Softly/Cantando Bajito* (1989), set in her native Puerto Rico, is unique in that it contains a good dosage of Spanglish.

You might suppose that by 1990 Latina lesbian literature would be easy to locate, but that was not the case. It took many years for some of the authors just named to become identified as lesbians within the "grapevine." Books were getting published one by one in different parts of the United States and the world in different genres and languages. You found out about them through friends, at the Latin American Lesbian Feminist Encuentros, or maybe you would never even know that they existed, or by the time you did, they were out of print. I did not know about many of these authors and titles *during* the time that the works were being published, and I was *actively looking*; in some cases I found out about them years later. Electronic communication had not taken off yet; access to such information was limited. In fact, the grapevine was often the best and sometimes the *only* source of this information. For the most part, these books were not being reviewed or examined by literary critics. This happened much later, in the mid-1990s. An excellent source for retrospective analysis of some Latin American and Caribbean lesbian literature is Elena M. Martinez's *Lesbian Voices from Latin America: Breaking Ground* (1996).

In 1991, *esto no tiene nombre, revista de lesbianas latinas*, was launched in Miami, Florida, in part as a response to a lack of literary representation. I was one of the founders of *esto no tiene nombre*, which was followed by *conmoción, revista y red revolucionaria de lesbianas latinas,* in 1995. A total of nine editions of *esto* and three editions of *conmoción* were published and distributed on a national level. To date, these are the only Latina lesbian magazines of their kind in the United States. Several Latina lesbian groups, such as Las Buenas Amigas (New York City), Mujeria (San Francisco), Ellas (San Antonio), and Lesbianas Unidas (Los Angeles) published regional newsletters, but none of these had a national focus or distribution.

The fine print in *esto's* editorial box reads, "*esto* publica material de lesbianas latinas que refleja nuestra diversidad y rompe con los estereotipos que nos han clavado. Nuestro objetivo es crear un foro donde las ideas y las imágenes contribuyan a la fortaleza y orgullo de nuestra comunidad."[4] We were aware that the published word was a reflection of us and we were hopeful that our magazine would stimulate organic dialogue between us. *conmoción* went even further, though. The editorial box states that "*conmoción* is an international latina lesbian vision que utiliza la palabra publicada para apoderar y aterrorizar, para derrotar y crear. publicamos, apoyamos y desarollamos cualquier tipo de actividad que conlleve al mejoramiento y a la mayor visibilidad de la lesbiana latina." *conmoción* was a raging Latina lesbian magazine; we wanted to rock the world with our published selves, and we did it in sinvergüenza style.[5]

We published poetry, reviews, essays, cuentos, interviews, commentary, news, photography, and graphics in *esto* and *conmoción*, all with a Latina lesbian vision, in Spanish, English, and Spanglish. For the sake of herstory, I will name some of the writers we published in these magazines: Carmen Corrales, Olga Melania Ulloa, Luz María Umpierre, Rosamaría Roffiel, Rosita Libre de Marulanda, Mariana Romo-Carmona, Margarita Castilla, Vanessa Cruz, Maria de los Ríos, Cristina Peri Rossi, Karleen Pendleton-Jimenez, Marcia Ochoa, Loana

Valencia, Susana Cook, Naomi Morena, Tina D'Elia, Cherríe Moraga, Amy Concepción, Terri de la Peña, Carla Trujillo, Lesley Salas, Juana Maria Rodriguez, Josi Mata, Teresa Mendoza, Roberta Almerez, Karla E. Rosales, Maya Alba, Ana Inés Rubinstein, Gina Anderson, Miriam Lavandier, Lori Cardona, Nena Cammarano, Lourdes Pérez, Ananda Esteva, Naomi Morena, Doralisa Goitía, Kimberly Aceves-Denyer, Yvette Colón, Nora F. Kerr, Theresa Becerril, Odette Alonso, Annette Gaudino, Dolissa Medina, and the one and only Erotiza Memaz. I consider *esto no tiene nombre* and *conmoción* to be examples of activist and survival publishing. These magazines were tools that we used to establish a dialogue within our community. They palpated with the poetry and politics of the moment. And unfortunately, there is no contemporary equivalent to these publications.

Latina lesbian texts by individuals continued to be produced and published, however. Fiction took off in the early 1990s in the United States with the publishing of novels and short story collections by authors such as Ibis Gómez-Vega, Sara Levi Calderón, Terri de la Peña, Emma Pérez, Alicia Gaspar de Alba, Achy Obejas, Kleya Forte-Escamilla, Mariana Romo-Carmona, and authors from América Latina. Also, the anthology, *Chicana Lesbians*, was published in 1991.

There has been a noticeable "boom" in Latin@ lesbian and gay publishing from the mid-1990s to the present, particularly in the academic arena. As queer Latinos move through the academy, we are leaving a noticeable publishing trail in our wake. Today's books have transgressive, telling titles such as, *Coraje y Corazón: Rhizomatic Readings of Queer Latinidad* (Rodriguez, forthcoming); *Reading and Writing the Ambiente: Queer Sexualities in Latino, Latin American, and Spanish Culture* (Chávez-Silverman 2000); *Tropics of Desire: Interventions from Queer Latino America* (Quiroga 2000); *Disidentifications: Queers of Color and the Performance of Politics* (Muñoz 1999); and *Eminent Maricones: Arenas, Lorca, Puig, and Me* (Manrique 1999). Among the queer Latin scholars who are researching and re-thinking literature, social sciences, queer theory, and cultural studies are Chela Sandoval, Bernardo Garcia, Emma Pérez, Lourdes Torres, Juana Maria Rodriguez, Alicia Gaspar de Alba, David Román, José Esteban Muñoz, Maria Lugones, Sylvia Molloy, Deena González, Michael Hames-García, Catriona Rueda Esquivel, José Quiroga, Marta Cecilia Vélez Saldarriega, Yolanda Leyva, Osa Hidalgo, Ramón Garcia, Mary Pat Brady, Ondine Chavoya, Tomás Almaguer, Yvonne Yarbro-Bejarano, Juanita Ramos, and Ellie Hernández. And the Latin@ lesbian and gay canon is in the process of being redefined as academics explore the works of some of our antepasados, including writers such as Porfirio Barba Jacob, Luis Cernuda, Gabriela Mistral, Federico García Lorca, Xavier Villaurrutia, Sor Juana Inés de la Cruz, Salvador Novo, Reinaldo Arenas, and Manuel Puig.

Although I appreciate my literary herstory and I have my own favorites (such as Reinaldo Arenas's autobiography, *Antes que anochezca* [1992]), what garners my attention now are new works by contemporary authors such as Angel Lozada, Gloria Anzaldúa, Alina Troyano, Rafael Campo, Gustavo Álvarez Gardeazábal, Fernando Vallejo, Francisco X. Alarcón, Erasmo Guerra, and two notable españolas, Lucia Etxebarría and Lola Van Guardia. Gay and lesbian books in Spanish are being published with greater frequency today due to translations and a proliferation of Spanish publishers that focus on this market, such as Horas y Horas, Ediciones Destino, and Editorial Gay y Lesbiana (EGALES).

There are good signs for queer titles in other countries as well. In México, for instance, Grijalbo published Rinna Riesenfeld's *Papá, mamá, soy gay* (2000), an authentic and instructive Mexican coming out book, and Sentido Contrario has in recent years published established lesbian writers such as Nancy Cárdenas and Rosa Maria Roffiel. Las editoras of the lesbian magazine, *LeS VOZ*, published the winners of an erotic lesbian poetry contest in the book *Poesía erótica lésbica* (2000) as part of their Visibility Series. El Armario Abierto, a gay bookstore from Mexico City, was present at the Guadalajara International Book Fair 2000 as an exhibitor selling openly gay materials. All of this points to the possibility of greater publishing and distribution opportunities for Latin@ gay and lesbian writers.

The same seems to be true for U.S. writers, where queer escritor@s are making it to the bookshelves. Several Cuban writers stand out. Achy Obejas is notable, not only for her talent, but also for her success. Her novel, *Days of Awe* (2001), which features a bisexual narrator, was published by Ballantine Books, a division of Random House, making her the first "out" Latina lesbian to be published by a mainstream press. Sonia Rivera-Valdés had her fiction collection, *Las historias prohibidas de Marta Veneranda/The Forbidden Stories of Marta Veneranda* (2000), published in Spanish and in English by Siete Cuentos/Seven Stories Press. And yet another cubana, Alina Troyano, had her dramatic *I, Carmelita Tropicana* (2000) published by Beacon Press. Each of these books are significant, especially considering the current difficult and uncertain state of the publishing industry.

Anthologies are another notable publishing venue for queer writers, some of whom are frequently anthologized but don't have their own books published. In the usual scenario, there is, at best, one Latin apellido (last name) in otherwise Anglo collections. Two gay Latin anthologies were published in 1999, *Bésame Mucho* (Manrique) and *Virgins, Guerrillas & Locas* (Cortez). These anthologies are also a sign of the times; they exemplify the fact that anthologies are able to showcase a multiplicity of voices that are *not* getting published outside of anthologies, including writers such as: Monica Palacios, Roger Schira, Miriam Sachs-Martin, Robert Vásquez-Pacheco, Luis Alfaro, Jorge Ignacio Cortiñas, Lisa Gonzales, Joel Antonio Villalón, Ramón Garcia, Maria de los Rios, Al Lujan, Ricardo A. Bracho, Adán Griego, Lito Sandoval, James Cañón, Horacio Roque Ramírez, and myself.

I will stop naming names now, but I want to point out that there are more names to add to the lists that I have presented in this overview. Through the naming, I have wanted to show that there is an abundance of names. We are definitely out there, working, writing, researching, and getting published, and this has been the case for some time.

However, there are serious problems with finding many of these titles in library catalogs, including inadequate cataloging and inappropriate and outdated sexual and ethnic identifiers ("Hispanic" versus Latino and Latina; "Mexican American" versus Chicano and Chicana, etc.). Also, the Library of Congress did not recommend assigning subject headings for works of literature until recent years, leaving most of our literature completely inaccessible via subject and keyword searches. And it is difficult to locate writers getting published in anthologies, as most cataloguers only enter the editor's name, leaving the twenty or so contributors lost in the bibliographic wind.

Librarians should work to bring greater visibility to queer Latin materials. We should employ third-level cataloging with appropriate subject headings and the names of all contributors in anthologies. We should use retrospective and contemporary bibliographies. We should review books as they get published, add them to our collections, give the writings their due space on the bookshelves, and give the authors their due space in libraries by organizing readings and exhibits. We should teach patrons how to conduct research that will lead to the published works.

We must remember that bibliographic invisibility disempowers the entire Latin community. We must be conscious that the library is not just a place that stores and serves information; it is a politicized space and we are the gatekeepers. We must think about the teenagers who are coming out, the compañeras, las locas, the pretty boys and the stone butches that expect and deserve representation, respect, and visibility in the library.

Notes

1.   This is from "Lesbian Literature"; it is an excerpt from *Lesbian Phenomenology/ Fenomenología Lesbiana,* which is my unpublished collection of poetic prose. All subsequent excerpts in this chapter are also from this same piece in *Lesbian Phenomenology.*

2.   Although I am aware that others may use certain "queer" Latin words in a derogatory fashion, I use maricona and other such terms as an affirmation and celebration of lesbian and gay culture. Also, I do not italicize words in Spanish; I will not marginalize my native language and I believe that Spanglish is a natural and valid linguistic hybrid and should be visually treated as such.

3.   The symbol "@" is used here and elsewhere to symbolize both of the feminine/masculine identifiers, a/o, of "gendered" Spanish words; this "wild card" function has mostly a symbolic visual effect, as there is not yet an accepted way to verbalize @. I came to use this symbol as a result of participating in Arenal, a Latin@ lesbian and gay electronic list; I've known @ to be employed as "a/o" since approximately 1996.

4.   *esto no tiene nombre: revista de lesbianas latinas* (1991–1994)

5.   *conmoción, revista y red revolucionaria de lesbianas latinas.* (1995–1996).

Selected Bibliography

Álvarez Gardeazábal, Gustavo. 1998. *El divino.* Santafé de Bogotá: Plaza & Janes.

Ángel, Albalucia. 1984. *Las andariegas.* Barcelona: Editorial Argos Vergara.

Anzaldúa, Gloria. 1999. *Borderlands/La frontera: The new mestiza.* 2d ed. San Francisco: Aunt Lute.

———. 2000. *Interviews/Entrevistas.* Edited by AnaLouise Keating. New York: Routledge.

Ardín, Aixa A. 1998. *Batiborrillo.* San Juan, PR: Calzado Ajena Editoras.

Arenas, Reinaldo. 1998. *Antes que anochezca.* 2d ed. Barcelona: Tusquets.

———. 1994. *Before night falls.* Translated by Dolores M. Koch. New York: Penguin.

Arrizón, Alicia. 1999. *Latina performance: Traversing the stage.* Bloomington: Indiana University Press.

Barba Jacob, Porfirio. 1998. *Poesía completa.* México, D. F.: Consejo Nacional para la Cultura y las Artes, Dirección General de Publicaciones.

Barquet, Jesus J. 1998. *Naufragios: Transacciones de fin de siglo, 1989-1997.* Chihuahua, México: Ediciones del AZAR A. C.

Batista, Adriana. 1998. *Nihilismos epidérmicos/Epidermic nihilisms.* México/USA: Ediciones Quiero Más Press.

Bergmann, Emilie L., and Paul Julian Smith, eds. 1995. *¿Entiendes? Queer readings, Hispanic writings.* Durham, NC: Duke University Press.

Campo, Rafael. 1999. *Diva.* Durham, NC: Duke University Press.

Cárdenas, Nancy. 1994. *Cuaderno de amor y desamor.* México, D.F.: Sentido Contrario.

Chávez-Silverman, Susana, and Librada Hernández, eds. 2000. *Reading and writing the ambiente: Queer sexualities in Latino, Latin American, and Spanish culture*. Madison: University of Wisconsin Press.

conmoción: revista y red revolucionaria de lesbianas latinas. 1995–1996. Miami Beach: Lambda Community Center of Greater Miami.

Cortez, Jaime, ed. 1999. *Virgins, guerrillas & locas: Gay Latinos writing on love*. San Francisco: Cleis Press.

De la Cruz, Sor Juana Inés. 1994. *Respuesta a Sor Filotea de la Cruz/The answer: Including a selection of poems*. New York: Feminist Press at City University of New York.

———. 1996. *Poesía lírica*. 2d ed. Madrid: Cátedra.

———. 1997. *Sor Juana's love poems*. Translated by Joan Larkin and Jaime Manrique. New York: Painted Leaf Press.

———. 1999. *Obras completas*. 10th ed. México, D. F.: Editorial Porrúa.

De la Peña, Terri. 1999. *Faults*. Los Angeles: Alyson Publications.

De la Tierra, Tatiana. Lesbian phenomenology/Fenomenología lesbiana. Unpublished.

esto no tiene nombre: revista de lesbianas latinas. 1991–1994. Miami Beach: Lambda Community Center of Greater Miami.

Etxebarría, Lucía. 1998. *Beatriz y los cuerpos celestes: Una novela rosa*. Barcelona: Ediciones Destino.

Foster, David William, and Emmanuel S. Nelson, eds. 1999. *Chicano/Latino homoerotic identities*. New York: Garland.

Garcia, Bernardo. 1998. *The development of a Latino gay identity*. New York: Garland.

García Lorca, Federico. 1998. *Poet in New York*. Rev. ed. Translated by Greg Simon and Steven F. White. Edited by Christopher Mauer. New York: The Noonday Press.

Gaspar de Alba, Alicia. 1999. *Sor Juana's second dream*. Albuquerque: University of New Mexico Press.

Gómez, Alma, Cherríe Moraga, and Mariana Romo-Carmona, eds. 1983. *Cuentos: Stories by Latinas*. New York: Kitchen Table: Women of Color Press.

Guerra, Erasmo. 2000. *Between dances: A novel*. New York: Painted Leaf Press.

Lemebel, Pedro. 2000. *Loco afán: Crónicas del sidario*. Barcelona: Editorial Anagrama.

Leyland, Winston, ed. 1979. *Now the volcano: An anthology of Latin American gay literature*. San Francisco: Gay Sunshine Press.

Lezama Lima, José. 2000. *Paradiso*. La Habana: Editorial Letras Cubanas.

Lozada, Ángel. 1998. *La patografía*. México, D.F.: Editorial Planeta Mexicana.

Manrique, Jaime. 1999. *Eminent maricones: Arenas, Lorca, Puig, and me*. Madison: University of Wisconsin Press.

———. 1999. *Maricones eminentes: Arenas, Lorca, Puig, y yo*. Madrid: Editorial Síntesis.

Manrique, Jaime, and Jesse Dorris, eds. 1999. *Bésame mucho: New gay Latino fiction*. New York: Painted Leaf Press.

Martínez, Elena M. 1996. *Lesbian voices from Latin America*. Hamden, CT: Garland.

Mogrovejo, Norma. 2000. *Un amor que se atrevió a decir su nombre: La lucha de las lesbianas y su relación con los movimientos homosexual y feminista en América Latina*. México, D.F.: Centro de Documentación y Archivo Lésbico.

Molloy, Sylvia. 1981. *En breve cárcel*. Barcelona: Seix Barral.

———. 1989. *Certificate of absence*. Edinburgh: Polygon.

Molloy, Sylvia, and Robert Mckee Irwin, eds. 1998. *Hispanisms and homosexualities*. Durham, NC: Duke University Press.

Monteflores, Carmen de. 1989. *Singing softly/Cantando bajito*. San Francisco: Spinster/ Aunt Lute.

Moraga, Cherríe. 2000. *Loving in the war years: Lo que nunca pasó por sus labios*. 2d ed. Cambridge, MA: South End.

Moraga, Cherríe and Gloria Anzaldúa, eds. 1981. *This bridge called my back: Writings by radical women of color*. New York: Kitchen Table.

———. 1988. *Esta puente, mi espalda: Voces de mujeres tercermundistas en los Estados Unidos*. Translated by Norma Alarcón and Ana Castillo. San Francisco: ISM Press.

Muñoz, José Esteban. 1999. *Disidentifications: Queers of color and the performance of politics*. Minneapolis: University of Minnesota Press.

Obejas, Achy. 2001. *Days of awe*. New York: Ballantine.

Ortiz Taylor, Sheila. 1982. *Faultline*. Tallahassee: Naiad.

———. 1991. *Terremoto,* Translated by Heide Braun. Madrid: Horas y Horas.

Pendleton Jiménez, Karleen. 1999. *Are you a boy or a girl?* Toronto: Green Dragon Press, 2000.

Pérez, Emma. 1999. *The decolonial imaginary: Writing Chicanas into history*. Bloomington: Indiana University Press.

Pérez Ocaña, Mariana, ed. 2000. *Poesía erótica lésbica: Compilación de la 1er Convocatoria.* México, D.F.: Prensa Editorial LeS VOZ.

Peri Rossi, Cristina. 1994. *Evohé.* Bilingual ed. Washington, DC: Azul Editions.

Quiroja, José. 2000. *Tropics of desire: Interventions from queer Latino America.* New York: New York University Press.

Ramos, Juanita, ed. 1994. *Compañeras: Latina Lesbians (an anthology).* 2d ed. New York: Routledge, Chapman & Hall.

Ramos Otero, Manuel. 1998. *Tálamos y tumbas: Prosa y verso.* Guadalajara, México: Universidad de Guadalajara.

Riesenfeld, Rinna. 2000. *Papá, mamá, soy gay: Una guía para comprender las orientaciones y preferencias sexuales de los hijos.* México, D.F.: Grijalbo.

Reyes, Guillermo. 1999. *Men on the verge of a His-panic breakdown: A play in monologues.* Woodstock, IL.: Dramatic Publishing.

Rivera-Valdés, Sonia. 2000. *Las historias prohibidas de Marta Veneranda.* New York: Siete Cuentos Editorial.

———. 2000. *The Forbidden Stories of Marta Veneranda.* New York: Seven Stories.

Rodriguez, Juana Maria. Forthcoming. *Coraje y Corazón: Rhizomatic Readings of Queer Latinidad.* New York: New York University Press.

Roffiel, Rosa Maria. 1997. *Amora.* Madrid: Horas y Horas.

Román, David. 1998. *Acts of intervention: Performance, gay culture, and AIDS.* Bloomington: Indiana University Press.

Sandoval, Chela. 2000. *Methodology of the oppressed.* Minneapolis: University of Minnesota Press.

Svich, Caridad, and Maria Teresa Marrero, eds. 2000. *Out of the fringe: Contemporary Latina/Latino theatre and performance.* New York: Theatre Communications Group.

Tejada, Roberto. 1999. *Gift and verdict.* San Francisco: Leroy.

Troyano, Alina. 2000. *I, Carmelita Tropicana: Performing between cultures.* Boston: Beacon Press.

Trujillo, Carla, ed. 1991. *Chicana lesbians: The girls our mothers warned us about.* Berkeley: Third Woman.

Vallejo, Fernando. 1999. *La virgen de los sicarios.* México, D. F.: Alfaguara.

Van Guardia, Lola. 1997. *Con pedigree: Culebrón lésbico por entregas.* Barcelona: Editorial Gay y Lesbiana.

———. 1999. *Plumas de doble filo.* Barcelona: Editorial Gay y Lesbiana.

Vélez Saldarriega, Marta Cecilia. 2000. *Los hijos de la Gran Diosa*. Medellín, Colombia: Universidad de Antioquia.

Villaurrutia, Xavier. 1999. *Nostalgia de la muerte*. Madrid: Huerga & Fierro.

Viñuales, Olga. 2000. *Identidades lésbicas: Discursos y prácticas*. Barcelona: Ediciones Bellaterra.

Xavier, Emanuel. 1999. *Christ-like*. New York: Painted Leaf Press.

Yarbro-Bejarano, Yvonne. 2001. *The Wounded Heart: Writing on Cherríe Moraga*. Austin: University of Texas Press.

Part 6

Conference Farewell Speech

The Power of Language

To Imagine, to Learn, to Act

El poder del idioma: Para imaginar, aprender y actuar

Oralia Garza de Cortés

As President Oralia Garza de Cortés brought the Second REFORMA National Conference to a close, she gave a dynamic farewell speech, calling upon all the attendees to carry forward what they had learned. She reminded the audience that Reformistas, change agents, can help to create a society that respects language rights, promotes literacy, and ensures access to knowledge and to power for Latinos and the Spanish speaking.

> Oralia Garza de Cortés is a writer and Latino children's literature and library services consultant living in Austin, Texas.

Have you felt it yet? Have you felt the strength and power of language in the talent of the incredible speakers who have sparked our imagination in the course of the last few days? Have you felt the power of language in this assembly of talent, of all of us gathered at this incredible conference?

I know I have felt the power and the calling of these words that speak to me. I have felt the calling of this theme from the very first day I read it and uttered it aloud. What does it mean for Reformistas today, in the twenty-first century? Let me tell you what it says to me. In the last few years I have been spending some time in the City of Angels, Los Angeles, the city with the largest concentration of Mexicans outside of Mexico City, the city with the largest concentration of Latinos in the United States. I have been blessed to meet people who have been in this country three, four, five, eight, ten, fifteen years. Immigrants. Marginalized people who left homelands ridden with war, poverty, and injustice to come to the Land of Opportunity, only to discover that this great country also offers them poverty, injustice, and all too often, violence. They suffer undue discrimination because the language they speak is different from the language of the dominant culture.

A young woman tells me that she wants to further her education, but there are barriers everywhere she turns. Young men and women, Spanish native speakers, have come to this country to forge a better life for themselves and for their families. But everywhere they turn they run into barriers, roadblocks in the form of laws and propositions, preventing them from accessing institutions of learning, from pursuing degrees in higher education. Citizenship laws prevent them from accessing systems, institutions, and tools that can help them to reinvent themselves. Many of these immigrants—and you know who they are—work very hard, many of them two, even three jobs. All they want is peace and a chance to give their children opportunities they never had.

But what do their children encounter when they go to school? Adults in power who bully them and intimidate them and prevent them from learning by denying them the language tools they need to become proficient Spanish language readers, which in turn prevents them from being truly successful English-language learners with critical learning skills. These same laws are being used to negate proven theories of oral language acquisition and native language learning. They are being used to manipulate data and to intimidate administrators who do not allow native language learning to occur for fear of legal reprisals. Are these children being denied the right to read? I would say so. Is that a first amendment infringement? Absolutely. Yes. Is this censorship? ¡Sí! ¡Sí! ¡Sí!

REFORMA. As a professional organization committed to serving Latinos and the Spanish speaking, as an organization affiliated with a powerful organization that fervently defends the right to read, we must affirm the rights of everyone to read and learn in their mother tongue, in English, in Spanish, or the language of their choice. In a free society, no government should dictate what certain members of a society should or should not read or learn. In a free society where choice is the order of the day, we should not allow segments of our society to have all the learning tools that they desire at the expense of a population that needs vital learning tools, for learning, for life, *para vivir*. As professionals, we have the responsibility to ensure that everyone has access to libraries, books, programs, services, and the information tools and resources that will help them develop to their fullest.

I want to take this opportunity to announce at this conference my presidential theme. *Con su permiso*, with your permission, I want to build upon the conference theme lest we forget what we have learned here at this conference. Hopefully, the theme shall serve as a reminder of all the wonderful things we have learned at the Second REFORMA National Conference. It will challenge us to re-create our library institutions and make them work for *nuestra gente*, for our people.

My presidential theme, "The Power of Language: To Learn, to Imagine, to Act," challenges us in many ways. It challenges us to learn how to do things differently to effect change. It challenges us to learn how to restructure services and programs to better serve the needs of our constituents. It challenges us to constantly learn new ways of tackling chronic, nasty policies that serve as barriers and hindrances to quality, effective service. I hope that we can develop a vision for library services that entails the best that a public institution built upon a system of democracy, not bureaucracy, can offer.

Imagine every library with friendly, Spanish-speaking librarians and staffs. Imagine children's programs that include weekly Spanish story hours, bilingual story hours, and English story hours; Born to Read Programs for babies and moms and dads in Spanish. Every document a readable document, forms equally accessible in English and Spanish. Imagine access tools like the electronic catalog, not just with Spanish interfacing that might just happen to be switched on at your branch even when you are not there, but with full bibliographical data available to the public in Spanish as well as English. Imagine a library system that goes beyond a program or two, that does more than pay lip service to the Spanish-speaking users, and that does not limit access to reading by limiting the size of the Spanish-language collection. Imagine libraries with policies that say, "We will develop the Spanish-language children's collection, and we will buy books in all categories, picture books, novels, and information books; we will develop Spanish-language collections for all ages, pre-school, elementary, young adults, adults, and even for *nuestros ancianos;* we will buy books from all Spanish-speaking countries of the world, not just translations of English language books into Spanish."

Imagine if you will a library organization, REFORMA, with state chapters that meet during your state library's annual conference. Imagine REFORMA at the table of power, at the White House speaking for us and on behalf of our communities; as a representative of ALA, showcasing our contributions to bring Latino children closer through reading by the creation of the Pura Belpré Award. Imagine if you will for a moment your favorite library organization, REFORMA, with a national office and the ability to leverage the Kellogg Foundation, or De Witt Wallace, or Carnegie, or the Ford Foundation, or the Casey Foundation; in partnership with PLA, ALA, or the Urban Libraries Council, or state libraries, further developing and implementing the types of models or programs that we have built with our knowledge and expertise over thirty years. We know what works best for our communities.

If there is anything I have learned from these few days here in Tucson, it is that the collective wealth, knowledge, and talent of all of the Reformistas are our greatest asset. You are our *tesoros*. So how can we transform that collective asset and make it work for the organization and make it work for the benefit of our communities? As we so fondly like to say: *ahí está el chiste. Ahí está el detalle.* (Therein lies the trick; therein lie the details.)

As you go back home today to your families and to your communities, enriched and energized by all that you have seen and heard here, I hope that you will do one thing for yourself and for your community. I hope that you will think about creating your own vision for what matters most to you, what is dearest and nearest to your heart, that you wish were different. Determine that you will work to make those goals, that vision, a reality, and then *actuar*—act—to make it happen. Think about those people who have impressed you the most. Think about how you can work with them through REFORMA to create the broader vision. But remember, it is only when we act on our vision and stay with it, and nurture it, and carve out that vision like a statue, *poco a poco, día tras día*, that we will carve out the public spaces—the democratic spaces in our communities that can enable people to read, to learn, to claim their place in the world. Only then will they have the power—*el poder*.

We cannot empower people; we cannot give them the power. They must find it within themselves, nurture it and use it for themselves. So many have the wrong idea of power. But you must remember what was said yesterday in the discussion on the Digital Divide: It is all about power. In Spanish the word is *poder*—to be able to. If we believe that knowledge is power, then we know that those who have the knowledge have the power and those who do not will be powerless. So, it is about people being able to access the tools and the systems that will enable them to be full participants, so that they can develop the ability, the power to change their lives. It's not just about information—it is about power.

So take your vision home with you today—and nurture it. It is only when you are able to act on your vision and collaborate with others to make it happen that you will be able to gain the power that is required to make change happen. So Reformistas—and I hope by now all of us are Reformistas, *todos somos Reformistas,* we are all change agents—take your dreams home today with you, create a vision, and find some people who will help you make a difference in your library system, or branch, or local community, or REFORMA chapter. Then get to work. Act. Whatever you do, do not lose sight of that vision; it will give you the power to change and to make a difference.

Is it doable? Yes! Will it be easy? Maybe. Will you encounter difficulty? *Por supuesto.* Is it worth it? You bet it is. *¿Pero se puede? ¡Sí, se puede!* I wish you Godspeed on your journeys home today, and on the Long Journey.

Index

Abif, Khafre, 145

Alire, Camila, 30–31, 33–34, 44, 46

Annotated catalogs. *See* Spanish-language publishers and distributors, services to libraries

Anthropology of Whiteness (Seminar, University of Massachusetts), 133

Approval plans. *See* Spanish-language publishers and distributors, services to libraries

Archivo Rodrigo Reyes, 182, 185–93. *See also* Reyes, Rodrigo

Ayala, Jacqueline, 44, 47

Baeza Ortego, Gilda, 44

Balderrama, Sandra Ríos, 30, 32, 44–45, 47

Baza, Ron, 44, 48

Betancourt, Ingrid, 44–47

Bicultural staff. *See* Bilingual-bicultural library employees

Bilindex, 68

Bilingual-bicultural library employees, 122–23, 125. *See also* Spanish-speaking library employees

Bilingual education, California, 13–22

Bilingual storytelling. *See* Storytelling, bilingual

Binding reinforcement. *See* Spanish-language publishers and distributors, services to libraries

Bissessar, Toni, 44, 47

Bounds vs. Smith (1977), 87, 97

California Proposition 209 of 1997, 13, 20

California Proposition 227 of 1998, 13–22

Carnegie Public Community Library, 116, 188, 168–77

Casey vs. Lewis (1996), 88

Castiano, Judith, 44, 46–47

Castillo-Speed, Lillian, 140

Center for Latino Policy Research, University of California, Berkeley, 5, 21

Center for Virtual Research, 62

Centro Cultural de la Misión. *See* Mission Cultural Center for Latino Arts

Chabrán, Richard, 58, 60

Chávez, Betty, 95–96

Chicano Database, 68

Chicano Thesaurus, 68

Children's literature, bilingual, 155

Chu, Clara, 37–41

Circulation statistics. *See* Library circulation statistics

Code switching (linguistics), 156

Collaboration among organizations. *See* Organizational partnerships

Collection development (libraries), 104–5

evaluation and selection, 106–7

See also Public libraries, collection development

Collection development objectives. *See* Collection development (libraries)

221